THE EU AND THE EUROZONE CRISIS

The Eurozone crisis is perhaps the most relevant event in European politics since the end of World War II. This book is an important contribution to understand the current path of the European integration process, not only in relation to this crisis, but in other policy areas. It is a valuable contribution for students and scholars of European politics.

Susana Borrás, Copenhagen Business School, Denmark

T0353063

The International Political Economy of New Regionalisms Series

The International Political Economy of New Regionalisms Series presents innovative analyses of a range of novel regional relations and institutions. Going beyond established, formal, interstate economic organizations, this essential series provides informed interdisciplinary and international research and debate about myriad heterogeneous intermediate level interactions.

Reflective of its cosmopolitan and creative orientation, this series is developed by an international editorial team of established and emerging scholars in both the South and North. It reinforces ongoing networks of analysts in both academia and think-tanks as well as international agencies concerned with micro-, meso- and macro-level regionalisms.

Recent titles in the series (continued at the back of the book)

The European Union Neighbourhood
Challenges and Opportunities
Edited by Teresa Cierco

The New Democracy Wars
The Politics of North American Democracy Promotion in the Americas
Neil A. Burron

The European Union after Lisbon
Polity, Politics, Policy
Edited by Søren Dosenrode

The EU and the Eurozone Crisis
Policy Challenges and Strategic Choices

Edited by

FINN LAURSEN
Canada Research Chair in EU Studies and
Professor of Political Science, Dalhousie University,
Halifax, NS, Canada

This book is published under the auspices of the EU Centre of Excellence at Dalhousie University with financial support from the European Commission

LONDON AND NEW YORK

First published 2013 by Ashgate Publishing

2 Park Square, Milton Park, Abingdon, Oxon OX14 4RN
711 Third Avenue, New York, NY 10017, USA

Routledge is an imprint of the Taylor & Francis Group, an informa business

First issued in paperback 2016

British Library Cataloguing in Publication Data
The EU and the eurozone crisis : policy challenges and
  strategic choices. -- (The international political economy of new regionalisms series)
  1. Monetary unions--Europe. 2. Financial crises--European Union countries. 3. European Union countries--Economic policy. 4. Intergovernmental fiscal relations--European Union countries. 5. Economic and Monetary Union. 6. European Union countries--Politics and government--21st century.
  I. Series II. Laursen, Finn.
  339.5'094-dc23

The Library of Congress has cataloged the printed edition as follows:
The EU and the Eurozone crisis : policy challenges and strategic choices / [edited] by Finn Laursen.
     pages cm
  Includes bibliographical references and index.
  ISBN 978-1-4094-5729-9 (hardback)   1. Financial crises--European Union countries. 2. European Union. 3. Eurozone. 4. Monetary policy--European Union countries. 5. European Union countries--Economic policy. I. Laursen, Finn.

  HB3782.E85 2013
  330.94--dc23

                                                        2012043453

ISBN 978-1-4094-5729-9 (hbk)
ISBN 978-1-138-26717-6 (pbk)

Contents

List of Figures	*vii*
List of Tables	*ix*
Notes on Contributors	*xi*
Preface	*xv*
Acknowledgements	*xvii*
List of Abbreviations	*xix*

PART I: INTRODUCTION

1   The Eurozone Crisis and Other Policy Challenges in the EU   3
Finn Laursen

PART II: THE EUROZONE CRISIS

2   Eurozone: Creeping Decay, Sudden Death or Magical Solution?   25
Kurt Hübner

3   The Eurozone Crisis and the Fiscal Treaty:
Implications for the Social Dimension and Democracy   45
Robert Finbow

4   Britain and Monetary Union   65
Alasdair Blair

PART III: OTHER POLICY DEVELOPMENTS AND CHALLENGES

5   The Common Agricultural Policy:
The Right Path versus Blind Alleys   85
Jacek Chotkowski and Benon Gaziński

6   New Challenges for EU Trade Policy-making:
Why is the EU Pursuing a Comprehensive Economic and
Trade Agreement with Canada?   107
Stefanie Rosskopf

PART IV: DEEPENING, WIDENING OR MULTISPEED INTEGRATION?

7   Direct Democracy: Remedying the Democratic Deficit?   125
    Ece Ozlem Atikcan

8   Europe After the Greek Default:
    Widening, Deepening, or Splitting?   143
    Imtiaz Hussain

9   Chronic Anxiety: Schengen and the Fear of Enlargement   161
    Ruben Zaiotti

10 Crossroads of Integration?
    The Future of Schengen in the Wake of the Arab Spring   177
    Kiran K. Phull and John B. Sutcliffe

PART V: CONCLUDING CHAPTER

11 Equilibrium, Further Deepening or More 'Variable Geometry':
    Reflections on the Future of European Integration   199
    Finn Laursen

Index   *209*

List of Figures

1.1   Dimensions of integration   6
1.2   Deepening versus widening   17

2.1   Composition of total debt, % of GDP, 2Q 2011   29
2.2   Crises cycle   32

11.1   Future of deepening and widening   203
11.2   Variable geometry of European integration   205

List of Tables

1.1   Expanding functional scope of European integration   7
1.2   Expanding membership of the EC/EU   14

5.1   Polish agricultural trade during the period 2003–2010   95
5.2   Major EU-15 potato starch producers   98
5.3   Balance of exports, imports and production of starch and starch products in Poland during the period 2001–2008, thousand tons   99
5.4   Evaluation of some of the proposed CAP reforms from the Polish perspective   100

Notes on Contributors

Ece Ozlem Atikcan is an Assistant Professor at the Department of Political Science, Université Laval. She completed her B.S. in International Relations at the Middle East Technical University before obtaining her M.A. in European Law at the University of Sussex, and her Ph.D. in Political Science at McGill University. Her research interests include international organizations, public opinion, referendums, political parties, transnational social movements, and nationalism.

Alasdair Blair is Jean Monnet Professor of International Relations and Head of the Department of Politics and Public Policy at De Montfort University, UK. He is author of a number of books and articles on European integration and British foreign policy, as well as articles on teaching and learning in Higher Education. Recent books include *The European Union: A Beginner's Guide* (Oneworld, 2012) and *The European Union since 1945* (2nd edition, Longman, 2010). Forthcoming books include *Britain and the World: British Foreign Policy since 1945* (Longman, 2013) and *The Routledge Companion to International Relations* (Routledge, 2013).

Jacek Chotkowski is Senior Research Worker, member of the Staff of the Plant Breeding and Acclimatization Institute, National Research Institute in Bonin near Koszalin (Poland). For three decades, he has been involved in research on the food market, including seed and potato market. He is also a Lecturer of the Koszalin University of Technology (market analysis and marketing).

Robert Finbow, Professor and Chair of Political Science at Dalhousie University, received his doctorate from the London School of Economics. A recipient of SSHRC and Fulbright fellowships, he has published books and articles on trade, labour and environmental policies in NAFTA and the EU, comparative political cultures, health care and social policy in North America and regionalism in Atlantic Canada.

Benon Gaziński, Jean Monnet Professor, is a research worker and academic teacher at the Institute of Political Sciences, Faculty of Social Sciences, Warmia and Mazury University of Olsztyn, Poland, involved in research and teaching on European integration. He has been engaged – for many years – in a number of international projects, mainly under the European Community framework (RSS – Central European University, Prague, TEMPUS, ACE, COPERNICUS, PHARE-FIESTA II, Pro-European Initiatives, J. Monnet – LLP, etc.). He has published 12 books and some 200 articles on the European integration.

Kurt Hübner holds the Jean Monnet Chair for European Integration and Global Political Economy at the Institute for European Studies Department of Political Science, the University of British Columbia (UBC). Central to Hübner's research are topics of global and European currency regimes, European trade policies and the relationship between innovation, global competitiveness and sustainability. His latest research focuses on the economic and socio-political base for the ongoing negotiations about the Comprehensive Economic and Trade Agreement (CETA) between the EU and Canada; his most recent book on CETA has been released with Routledge in 2011. Currently he is working on a project on currency competition and currency co-operation, which analyses the relations between the US Dollar, the Euro and the Chinese Rinminbi. This research will be published in 2013.

Imtiaz Hussain is an International Relations Professor at Universidad Iberoamericana (Mexico). His publications include *Re-evaluate NAFTA* (Palgrave, 2012), *Afghanistan-Iraq and Post-conflict Governance* (Brill, 2010), *The Impact of NAFTA on North America* (Palgrave, 2010), *North American Homeland Security* (Praeger, 2008), *Community, Diffusion, and North American Expansiveness* (UIA, 2008), *Running on Empty Across Central America* (UPA, 2006), and *Globalization, Indigenous Groups, and Mexico's Plan Puebla Plan* (Edwin Mellen, 2006). Published articles in *FIU Law Review*, *Voices of Mexico*, *Handbook of Global Security and Intelligence*, *South Asian Survey*, *Politics & Policy*, *Journal of the Asiatic Society of Bangladesh*, and *Norteamérica*. A recipient of several fellowships and teaching awards, he graduated from University of Pennsylvania (Political Science, 1989), and is from Bangladesh.

Finn Laursen, Canada Research Chair in EU Studies at Dalhousie University, Halifax. He also holds an *ad personam* Jean Monnet Chair. Previously he has been professor at the European Institute of Public Administration, Maastricht, 1988–1995, and Professor of International Politics at the University of Southern Denmark, Odense, 1999–2006. Recent edited books include: *Comparative Regional Integration* (Ashgate, 2010), *The EU and Federalism* (Ashgate, 2011), *The Making of the Lisbon Treaty* (P.I.E Peter Lang, 2012), and *The EU's Lisbon Treaty: Institutional Choices and Implementation* (Ashgate, 2012). Two forthcoming books on Transatlantic Relations will be published by P.I.E. Peter Lang in late 2012 and early 2013.

Kiran K. Phull graduated from the Academy for Gifted Children P.A.C.E. in Oak Ridges, Ontario, in 2003. From there, she went to the Schulich School of Business in Toronto, Ontario, where she obtained an International Bachelor of Business Administration degree in 2007 with a joint study at the Université Catholique de Louvain, Belgium. After working in public opinion research for two years, she completed a Master of Arts Degree in Political Science from the University of Windsor, Ontario in 2012. Currently, she is working towards obtaining a Ph.D. in Political Science.

Stefanie Rosskopf holds an M.A. in Political Science from Memorial University of Newfoundland. She is currently a Programme Coordinator for the Edmonton Branch of the Canadian International Council. Her research interests include transatlantic relations and global governance.

John B. Sutcliffe is an Associate Professor and Department Head of Political Science at the University of Windsor. His research focuses on the role of municipal governments and multi-level governance in the European Union and North America. A current research project focuses on the reform and operation of borders in these two settings. He has published articles on these and other topics in journals such as the *American Review of Canadian Studies*, *Regional and Federal Studies*, *Local Government Studies*, and the *Journal of European Public Policy*.

Ruben Zaiotti is an Assistant Professor in the Department of Political Science at Dalhousie University (Canada). He holds a Ph.D. from the University of Toronto, a Master of Studies from the University of Oxford and a B.A. from the University of Bologna. His main areas of interest are international relations theory, international security, border control and European Union politics. Recent publications include the monograph *Cultures of Border Control: Schengen and the Evolution of European Frontiers* with University of Chicago Press, 2011 and articles for *Review of International Studies*, *European Security*, *Journal of European Integration*, *International Journal of Refugee Law*, *Cultures & Conflicts*. He is the former Editor-in-chief of the *Journal of International Law and International Relations*.

Preface

The European Union faces a serious crisis, especially the eurozone, which is the group of member states that have adopted the single currency, the euro. But the crisis affects the union as such, including other policy areas. The relationship between the 17 countries that are currently in the eurozone and the 10 member states that are outside is affected, complicating decision-making in general. All in all the current situation makes it more difficult to deal adequately with other issues that need attention.

This book tries to deal with some of these issues. It is the outcome of a project entitled 'Widening and Deepening of European Integration: Challenges and Strategic Choices Facing the European Union'.

In a call for proposals issued in November 2011 we stated *inter alia*:

> "The EU faces a number of internal challenges, especially the eurozone financial crisis, and more broadly an employment crisis. What steps are needed to overcome these crises? Was the Maastricht EMU set-up faulty? Is an economic government needed in the EU? Will more fiscal federalism be required?"

> "Linked with the current challenges are questions of decision-making and leadership in the post-Lisbon-Treaty EU. Is there a tendency to increasingly revert to intergovernmentalism [...]? Should the application of the Community method, with enhanced roles for the Commission and the European Parliament, be the way forward [...]? Will another treaty change be required to allow for imposition of economic policies on member states [...]? And if economic governance is tightened among eurozone members, how will this affect EU member states not taking part in the euro? With all the challenges facing the EU will we get even more multi-speed integration than we currently have?"

These are big questions. The chapters in this book try to answer at least some of them. Papers dealing with enlargement issues also received, presented and discussed as part of the project will be published in another volume.

The editor is happy that this book is published by Ashgate's *International Political Economy of New Regionalisms* Series, which previously published two books he edited on *Comparative Regional Integration*, in 2003 and 2010 respectively. Ashgate has also published two of his other books, one on *EU and Federalism* (2011) and one on *The Lisbon Treaty* (2012).

Finn Laursen,
Halifax

Acknowledgements

This book is published under the auspices of the EU Centre of Excellence (EUCE) at Dalhousie University, Halifax, Nova Scotia, Canada. The EUCE is co-financed by a three-year grant from the European Commission. Without the support from the Commission, the production of this book would not have been possible. The grant period during which this book was produced expired on 4 December 2012.

The editor, who has directed the EUCE at Dalhousie since the beginning in 2006, also wants to acknowledge the contributions of Danijela Juric, the Administrative Secretary of EUCE. She assisted with the logistics in connection with the research project, including the 11–13 April 2012 gathering, where early versions of the chapters were first presented and discussed. Also thanks to Karen Snaterse and Faton Tony Bislimi for practical assistance in connection with the project.

I want to thank Dr. Robert Summerby-Murray, Dean, Faculty of Arts and Social Sciences, Dalhousie University for welcoming the participants on the 11th of April and Dr. Donna Rogers, Associate Dean Academic, Faculty of Arts and Social Sciences, for addressing the opening session on the 12th April. Special thanks go to His Excellency Ambassador Matthias Brinkmann, Head of the European Delegation to Canada, for coming to Halifax on this occasion and giving a very substantial opening address. Finally I want to thank Kasper Gimsing, Policy Advisor, the Danish Embassy, Ottawa, for presenting the programme of the Danish Presidency. The recognition given by the Dalhousie and EU leaderships was much appreciated.

Carolyn Ferguson is thanked for her diligent work as language checker and copy editor. Professor Timothy Shaw, Series Editor of Ashgate's *International Political Economy of New Regionalisms* Series, is thanked warmly for his continued support and encouragement. Finally, Kirstin Howgate, Publisher in Politics and International Relations at Ashgate Publishing Limited, is thanked for excellent and efficient cooperation.

Finn Laursen,
Halifax

List of Abbreviations

AAA	Authentication, Authorization and Accounting
AFSJ	Area of Freedom, Security and Justice
ATTAC	Association for the Taxation of Financial Transactions for Citizens' Action
BCU	Benelux Customs Union
BPS	Basic Payment Scheme
Buba	German *Bundesbank*
CAP	Common Agricultural Policy
CCC	Community Customs Code
CDA	Christian Democratic Appeal
CEE	Central and Eastern Europe
CEECs	Central and Eastern European Countries
CETA	Comprehensive Economic and Trade Agreement
CFSP	Common Foreign and Security Policy
CG	Cairns Group
CGT	General Workers' Confederation
CIC	China Investment Company
COES	Cabinet Office European Secretariat
COPA-COGECA	Agri-Cooperatives-European Agri-Cooperatives
CRAs	Credit Rating Agencies
CSDP	Common Security and Defence Policy
CSO	Central Statistical Office
CSV	Christian Social People's Party
CUFTA	Canada-US Free Trade Agreement
DM	*Deutschmark*
DP	Democratic Party
DPP	Danish People's Party
DTI	Department of Trade and Industry
DTR	Declaration on Transatlantic Relations
EAEC	European Atomic Energy Community
EC	European Community/ies
ECB	European Central Bank
ECJ	European Court of Justice
ECOFIN	Economic and Financial Affairs Council
ECSC	European Coal and Steel Community
ECU	European Current Unit
EEC	European Economic Community

EFSF	European Financial Stability Facility
EFTA	European Free Trade Association
EIB	European Investment Bank
EMS	European Monetary System
EMU	Economic and Monetary Union
EP	European Parliament
EPC	European Political Cooperation
EPP	European Peoples Party
ERM	Exchange Rate Mechanism
ESM	European Stability Mechanism
EU	European Union
EUAFR	European Union Agency for Fundamental Rights
EUB	European Union Bill
EUTC	European Union Trade Confederation
FACEC	Framework Agreement for Commercial and Economic Cooperation
FCO	Foreign, Commonwealth Office
FN	Front National
FSJ	Freedom, Security and Justice
FTAs	Free Trade Agreements
GATT	General Agreement on Tariffs and Trade
GDP	Gross Domestic Product
GEAC	German Economic Advisory Council
HEP	Harvest Experience programme
IACS	Integrated Administration and Control System
ICV	Initiative for Catalonia Greens
IGC	Intergovernmental Conference
IIF	Institute of International Finance
IMF	International Monetary Fund
IPR	Intellectual Property Right
IST	Income Stabilization Tool
JCC	Joint Cooperation Committee
JHA	Justice and Home Affairs
LFAs	Less Favoured Areas
LN	Lega Nord
LSAP	Luxembourg Socialist Workers' Party
LTROs	Long-term Refinancing Operations
MENA	Middle East and North African
MEP	Member of the European Parliament
MP	Member of Parliament
NAFTA	North American Free Trade Agreement
NDP	New Democratic Party
NTBs	Non-Tariff Barriers

OECD	Organization for Economic Co-operation and Development
PASOK	Panhellenic Socialist Movement
PCF	French Communist Party
PIIGS	Portugal, Ireland, Italy, Greece and Spain
PP	Spanish Popular Party
PS	French Socialist Party
PSOE	Spanish Socialist Workers' Party
PTAs	Preferential Trade Agreements
PvdA	Dutch Labour Party
QMV	Qualified Majority Vote
SAPS	Single Area Payment Scheme
SBC	Schengen Borders Code
SCH/C	Schengen Co-operation
SEA	Single European Act
SEG	Schengen Evaluation Working Group
SEM	Schengen Executive Committee
SGP	Schengen Governance Package
SIC	Schengen Implementing Convention
SIS	Schengen Information System
SMU	Scandinavian Monetary Union
SP	Dutch Socialist Party
S&P's	Standard & Poor's
SPS	Single Payment Scheme
TBTs	Technical Barriers to Trade
TCE	Treaty Establishing a Constitution for Europe
TCNs	Third Country Nationals
TEP	Transatlantic Economic Partnership Agreement
TEU	Treaty on European Union
TFEU	Treaty on the Functioning of the European Union
TIEA	Trade and Investment Enhancement Agreement
TSCG	Treaty on Stability, Coordination and Governance
UK	United Kingdom
USA	United States of America
USD	US-Dollar
UMP	Union for a Popular Movement
UNHCR	United Nations High Commissioner for Refugees
VVD	People's Party for Freedom and Democracy
VAT	Value Added Tax
WTO	World Trade Organization
WRR	Dutch Scientific Council for Government Policy
WWI	World War I
WWII	World War II

PART I
Introduction

Chapter 1

The Eurozone Crisis and Other Policy Challenges in the EU

Finn Laursen

Introduction

The European Union (EU) is facing a fundamental crisis, which especially affects the countries that take part in the single currency, the euro. The group is usually referred to as the eurozone, and when the ministers of finance from these countries meet they are referred to as the Euro Group. This group has its own president, currently Jean-Claude Juncker from Luxembourg. It can be seen as a subgroup of the Economic and Financial Affairs Council (ECOFIN) of the Council of the EU. The current 17 members of the eurozone are Austria, Belgium, Cyprus, Estonia, Finland, France, Germany, Greece, Ireland, Italy, Luxembourg, Malta, the Netherlands, Portugal, Slovakia, Slovenia and Spain. It means that there are 10 member states of the EU which are not members of the eurozone, namely Bulgaria, the Czech Republic, Denmark, Hungary, Latvia, Lithuania, Poland, Romania, Sweden and the United Kingdom. This kind of situation, where not all member states take part in a certain policy, in this case Economic and Monetary Union (EMU), has been referred to by many names, such as 'flexibility' or 'variable geometry'. Assuming that those which are 'out' will eventually join those which are 'in', it can also be seen as two-speed or multispeed integration. The literature on European integration is full of discussions about the pros and cons of flexibility (e.g. CEPR 1995; Stubb 2002a, 2002b). In the academic literature it is also sometimes referred to as 'differentiated integration' (Kölliker 2006).

At the outset of European integration in the 1950s the idea was that all member states should take part in all common policies and institutions. New member states were expected to accept all existing rules, treaties and legislation, known as the *acquis communautaire*. No permanent exceptions were on offer, only transition periods of varying lengths.

Sometimes a smaller group of member states would start closer cooperation outside the treaties which had established the three European Communities (EC) in the 1950s, such as for instance when France, Germany and the Benelux Countries started the so-called Schengen cooperation in the 1980s with the view of abolishing border controls. The membership of Schengen would grow the following years, and eventually the Schengen *acquis* was incorporated into the EU by the Amsterdam Treaty, which entered into force in 1999, although the United Kingdom (UK) and Ireland remained outside the Schengen cooperation.

EMU was first outlined as part of the Maastricht Treaty, which established the EU in 1993. It outlined three stages towards EMU, which would establish the single currency, the euro, and the European Central Bank (ECB) in 1999, among 11 member states at the time. The treaty included so-called convergence criteria, basically economic conditions, for participation. This sanctioned two-speed integration in the monetary area. Further, the UK and Denmark got opt-out clauses in protocols to the treaty, although other member states are in principle expected to join the eurozone once they fulfil the criteria.

The Maastricht Treaty also included a second pillar in the form of cooperation on Common Foreign and Security Policy (CFSP) and Justice and Home Affairs (JHA). Cooperation in these areas had taken place outside the Community framework prior to the establishment of the EU.

The Lisbon Treaty, in force since December 2009, abolished the pillar structure, but CFSP has retained its own decision procedures, basically remaining as intergovernmental cooperation, while JHA has become more integrated under the so-called Community method, where decisions can be made by a qualified majority vote (QMV) in the Council, and the European Commission, and the European Parliament (EP) and the European Court of Justice (ECJ) play stronger and more important roles.

The treaty has an article now sometimes referred to as the 'flexibility clause' (Art. 352 TFEU, ex-Art. 308 TEC).[1] This article actually goes back to Article 235 in the Treaty of Rome establishing the European Economic Community (EEC) in 1958. It allowed the Council of Ministers to take action not explicitly foreseen by unanimity as long as they were necessary to attain one of the objectives of the Community. It got the name 'flexibility clause' in the defunct draft Constitutional Treaty (Art. I-18) (Piris 2006). Its scope was extended to include CFSP and JHA and the consent of the European Parliament (EP) was required. The clause survived in the Lisbon Treaty, but the name 'flexibility clause' was dropped. It refers to the objectives of the treaties, since the term 'Community' has been abolished in the treaty (Piris 2010).

This kind of 'flexibility' is different from the multispeed variant we see in the case of EMU. Apart from EMU and a few explicit opt-outs eventually accepted – mostly for the UK and Denmark – the treaty introduced provisions on 'closer cooperation' by the time of the Amsterdam Treaty in 1997 (Stubb 2002a, 2002b), subsequently amended by the Treaty of Nice, which entered into force in 2003, to make their application easier. At the same time the name was changed to 'enhanced cooperation' (Olsen 2006). So 'enhanced cooperation', as it is now officially called, can take place on the basis of the treaties, on certain conditions which are

---

1   Since the entry into force of the Lisbon Treaty the treaty has two parts: the Treaty on European Union (TEU) and the Treaty on the Functioning of the European Union (TFEU).

outlined in the treaty. Enhanced cooperation post-Lisbon Treaty requires at least nine member states to participate (Art. 20 TEU).

Dimensions of Integration

European integration, the process associated with the three European Communities created in the 1950s and continuing with the EU from 1993, can be seen as a process of creating common institutions and developing common policies among a certain group of states. It started with the European Coal and Steel Community (ECSC) in 1952. Basically, six countries pooled their coal and steel sectors and set up an independent supranational body called the High Authority to manage these sectors jointly. The institutional set-up also included a Council where the ministers from the member states would meet and make certain decisions. The purpose of the Council was to create a degree of political accountability. From the beginning a strong European Court of Justice (ECJ) was created. However, the original parliamentary assembly was relatively weak. The following two communities, the European Economic Community (EEC) and European Atomic Energy Community (EAEC, or EURATOM), created by the Treaties of Rome in 1958, established two independent, but slightly less supranational, 'executives' – called 'Commissions' in both cases – as well as two separate Councils of Ministers. The Assembly and the ECJ were common for the three Communities from the beginning. Eventually the Merger Treaty in 1967 merged the 'executives' and Councils to form a single Commission and a single Council. The latter could meet in separate configurations though.

The important institutional part of the three Communities was an independent European 'executive' representing the 'Community' interest with a right of initiative, sometimes an exclusive right, and a high degree of autonomy. Further, in the Council some decisions could be made by a qualified majority vote (QMV). The Court was a real court that made binding decisions. So Community law started resembling federal law. This decision-making system became known as the Community method. Arguably, it has served Europe well. The alternative is the much weaker intergovernmental cooperation, which has also been used in Europe, especially in the area of foreign policy cooperation, where the attachment to national sovereignty has been too strong for adoption of the Community method. When the Maastricht Treaty created the EU, intergovernmental cooperation was retained in CFSP and JHA. The Lisbon Treaty still retains it for CFSP.

Figure 1.1 suggests three important dimensions of European integration. Over time more and more countries joined the process, and more and more policy areas were included. That more and more countries have chosen to do more and more together suggests a certain degree of success for European integration. Developing good common institutions arguably has been one of the reasons for this success.

Institutional capacity

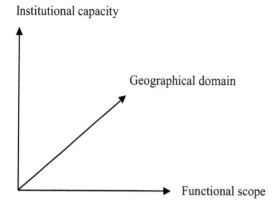

Figure 1.1   Dimensions of integration
Source: Compiled by the author.

Expanding Policy Scope

Table 1.1 provides an overview of the functional scope of European integration. The focus is on the addition of formal policy chapters in the treaties establishing the EC/EU. Some policies were gradually included even before they were formally mentioned in the treaties. Such is the case with environmental policy. By the time that this was formally included by the Single European Act (SEA) in 1987, a number of environmental directives had already been adopted using various articles in the treaties, including Article 235 in the EEC Treaty, which, as mentioned, allowed the Council by unanimity to adopt measures considered necessary to reach the objectives of the Community.

During the first four decades the focus was on the four freedoms of the internal market: free movement of goods, services, capital and people. Since the necessary harmonization of national legislation, according to the Treaty of Rome (Art. 100), required unanimity, it was necessary to improve the institutional capacity by introducing QMV for this harmonization. When this happened through the SEA, it gave integration a new momentum (Laursen 1990). Thus institutions clearly matter.

Table 1.1   Expanding functional scope of European integration

Treaty of Paris (1952)	Treaties of Rome (1958)	Single European Act (1987)	Maastricht Treaty (1993)	Amsterdam Treaty (1997)	Nice Treaty (2003)	Lisbon Treaty (2009)
						Space
						Energy
						Tourism
					Defence	
				Employment		
				Schengen *acquis*		
				UK joins Social Policy		
			EMU			
			Visa policy			
			Public health			
			Consumer protection			
			Industry			
			Trans-European networks			
			Development cooperation			
			Education			
			Culture			
			Social policy (UK opt-out)			
			CFSP			
			JHA			
		Completion of Internal market				
		Environment				
		Economic and Social cohesion				
		R&D				

Table 1.1   Continued

	Common Market					
	Trade					
	Competition					
	Agriculture					
	Transport					
	Atomic energy					
Coal						
Steel						

Source: Compiled by the author. For details on the different treaties, see Laursen 2012c.

The functional scope received the biggest boost with the Maastricht Treaty, which was to a large extent the response to the end of the Cold War (Laursen 1992). It included EMU, which had been put on the agenda before the end of the Cold War. EMU was a radical upgrading of the European Monetary System (EMS) which dated back to 1979. The treaty changes since Maastricht also increased the policy scope, but less so. They were mostly about upgrading the institutional capacity considered necessary to accommodate new member states, especially Central and Eastern European Countries (CEECs), which wanted to join the EU after the end of the Cold War.

The Eurozone: A Step Too Far?

Given the central importance of the eurozone crisis at the moment, EMU deserves extra space in this introduction. Arguably, it was the most important novelty of the Maastricht Treaty, and it was controversial among politicians as well as professional economists, who asked the question whether Europe constituted an 'optimal currency area' and whether the institutional aspects of EMU were adequate.

The theory of optimum currency areas was mainly developed by the Canadian economist Robert Mundel at Columbia University in the 1960s. Mundel saw mobility of production factors as most important (Geza and Vasilescu 2011). Along this line of thinking, the four freedoms in the EC could be seen as contributing to making the EC/EU an optimum currency union. Free movement of capital was slow to be realized in the EC, but it eventually was realized from the late 1980s. Free movement of labour existed on paper, but many unemployed people hesitated to move to another member state, where they might not know the language, for instance. Other economists have looked at a host of factors, including openness of the economy, degree of diversification of production, financial integration, similarity of inflation rates, flexibility of prices and salaries, and finally degree of political integration. Compared on these factors, the EU obviously scores lower than the US or Canada. Therefore the big question when the EU set out to create the EMU was whether it could sustain so-called asymmetrical shocks, where member states face different economic policy developments and challenges, but have lost their monetary policy autonomy. Low labour mobility and real wage inflexibility are problems in the EU. This leaves fiscal transfers as a possibility, but the EU budget is relatively small (Dyson 2000: 193–5). Further, the Maastricht Treaty has a no-bailout clause, which put strict limits on transfer possibilities through the European Central Bank (ECB) to the member states.

There had been monetary cooperation among EC states before Maastricht. The Treaty of Rome called for macroeconomic cooperation, especially concerning conjunctural policy (Art. 103) and balance of payments (Art. 104) and established a Monetary Committee with advisory status (Art. 105). According to Article 104, it was up to the member states to 'pursue the economic policy needed to ensure the equilibrium of its overall balance of payments and to maintain confidence in its currency, while taking care to ensure a high level of employment and a stable level of prices'.

The idea of EMU was subsequently proposed at the Hague Summit in 1969 and a plan, the Werner Plan, was worked out. It foresaw the establishment of EMU over the following decade. This was at about the time that the Bretton Woods system was starting to crumble. However, the Werner Plan was too ambitious at the time and the energy crisis in the 1970s had a negative effect on the possibilities. In 1972 some member states did start cooperating on limiting currency fluctuations, within the so-called 'snake', limiting exchange rate fluctuations to a maximum of ± 2.25%. This cooperation had its limits and flaws, so in 1979 the European Monetary System (EMS) was initiated. EMS established an Exchange Rate Mechanism (ERM) and a European Currency Unit (ECU) based on a basket of currencies. Currency movements were limited to 2.25% around parity (Hodson 2010; Verdun 2011).

EMS was successful in creating macroeconomic convergence in the 1980s and EMU got on the agenda again, as a next step. The SEA added a new Article 102a about cooperation in economic and monetary policy. It mentioned 'Economic and Monetary Union' for the first time in the treaty, but in a bracket. Although EMU was on the agenda, the member states were not yet ready for treaty-based commitments. In regard to cooperation, the SEA stated that 'In order to ensure the convergence of economic and monetary policies which is necessary for the further development of the Community, Member States shall cooperate ...' (Art. 102a). The experience acquired within the EMS should be taken into account. Should institutional changes be necessary, it would require another treaty amendment, it was said.

The treaty amendment followed with the Maastricht Treaty. In the meantime a committee chaired by Commission President Jacques Delors had prepared a report in 1988, which outlined three phases towards EMU. These phases became part of the Maastricht Treaty. The third phase saw the creation of the European Central Bank (ECB) and the introduction of the common currency, the euro, in 1999.

To qualify for taking part in the euro the member states had to fulfil the following convergence criteria:

- *Price stability*: Inflation rate may not be higher than 1.5% of the average inflation rate of the three best performing member states;
- *Sound public finance*: The government deficit may not exceed 3% of the GDP;
- *Sustainable public finance*: The government debt may not exceed 60% of GDP;
- *Durable convergence*: The nominal long-term interest rate may not be higher than 2% of the average of the three best performing member states in terms of price stability;
- *Exchange rate stability*: Observance of normal fluctuation margins in the European Exchange Rate Mechanism (ERM), without devaluation for at least two years (Art. 109j and Protocol no. 6 on the Convergence criteria; Hodson 2010: 162).

After the entry into force of the Maastricht Treaty, the Germans in particular wanted to establish stricter rules for fiscal policy, which basically remained a national responsibility according to the Maastricht Treaty. Some governments hesitated, including the French government. These governments wanted to be able to use fiscal policy to create jobs, especially as they lost their monetary policy autonomy. The outcome was the adoption of the Growth and Stability Pact at the time when the negotiations of the Amsterdam Treaty were concluded in June 1997. The main elements were:

- Governments will aim to achieve a balanced budget;
- Countries with a budget deficit exceeding 3% of GDP will be fined up to 0.5% of GDP;
- These fines will not be applied if there are exceptional circumstances, such as a natural disaster or a decline in GDP of more than 2% in one year;
- In cases where the drop in GDP is between 0.75% and 2% the application of the fine will be decided by ECOFIN by a QMV.[2]

The Growth and Stability Pact was not part of the treaty, but a separate resolution. Subsequently, it was complemented by two Regulations (McNamara 2005). Regulations are legally binding. However, the commitments were insufficient. In connection with the economic slowdown in 2001–2 several governments started

---

2   Additional information at: http://europa.eu/legislation_summaries/economic_and_monetary_affairs/stability_and_growth_pact/l25021_en.htm (accessed 18 February 2012).

borrowing in excess of 3%, including Germany and France. ECOFIN failed to act on Commission recommendations. A softer version was adopted in 2005, and excessive deficit procedures against Germany and France were revoked in 2007, after fiscal improvement in 2006 (Hodson 2010: 172–3).

Arguably, the current crisis started in the United States, but who knows whether the sovereign debt crisis in Europe would have happened anyway, maybe at a later stage. The response to the financial crisis on both sides of the Atlantic has been to increase governmental oversight by creating new institutions. The moment a crisis starts spreading from one country to another the collective action problem becomes an international problem. This explains why international institutions, especially the International Monetary Fund (IMF), got involved.

The EU responded to the financial crisis with a series of steps that are still ongoing, suggesting a trial-and-error process. The steps taken have been politically controversial; the interstate disagreements on what to do have their roots in domestic politics. The countries that needed to bail out their banks or needed bailouts themselves because of unsustainable public debt, the so-called PIIGS (Portugal, Ireland, Italy, Greece and Spain) in particular, were blamed for irresponsible fiscal policies, and other countries were not eager to step in. Had there been more solidarity between the member states more could have been done faster.

The ECB did assist the private sector, which was important (Mallaby 2012). But the no-bailout clause in the Treaty of Maastricht created problems, especially for assisting Greece, but also other eurozone countries with high public debt, such as Italy and Spain. These latter countries have much larger economies than Greece. Germany, arguably the regional paymaster in the EU, set strict conditions for assistance, which first led to the creation of a temporary bailout fund, the European Financial Stabilization Mechanism (EFSM) and then a permanent bailout fund, The European Stability Mechanism (ESM). This was referred to as a firewall in the debate. In parallel, private investors also had to take a loss. This in turn was referred to as a haircut. The ESM required an amendment of the Lisbon Treaty. Further, a Fiscal Stability Treaty involving all eurozone members and most other EU member states, except the UK and the Czech Republic, has been adopted. It was hoped that these and other measures would reduce the risks in the future. However, many observers remain sceptical. In addition, the challenge of competitiveness and growth remains to be addressed adequately. The situation in Greece after the elections in May 2012, which did not produce a government capable of carrying out the reforms requested by the IMF and European partners, created a serious situation for the eurozone. A second election took place in June. It has produced a three-party coalition government which is committed to carrying out austerity and structural reforms, but the austerity measures may be too tough and counterproductive.

The eurozone crisis has clearly demonstrated the asymmetrical nature of the EMU. The EMU has a centralized monetary policy, with a single currency for the 17 countries which have adopted the euro. However, fiscal policy has remained decentralized, with member states retaining the main responsibilities for taxation and expenditures (Verdun 2011: 254). Only about 1% of the EU's Gross Domestic Product (GDP) goes through the EU budget, so the possibilities for autonomous EU anti-cyclical policies are tiny, basically limited to money from the so-called Structural Funds, including the Cohesion Fund, which have transferred money to the poorer countries and regions in the EU in the past, especially Greece, Spain, Portugal and Ireland until the eastern enlargements in 2004 and 2007. The new member states from Central and Eastern Europe have now become the main recipients of money from the Structural Funds (Sbragia and Stolfi 2008). Beyond the Structural Funds there is also the European Investment Bank (EIB), which could potentially make bigger contributions to growth, short of a more active ECB issuing eurobonds, something not allowed at the moment but advocated by some member states, the Commission and many economists. The new French president, François Hollande, elected in May 2012 has insisted on the EU also developing a growth pact, and he has found some support. The meeting of the European Council at the end of June 2012 did agree to more stimuli and to bailing out banks in Spain and Italy. Nevertheless, the mutualization of sovereign debt through eurobonds has still not been accepted by the German Chancellor Angela Merkel, at least not without further movement towards political union.

Expanding Membership

In parallel with the expansion of policy scope, membership has also expanded. If we assume that it is more difficult to make decisions in a large group than in a small group (which is not necessarily always the case), this has implications for policies and institutions. This is the way many politicians see it, and that explains why widening has often happened in parallel with deepening – that is, the expansion of policy areas and efforts to improve the institutions.

The first enlargement in 1973 was decided by the Hague Summit in 1969, where the leaders agreed on what they referred to as 'completion, deepening, [and] enlargement'. Completion first of all required agreeing on how to finance the Common Agricultural Policy (CAP). An agreement on 'own resources' – that is, independent sources of revenue for the EC – was reached in 1970. At the same time a Budgetary Treaty, which strengthened the EP slightly in the budgetary process, was adopted. The deepening part also included decisions to start foreign policy cooperation in 1970 in the form of European Political Cooperation (EPC), the predecessor of CFSP, as well as EMU, which was supposed to be realized in a 10-year period, but failed to be realized at the time (Dinan 2010).

The Mediterranean enlargements in the 1980s led to greater emphasis on regional policy, including the concept of 'economic and social cohesion' which was added into the treaty in 1987 by the SEA and eventually led to an important increase in funding of the Structural Funds. Institutionally, the new Article 100a, which introduced QMV for harmonization of much of the legislation needed to complete the internal market, was very important.

The accession of three former members of the European Free Trade Association (EFTA) in 1995 may have had less impact. They were small, rich countries. But as formerly neutral countries there was some concern about the impact on CFSP. Subsequently, Sweden and Finland played an active role in getting the so-called Petersberg tasks explicitly mentioned in the Amsterdam Treaty, the first treaty reform they took part in. Basically, these tasks give a 'soft security' definition of EU defence policy, such as peacemaking, peacekeeping, conflict resolution and so on.

The subsequent 2004 enlargement was much larger and required more preparation both inside the EU and in the applicant states. The deepening versus widening aspect was quite clear during the process. Deepening now especially meant making the EU ready institutionally to function with many more member states. The first effort in the form of the Amsterdam Treaty was not very successful. The next effort, the Treaty of Nice, did produce a reweighting of the votes in the Council, with bigger member states getting relatively more votes than the smaller member states than previously. This was requested by the larger member states to avoid a situation where the smaller member states would be able to dominate after enlargement (Laursen 2006).

However, the outcome of Nice was messy and many political actors felt that more was needed. This explains that reform efforts continued after Nice, first in the form of a so-called European Convention, which involved members of the EP (MEPs) and members of national parliaments (MPs), in the hope of producing a more legitimate treaty. The Convention duly drafted a so-called Constitutional Treaty, which was slightly amended by the member states in a 2003–4 Intergovernmental Conference (IGC). However, this draft treaty was rejected by the French and Dutch voters in referendums in 2005. After a reflection period the Lisbon Treaty was negotiated in much greater secrecy. It took over most of the content of the Constitutional Treaty, but changed the terminology away from explicit 'constitutionalism' (Laursen 2008, 2012a, 2012b).

Enlargements are set to continue in the future for some years at least. Croatia will join in 2013. There are other official candidates: Turkey, Macedonia, Montenegro, Serbia and Iceland, and the remaining states in the Western Balkans have the membership perspective, conditioned upon political, administrative and economic reforms: Albania, Bosnia and eventually Kosovo.

However, it seems there is enlargement fatigue in the EU at the moment. Negotiations with Turkey are barely moving. Negotiations with Macedonia cannot start because of the name dispute with Greece. Eventually, the EU will have to get its act together and get serious about its promises. Were it to pull through the eurozone crisis, it might have time and energy for other urgent matters.

Table 1.2   Expanding membership of the EC/EU

Number of members	Original members (1952)	1st enlargement (1973)	2nd enlargement (1981)	3rd enlargement (1986)	4th enlargement (1995)	5th enlargement (2004)	6th enlargement (2007)	7th enlargement (expected 2013)
28								Croatia
27							Bulgaria	
							Romania	
25						Estonia		
						Latvia		
						Lithuania		
						Poland		
						Czech Republic		
						Slovakia		
						Hungary		
						Slovenia		
						Cyprus		
						Malta		
15					Austria			
					Finland			
					Sweden			
12				Portugal				
				Spain				
10			Greece					
9		Denmark						
		Ireland						
		UK						
6	Belgium							
	France							
	Germany							
	Italy							
	Luxembourg							
	Netherlands							

Source: Compiled by the author.

Improving the Institutional Capacity

I have referred to some of the treaty changes over time. These have been about adding new policies or reforming existing policies. They have also been about the institutions, where there have been two kinds of concerns: efficiency and legitimacy.

It is probably fair to say that efficiency was foremost on the mind of the founding fathers in the 1950s. The supranational High Authority, which was part of the ECSC in 1952, was considered most important by Jean Monnet, who inspired Robert Schuman to propose the so-called Schuman Plan in 1950, pooling the coal and steel sectors of the six original members and creating novel institutions.

The founding fathers also created a Parliamentary Assembly, weak at first, but subsequently the main institutional winner in most treaty reforms that followed. Arguably, this was the case because politicians concluded that, once more decisions were transferred to the supranational level, including budgetary powers from the 1970s, the supranational level required democratic legitimacy (Rittberger 2005).

It is often said that the Commissions of the EEC and EURATOM were less supranational than the High Authority of the ECSC, but still the Commissions had their own prerogatives. They were still supposed to exercise supranational leadership (Lindberg and Scheingold 1970). They were expected to assist the member states overcome collective action problems. Arguably, the very first treaty reform, the Merger Treaty in 1965 – in force in 1967 – was about increasing coordination and cutting down on transaction costs, thus increasing efficiency (Laursen 2012c). However, the increased budgetary powers given to the EP in the two Budgetary Treaties, in 1970 and 1975 respectively, were about democratic legitimacy as so-called 'own resources' were introduced. Customs duties, agricultural levies and a small part of the Value Added Tax (VAT) in the member states would now become EC revenue, escaping the control of national parliaments (Knudsen 2012).

The SEA adopted in the mid-1980s had both efficiency and legitimacy aspects. Most important for efficiency was the new Article 100a, which introduced QMV for much of the legislation required to complete the internal market. At the same time the EP's powers were increased slightly by a new procedure called the 'cooperation procedure', according to which internal market legislation should go through two readings in the EP. The EP also got a veto, known as 'assent' at the time, in respect to association agreements with third states and enlargement (Dinan 2010).

Similarly, the Maastricht Treaty creating the EU responded to a mix of concerns. QMV was extended to a number of new and existing policy chapters in the treaty, and the EP got a right of co-decision in some areas, especially for the internal market. Subsequently, through the Amsterdam, Nice and Lisbon Treaties, QMV and co-decisions were extended to more new and existing policy chapters. After Lisbon most decisions can be made by QMV and the EP has a right of co-decision in most areas, now called the ordinary legislative method (Beach 2005; Laursen 2012c). The EU has started looking more like a bicameral federal system.

The exception to this process of increasing QMV and empowering the EP has been CFSP, and its component the Common Security and Defence Policy (CSDP). CFSP was kept as a separate intergovernmental pillar by the Maastricht Treaty and so was Justice and Home Affairs cooperation (JHA) at the time; but whereas JHA has gradually become communitarized, CFSP retains its intergovernmental nature even in the Lisbon Treaty. This, arguably, is the major shortcoming of the EU as a foreign policy actor (Laursen 2009, 2012b).

The clear trend, over time, with ups and downs, has been a move towards increasing institutional capacity. Some of the more important steps have been taken in parallel with enlargements, sometimes with small time gaps. But the growths in membership continuously produced concerns about institutional capacity. The premise was: the larger the union, the greater the diversity of interests and political cultures, and the greater the difficulty of making decisions. Thus improving the institutions became a part of the deepening of integration together with the expansion of policy scope.

Deepening versus Widening

With the two dimensions of deepening and widening the EU can move in different directions, illustrated as four quadrants in Figure 1.2. Historically, one can argue that the EU has combined widening and deepening. This does not guarantee that the future will be like that. Widening seems to have grinded to a near halt, especially if we look at the situations of Turkey and Macedonia. After the debacle of the Constitutional Treaty it is also difficult see much deepening in the foreseeable future.

The big challenge for our predictions is the eurozone crisis. The Germans are calling for more union, especially fiscal and banking union. However, they may not be able to pull all member states in that direction. They may not even be able to pull all members of the eurozone in that direction. Some members are unhappy with the German insistence on fiscal discipline and austerity at a time when unemployment is high and growth very low or negative. They believe that more fiscal transfers and growth measures are necessary. In the end this has to do with the different member states and their political leaders having different economic doctrines. Political culture may be part of the problem, too. In the end you could argue that we have not yet arrived at that *solidarité de fait* which Robert Schuman spoke about when he made his famous declaration in 1950 that started the whole process of European integration.

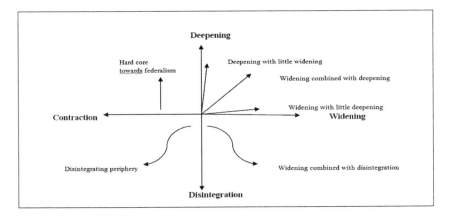

Figure 1.2   Deepening versus widening
Source: Adapted from Wessels 1996 and 2008.

Were Greece and/or other members to exit the eurozone, that might push a smaller eurozone, a kind of hard core, towards more federalism. It is difficult to predict the dynamic this might create. The internal market and some other common policies may well survive among 28 or more member states. A complete collapse of the EU or EMU does not seem likely. The EC/EU has faced serious crises before. The political investments – and economic interdependence – are too great. The EU will most likely move forward, muddling through, not taking the rational strategic decisions federalists would like. The outcome could well be even more variable geometry than today.

Overview of the Chapters in This Book

In Chapter 2 Kurt Hübner gives an economic analysis of the eurozone crisis. When European governments started rescuing banks, public debt increased. When these governments needed international assistance austerity measures were imposed, which in turn weakened growth. Weakened growth made it more difficult for these governments to finance their debt. Basically, a vicious circle set in. It is important to remember that much of the public debt started in the private sector. Hübner is very critical of the approach to the crisis taken by the eurozone leaders, Chancellor Merkel of Germany in particular. He discusses three scenarios, continued muddling through, a Greek exit possibly followed by other exits, and what he calls the 'magical' solution of simultaneously launching banking, fiscal and political union (the 'Three Us'). There is a high probability that the decision makers will continue to muddle through, which may also include a Greek exit. The likelihood of the 'Three Us' is the lowest. It will require time and may not have sufficient political support.

In Chapter 3 Robert Finbow looks at the eurozone crisis from the perspectives of the social dimension and democracy. Again, we get a very critical analysis of the austerity approach which has been run by technocratic political elites with little concern for the views of parliaments and civil society. More austerity has deepened the recession and affected the legitimacy of national governments and EU institutions negatively. There is a danger of a nationalist backlash. It is time for more openness, participation and accountability.

In Chapter 4 Alasdair Blair gives us an account of the United Kingdom's complex relation with EMU as well as the implications of British non-participation. The latest part of the narrative is Prime Minister Cameron's refusal to support the new fiscal treaty – together with the Czech government – which led to the treaty being adopted outside the EU treaty framework among 25 member states. The UK is increasingly ending up on the EU sidelines, thus complicating the situation inside the EU.

The next section looks at other policy developments and challenges. It deals with two of the original common policies, agriculture and trade, both of which were central policy areas in the Treaty of Rome establishing the EEC in 1958. The Common Agricultural Policy (CAP), in particular, became a controversial policy as it started taking a huge part of the Community budget and distorted international trade. Agriculture became a trade issue in the Uruguay Round in the 1980s and eventually international pressure forced the EU to agree on reforms, but from a rational, strategic point of view further reforms could be a good idea. Trade policy as such also faces challenges today in a very competitive environment. To what degree should the EU stick to a multilateral approach within the World Trade Organization (WTO)? To what degree should the EU go for bilateral trade agreements with major trading partners? Indirectly, the two policies are linked with the eurozone problems. A less expensive CAP could leave more money for job creation in other areas, and freer international trade can produce jobs.

In Chapter 5 Jacek Chotkowski and Benon Gaziński deal with the CAP. providing the historic background for the policy from the provisions in the Treaty of Rome of 1957 establishing the EEC to its more detailed development in the early 1960s. We learn how the policy eventually started to be a problem, becoming expensive both for the EEC budget and for consumers, producing surpluses that led to the dumping of farm products on the world markets and producing conflicts with trading partners. Reforms started slowly in the 1980s, were speeded up in the 1990s, and remained on the agenda prior to the big enlargement in 2004 and during its aftermath. The detailed account of the current policy suggests that it has become a bureaucratic monster in need of radical simplification. But can the Brussels bureaucracy carry out such a simplification? Can our political leaders exercise the necessary political leadership? The CAP still consumes about 40% of the EU budget. Might not some of that money be better spent elsewhere?

In Chapter 6 Stefanie Rosskopf studies the EU–Canada free trade negotiations, which should lead to a Comprehensive Economic and Trade Agreement (CETA). It is a test case for the European Commission's new global trade strategy which will have important ramifications for international trade. Important but also controversial issues on the agenda are public procurement, services, investments and enforcement. A joint report has found important benefits for both sides from the CETA. But as usual there are vested interests in the status quo that will require political leadership to overcome. EU trade commissioner Karel de Gucht has explicitly seen the EU's more ambitious bilateral trade agenda as part of an exit strategy for the financial crisis. There are both practical and symbolic reasons for adopting the CETA.

The next section turns to the deepening versus widening discussion. Where is the EU going? Can the democratic deficit be remedied? Will the eurozone split up, and, if so, what consequences will it have for the integration project? Can the EU – including the Schengen area – widen further despite enlargement fatigue and anxiety?

In Chapter 7 Ece Özlem Atikcan looks at direct democracy and its role in the EU. Using referendums for major EU decisions is a possible way to involve the citizens more, but this strategy is not without problems. When voting about a new treaty it can be argued that the 'no' side has an advantage over the 'yes' side. It is easy to produce scare scenarios, making claims that have no foundation in the treaty the voters are being asked to vote about. On the other hand, criticizing a European policy is often seen as opposing EU membership in these debates. Therefore an alternative and better strategy to encourage more involvement might be regular debate of EU issues within the member states, which basically means a greater politicization of the issues. Such a strategy depends on the politicians, political parties, governments, EU institutions and, not least, the media. Governments can often use the EU as a scapegoat for a particular problem, while some of the media are more concerned with sensationalism than with giving an accurate account of European issues. Getting balanced debates can be a challenge.

In Chapter 8 Imtiaz Hussain turns to the implications of a possible Greek default. He provides us with a lot of facts about the development of the crisis and the Greek situation. He is very critical of the role of the credit rating agencies, whose rankings have affected the financial markets to the detriment of solutions created by governments and international institutions. There are many other elements, including nationalism, asymmetry and external influence. Obviously, the role of Germany is important if the splitting up of the eurozone, and possibly the Union, is to be avoided.

In Chapter 9 Ruben Zaiotti traces the history of Schengen cooperation with an emphasis on enlargement, from the original five members in the 1980s to the current 26 members, which include four non-EU members, namely Norway, Iceland, Lichtenstein and Switzerland. These members of the European Free Trade Association (EFTA) all have close economic relations with the EU. Except Switzerland they take part in the European Economic Area (EEA), which makes them part of the single market. Two EU countries, the UK and Ireland, have chosen to stay outside Schengen, and three EU countries are waiting to join, namely Bulgaria, Romania and Cyprus. The Schengen cooperation started outside the European Community in 1985. It was consolidated with the Schengen Implementation Convention in 1990. The Schengen *acquis* was subsequently incorporated in the EU by the Amsterdam Treaty, which entered into force in 1999. Currently, the accession of Bulgaria and Romania is controversial since some member states feel that these countries cannot assure external border control well enough. Zaiotti draws attention to the role of anxiety in the development of the European project and we learn that such anxiety existed in the past, too. He focuses on Italy and Denmark as case studies. The core five members especially had doubts about the southern countries which subsequently joined. In the Italian case it was only in 1997 that the country was finally accepted. Refugees from the former Yugoslavia and Albania during the 1990s contributed to the anxiety, the fear that many illegal immigrants would get into 'Schengenland' via Italy. In the case of Denmark, the main complication was the Nordic passport union going back to the 1950s. When Sweden and Finland joined the EU in 1995 this still left Norway and Iceland outside. The three Nordic EU members could not accept reintroducing border controls for people entering from those two countries. Eventually, the Schengen members accepted all five Nordic countries as members.

In Chapter 10 Kiran Phull and John Sutcliffe turn to current developments within the Schengen area, with a focus on the closing of the Franco-Italian border in 2011when Italy gave temporary residence permits to immigrants from Libya. The French government closed the border to Italy for these new entrants, arguably in violation of Schengen rules. Eventually, a solution was found, but it included a modification of rules allowing for temporary border controls. The authors mention other cases where countries have reintroduced controls, including the Danish Liberal–Conservative government's introduction of border controls in the spring of 2011, under the influence of the anti-immigrant, nationalist party, the Danish People's Party. Luckily for the spirit of Schengen, the new Social Democratic-led government abolished these controls in September 2011. But the incidents suggest that borders have become – and remain – politicized and securitized, thus threatening one of the main achievements of European integration, the free movement of people.

Finally, in the conclusion the editor reflects on the future of European integration. Have we reached a certain plateau or equilibrium, or are we moving towards more 'variable geometry' where different groups of countries take part in different policies? Are decisions becoming more difficult in a larger union? Will we see a smaller group of countries moving forward, leaving the laggards on the sidelines? And might that create a new dynamic where the laggards eventually will conclude that the costs of exclusion are too high? Or will variable geometry produce *á la carte* integration with countries picking and choosing only what is best for themselves, not caring for the collective interest? For the EU to move forward and avoid collapse, leadership and solidarity are in high demand.

References

Beach, D. (2005), *The Dynamics of European Integration: Why and When EU Institutions Matter.* Houndmills: Palgrave Macmillan.

CEPR (1995), *Flexible Integration: Towards a More Effective and Democratic Europe.* Monitoring European Integration 6. London: Centre for Economic Policy Research.

Dinan, D. (2010), *Ever Closer Union: An Introduction to European Integration.* Houndmills: Palgrave Macmillan.

Dyson, K. (2000), *The Politics of the Euro-Zone: Stability or Breakdown?* Oxford: Oxford University Press.

Geza, P. and L. Giurca Vasilescu (2011), 'The Optimum Currency Area. Is the Euro Zone an Optimum Currency Area?' MPRA Paper No 29656. http://mpra.ub.uni-muenchen.de/29656/1/MPRA_paper_29656.pdf (accessed 15 August 2012).

Hodson, D. (2010), 'Economic and Monetary Union: An Experiment in New Modes of EU Policy-making', in Helen Wallace, Mark A. Pollack and Alasdair R. Young (eds), *Policy-making in the European Union*, 6th edn. Oxford: Oxford University Press, 158–80.

Knudsen, A.-C.L. (2012), 'The 1970 and 1975 Budget Treaties. Enhancing the Democratic Architecture of the Community', in Finn Laursen (ed.), *Designing the European Union: From Paris to Lisbon.* Basingstoke: Palgrave, 98–123.

Kölliker, A. (2006), *Flexibility and European Unification: The Logic of Differentiated Integration.* Lanham, MD: Rowman and Littlefield.

Laursen, F. (1990), 'Explaining the EC's New Momentum', in Finn Laursen (ed.), *EFTA and the EC: Implications of 1992.* Maastricht: European Institute of Public Administration, 33–52.

Laursen, F. (1992), 'Explaining the Intergovernmental Conference on Political Union', in Finn Laursen and Sophie Vanhoonacker (eds), *The Intergovernmental Conference on Political Union: Institutional Reforms, New Policies and International Identity of the European Community.* Maastricht: European Institute of Public Administration, 229–48.

Laursen, F. (ed.) (2006), *The Treaty of Nice: Actor Preferences, Bargaining and Institutional Choice.* Leiden: Martinus Nijhoff.

Laursen, F. (ed.) (2008), *The Rise and Fall of the EU's Constitutional Treaty.* Leiden: Martinus Nijhoff.

Laursen, F. (ed.) (2012a), *The Making of the EU's Lisbon Treaty: The Role of Member States.* Brussels: PIE–Peter Lang.

Laursen, F. (ed.) (2012b), *The EU's Lisbon Treaty: Institutional Choices and Implementation.* Farnham: Ashgate.

Laursen, F. (ed.) (2012c), *Designing the European Union: From Paris to Lisbon.* Basingstoke: Palgrave.

Lindberg, L.N. and S.A. Scheingold (1970), *Europe's Would-be Polity: Patterns of Change in the European Community*. Englewood Cliffs, NJ: Prentice-Hall, Inc.

McNamara, K. (2005), 'Economic and Monetary Union', in Helen Wallace, William Wallace, and Mark A. Pollack (eds), *Policy-making in the European Union*, 5th edn. Oxford: Oxford University Press, 141–60.

Mallaby, S. (2012), 'Europe's Optional Catastrophe: The Fate of the Monetary Union Lies in Germany's Hands', *Foreign Affairs* 91(4) (July/August), 6–10.

Olsen, L.L. (2006), 'Enhanced Cooperation: Lowering the Restrictions – and Creating the Basis of a Hard Core?', in Finn Laursen (ed.), *The Treaty of Nice: Actor Preferences, Bargaining and Institutional Choice*. Leiden: Martinus Nijhoff, 459–76.

Piris, J.-C. (2006), *The Constitution for Europe: A Legal Analysis*. Cambridge: Cambridge University Press.

Piris, J.-C. (2010), *The Lisbon Treaty: A Legal and Political Analysis*. Cambridge: Cambridge University Press.

Rittberger, B. (2005), *Building Europe's Parliament: Democratic Representation beyond the Nation State*. Oxford: Oxford University Press.

Sbragia, A. and F. Stolfi (2008), 'Key Policies', in Elizabeth Bomberg, John Peterson and Alexander Stubb (eds), *The European Union: How Does it Work?*, 2nd edn. Oxford: Oxford University Press, 115–37.

Stubb, A. (2002a), *Negotiating Flexibility in the European Union: Amsterdam, Nice and Beyond*. Houndmills: Palgrave.

Stubb, A. (2002b), 'Negotiating Flexible Integration', in Finn Laursen (ed.), *The Amsterdam Treaty: National Preference Formation, Interstate Bargaining and Outcome*. Odense: Odense University Press, 537–64.

Verdun, A. (2011), 'The EU and the Global Political Economy', in Christopher Hill and Michael Smith (eds), *International Relations and the European Union*, 2nd edn. Oxford: Oxford University Press, 246–74.

Verhelst, S. (2011), *The Reform of European Economic Governance: Towards a Sustainable Monetary Union?* Egmont Paper 47. Brussels: Royal Institute for International Relations.

Wessels, W. (1996), 'Evolution possible de l'Union européenne. Scénarios et stratégies pour sortir d'un cercle vicieux', *Politique Étrangère* 1, 139–50.

Wessels, W. (2008), *Das politische System der Europäischen Union*. Wiesbaden: VS Verlag für Sozialwissenschaften.

PART II
The Eurozone Crisis

Chapter 2

Eurozone: Creeping Decay, Sudden Death or Magical Solution?

Kurt Hübner

Patterning

Since the outbreak of sovereign debt default crises in a number of eurozone economies a pattern of interactions between financial markets, national governments and European Union (EU) agencies emerged that is being repeated time and again. When, after the disclosure of the Greek financial debacle in 2009, financial market actors began to be sensitive to the levels of public debt of some member economies in the eurozone by way of demanding higher risk premiums, it was up to national governments, and more so the EU and its respective political bodies, to calm this nervousness by putting policies in place that would address the underlying problems. However, for quite a while the majority of member governments, as well as the Commission and the European Council, decided to play dumb and to follow a strategy of procrastination (Hübner 2012) by responding slowly and hesitantly to the concerns of financial markets. When this hesitation triggered further increases of yields for some sovereign debtors, and consequently raised doubts regarding the viability of the eurozone and its political and financial architecture, it was eventually the European Council and the European Central Bank (ECB) that moved forward in May 2010 with the first bail-out attempt of Greece. Still, crisis resolution policies were packaged in small doses and were quickly rejected by financial market actors as insufficient to tackle the underlying problems. The ensuing increases in yields eventually pushed political bodies to demand even harsher austerity programs than the ones already in place. The political and economic implementation problems with these programs, as well as their negative effects on economic growth, contributed to the increasing nervousness of financial markets.[1] In order to calm these concerns, national governments were forced to introduce even harsher austerity programs that then met the resistance of broad sectors of the society, and in many cases resulted in elections that brought new governments into office; however, the result

---

1 Greece may easily be the case with the worst practice. Since its first troika program, the rate of implementation of agreed measures stays extremely low. Implementation failures add more hardship to society as creditors have the habit of imposing even harsher measures in case committed targets have been missed.

of this was that newly designed austerity programs were soon running into even more political trouble. Attempts to soften or delay imposed austerity measures on the side of national governments were seen as proof of institutionally embedded moral hazard, where some governments wanted to avoid the political fallout of the adjustment burden.[2] The emerging political conflict in those countries, and also between respective governments and the so-called 'troika' (the ECB, EU and the International Monetary Fund (IMF)), were understood by financial market actors as a confirmation of their overall skepticism towards adequate political crisis responses, and this triggered a further sell-off of government bonds. Critical increases in yields then kick-started the next round of high-level meetings, which resulted in new crisis programs and even in changes to the fundaments of the euro architecture – only to again fail to meet the expectations of financial markets.[3]

The most recent summit of June 28/29, 2012, very much confirmed this pattern. Brief euphoria about the summit statement was followed by deep skepticism, and eventually higher risk premiums for Spain and Italy as well as an even further slide of the euro exchange rate against top currencies. How long will this pattern last? Will this game continue or will it change either by finally overcoming the crisis or by the break-up of the eurozone?

Reminder

Let us not get it wrong. The sovereign debt crisis did not start with Greece and its roots are not public debt, at least not directly.[4] The sovereign debt crises of various eurozone economies are connected to the 'Great Crisis', which began as a mortgage crisis in the United States (US) and soon spread as a fully-fledged

---

2   The Spanish Conservative majority government recently asked for 'special treatment'. What it got was an extension of adjustment time of one year. Immediately after this deal the government came forward with further austerity measures that should amount to public savings of about 65 billion euro over two years. Briefly after this program passed a majority vote in the Parliament the risk premium for all sorts of Spanish government bonds climbed to new record heights.

3   Only a few weeks and further reforms and austerity measures of the Monti technocratic cabinet as well as the June 2012 Summit later, the rating agency Moody's continued to downgrade Italian government bonds that are now close to junk status. Refinancing costs in the first quarter 2012 amounted to 19 billion euro – an increase of 3 billion compared to the first quarter of 2011. If the risk premium stays at such a level the government needs to find additionally savings of 12 billion euro only to finance the increase in the premium. That means any 'austerity gains' are claimed by risk premiums of financial markets.

4   Having said that, it needs to be stressed that Greece indeed is the case where the political class has exploited the state (coffers) in order to save power. This resulted in a widening scissor effect between tax receipts and expenditures. After joining the eurozone, the gap was easy to finance as international banks saw Greece as a solvent and liquid creditor and thus was not asked for risk premiums.

financial capitalism crisis to other parts of the global economy. The burst of the real state bubble in the US that began in 2007 came with strong contagion effects, not least due to the securitization practices that came with the small-sizing and re-packaging of a broad range of assets that were then marketed across the global financial industry. When the underlying values of securitized financial products lost value or the quality was increasingly questioned by interconnected banks, contagion started to spread and began to threaten the viability of the global finance industry. Financial crises are well-known phenomena of capitalism, as are bank runs and sovereign debt defaults (Reinhart and Rogoff 2009). The huge rise in international banking since the 1980s laid the foundation for one of the most encompassing financial crises in recent history.[5] The driver of this process of financial globalization was the speed and depth of financial innovation that has been triggered by mature capitalist economies adopting encompassing policies of liberalization and de-regulation. Securitization and the launch of a broad variety of special purpose financial vehicles as well as processes of financial off-sharing, over-the-counter practices, and the emergence of shadow banking, made international finance the dominant feature of many advanced capitalist economies.[6] The launch of the euro gave the integration of European money and credit markets a huge push and moved it into a premier position of global finance:

> The elimination of currency risk among the member countries means that there is a much higher degree of substitutability between domestic and foreign securities, which has contributed to a substantial reduction in home bias and increased financial trade within the euro area. Moreover, the greater depth and liquidity of a single area-wide financial market has also boosted financial trade vis-à-vis non-member countries. (Indeed, the United Kingdom has been a primary beneficiary as a key center for euro-denominated financial trade, although it is not a member of the monetary union) (Lane and Milesi-Ferreti 2008: 327f).

---

5   I follow the definition given by the Committee on the Global Financial System (2010, 4f): '… we define international banking as intermediation activity that falls into one of the following categories. The extension of credit by a bank headquartered in a particular country to residents of another country can occur via: (i) cross-border lending; (ii) local lending by affiliates established in the foreign country; (iii) lending booked by an affiliate established in a third country … In addition, the BIS international banking statistics on a residency basis include the extension of credit by a bank headquartered in a particular country to residents of the same country but in a foreign currency. The underlying financial instruments could be loans, deposits or securities as well as derivatives contracts and contingent facilities'.

6   Equally important, and in some respect a requisite of the processes of financialization, was the transformation of traditional banking systems to the 'originate and distribute'-banking model. In this model loans are getting pooled, sliced and repackaged, mostly in forms of securitization.

Of course, in the case of the eurozone, aftershocks from the Great Crisis met an already weakened and highly flawed financial market liberalization project that had the common currency in its core. Not only did it turn out that the supposedly high substitutability between domestic and foreign but euro area-wide assets are actually low in times of turbulence, and consequently races to safe havens began to occur, but it also turned out that the passive character of financial integration, and thus the co-existence of under-powered national supervisory and regulatory bodies, were excellent ingredients for the accumulation of risky assets and liabilities that needed only a small push in order to generate fundamental banking and financial crises. Rescue operations for banks and the overall financial industry made it paramount for member states to take action, with the consequence that even in economies with relatively low public debt ratios pre-crisis, the situation was now reversed. Ireland and Spain are the most prominent examples in this respect. 'Sudden stops' of private capital inflows began to threaten the accumulation regimes, and generated various forms of public financial support flows in order to close the gap. The initial European Financial Stability Mechanism (EFSM), as well as the newly launched European Stability Mechanism (ESM), provide suffering governments with conditional funding which usually takes the form of new public debt. National programs to socialize bank losses resulted in further increases in public debt. Shattered national banking industries and the sudden cut-off from capital markets and thus access to credit further undermined the already weak growth regimes, and as a result tax receipts began decreasing. The result of this vicious cycle was a sudden increase in public debt, in particular in economies that had entered the crisis with relatively low levels. Despite all the attention that has been directed towards public debt, it is the still high level of private debt that rattles eurozone economies (Figure 2.1).

Households and non-financial sectors are deep in debt, as are the financial sectors of most of the troubled eurozone economies.[7] The few studies that deal with balance sheet adjustments of non-governmental financial sectors are by Ahearne and Wolff (2012), and Ruscher and Wolff (2012). These authors report much higher corporate debt levels to GDP for EU companies than for US companies. In particular, between 1999 and 2008 this ratio jumped by 40 percentage points and was at 105% in 2008, only to decline slightly as the outcome of strong deleveraging efforts of financial and non-financial corporations (Ahearne and Wolff 2012: 2ff).[8]

---

7   In the last two years those sectors started ambitious and 'successful' deleveraging in order to clean up their balance sheets. The resulting negative effects for economic growth were amplified by austerity programs, and eventually led to increasing public debt ratios.

8   Spain and Portugal belong to the group of economies with jumps of 70–80 percentage points in the period.

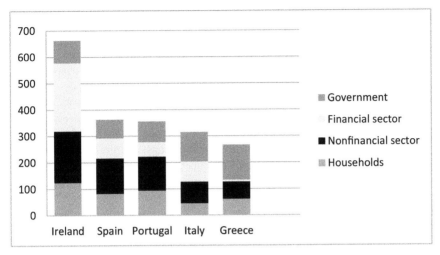

Figure 2.1   Composition of total debt, % of GDP, 2Q 2011
Source: McKinsey Global Institute 2012: 5.

This build-up of private debt, as already indicated, is closely linked to the common currency project and at the same time part of the global *wave of financialization* that swept the EU and the global economy during the 1990s.[9] Long before the new currency was put in place, the member economies of the EU were obliged to begin comprehensive liberalization programs of their financial industries which allowed for the free circulation of money and capital across the EU. European banks made ample use of financial innovations and participated heavily in international banking and the emerging global markets in structured derivatives. This resulted in a deeper integration of EU-wide financial markets and contributed simultaneously to the emerging narrative that with the abolition of exchange rate risks between the eurozone members all quality risks of financial assets and liabilities would also disappear. The eventual launch of the euro then offered the opportunity for easy access to relatively cheap credit in value-stable money, and economic actors, in particular those from economies that were catching-up, made ample use of this opportunity. Paradoxically, it was the unintended effects of actions by the ECB that provided an incentive for economic actors to go increasingly into debt. Imagine for a moment the eurozone as consisting of economies with varying inflation rates. In a common currency area an economy with an above-average inflation rate still enjoys identical nominal interest rates as any other member economy. This implies

---

9   The two most prominent cases of financialization are the US and the UK. Both economies deal with long-term negative repercussions of the debt-overhang, admittedly under different circumstances than eurozone economies.

that the real interest rates differ. Actors of economies with above-average inflation rates enjoy relatively lower, and in extreme cases even negative real interest rates. This is an incentive to use credit to finance consumption or investment activities that then helps to spur economic growth. The availability of credit fed housing booms in Spain and Portugal allowed Greek governments to make use of outside funds to finance public deficits, and was the source used to close the gap of current account deficit economies in the eurozone. Those funds were available and needed to be channeled into lucrative opportunities due to the current account surpluses of a few eurozone economies that required steady liquidity transfers in order to maximize the portfolios of the financial industry. Consequently Greece, Ireland, Italy, Spain, and Portugal made use of this opportunity and thus saw strong inflows of private capital that reached up to 50% of all inflows (Merler and Pisani-Ferry 2012: 9). This stopped in the aftermath of the Great Crisis, and private inflows were substituted by official capital inflows that simultaneously increased the share of public debt in the receiving economies. The possibility of systemic banking crises in troubled eurozone economies motivated governments to intervene and to inject capital into suffering banks, directly or indirectly; to acquire impaired bank assets; and to guarantee assets respectively bank liabilities. All these actions obviously jeopardized public finances. In cases such as Ireland and Spain it resulted in an explosion of public debt and public debt ratios, initially far below the eurozone-average, began to skyrocket. The already impaired public finances of Greece and Portugal experienced further instability, resulting in increased yields.

All this is well known and should guide the understanding as well as the solving of the ongoing crises. Yet, politics is a different beast. Public crisis discourse, as well as official crisis management, is all about public debt and not a word about the private credit orgies of the past. Unfortunately, this wrong-headed public discourse has rather serious consequences for the type of crisis management that is only about taming public deficits and debt. For non-experts this seems quite understandable from today's perspective, as most of the eurozone economies are indeed struggling with high public deficits and piles of public debt, and voters do not care much whether the deficits and debts are the outcome of spending sprees of government, the fiscal reflex of saving national banking industries or the result of fiscal stabilizers that worked so well during the Great Recession.[10]

---

10   The myth of a general public debt crisis is just a myth, but a powerful myth as it guides public conversations and also crisis management. It is not necessary, though, to consult critical academic reports to get a better and more adequate understanding of what happened. McKinsey Germany (2012: 12), for example, gives a good summary: 'However, if deficits are mainly run to fund consumption, public or private, or real estate expenditures, such deficits are less benign. ... This has happened in Southern European countries. In Greece, consumption was responsible for 92 per cent of GDP growth between 2000 and 2008, compared with 72 per cent in Northern European economies during the same period. Southern Europe had large, mainly private, foreign debts. Private debt levels increased even more dramatically than public debts, but, as the global banking crisis unfolded, a great

However, any sustainable solution to the crises will have to deal with *all* of the mechanisms and structures that caused the problem, and not solely with public finances. It only requires a brief 'counterfactual analysis' to figure out what the implications of a truly fiscal compact would look like. If a rather rigid version of the fiscal compact had been in place when the sovereign debt default crises began, then it would not have been possible to counter the effects of the imminent deleveraging of private sectors, and to offer rescue programs for ailing banking industries, at least not without a drastic reshuffling of state budgets, which would have destroyed any public support for such a policy approach. In other words, an existing (rigid) fiscal compact would have bounded economic policymaking in such a way that widespread bank failure and sovereign debt defaults would have become the norm.

The fact that governments of all political stripes were not constrained by a fiscal compact and therefore could act to maintain financial stability was critical, but it came with the price of a steep increase in public debt. In most cases this increase should not be seen as an indication of fiscal profligacy but rather as the reflex of failed growth regimes that were based on structures of strong financialization and weak (price and quality) competitiveness. Of course such an analytical view contradicts the well-established narrative of sovereign debt default crises as public finance crises, and thus opposes the popular crisis management recipe of 'pure austerity'. Unfortunately, such an analysis is not connected to a straightforward alternative crisis resolution policy. Besides some indispensable corrections of the eurozone architecture, it probably requires a case-by-case approach to adequately deal with the challenges on ground.

Bad Equilibrium

It is now well understood that economies plagued by sovereign debt default crises are trapped in bad equilibria. Bad equilibria are situations in which social actors are under the influence of self-fulfilling mechanisms that reinstate and reinforce the initial situation. Low trust and uncertainty feed expectations of economic and political actors; these are thus confirmed by the outcomes of the isolated actions of those agents. The various sovereign debt crises of eurozone economies, as well as the ensuing euro crisis, can best be understood as the perfectly functioning interplay of five types of crisis (see Figure 2.2) which characterizes a bad equilibrium.

---

deal of this private debt became public due to public bailouts of ailing financial institutions aimed at containing systemic externalities. Sovereign debt levels, which had been relatively stable before the banking crisis and, in some cases, even improved, now increased strongly. Some countries were more severely affected than others. For example, in Ireland, where the government was forced into a large-scale bailout ... public debt increased from less than 30 per cent to more than 90 per cent and is likely to reach more than 110 per cent in 2012'.

Figure 2.2   Crises cycle
Source: Author.

During this critical situation it turned out that the governance structure of the eurozone was not at all prepared to deal with the challenges ahead. 'Muddling through' became the rule of the day, and from Council meeting to Council meeting only band-aid solutions were provided, until the next wound was detected. The national governments of troubled economies tried to make use of their (shrinking) negotiation powers but overall were willing to accept the austerity 'medicine'. In cases such as Greece, Spain, Portugal, Ireland and Italy, this led to the discharge of governments, only to bring in new governments that were sticking to the prescribed 'treatment'. The political situation differs between members, but it would not be an exaggeration to conclude that the level of 'political legitimacy' that governments have is in decline. Even if we – probably falsely – assume that the political protest comes only from marginal sectors of society, it is still obvious that one-sided austerity programs are running against the political and social limits of troubled nation-states. Maybe just as important is the fact that the European Council's crisis responses are increasingly generating legal concerns as, for example, in the case of Germany where the Constitutional Court has to deal with a collection of law suits that question the constitutionality of newly created mechanisms like the ESM, or the bond-buying activities of the European Central Bank. In countries such as Finland and the Netherlands, rescue operations run up against the political limits of vast sectors of the electorate who refuse to send more 'good money' to economies that are widely seen as 'failed states'. Aglietta (2012: 24) recently stressed that the history of monetary unions indicates two opposing paths of development: they can either disappear, or can move towards constitutional political sovereignty. Even though his examples are technically not applicable, as the EMU is neither a multinational currency union (like, for example, the Scandinavian Monetary Union) nor a national currency union (like, for example, the United States of America) but rather a currency union *sui generis* (Eichengreen 2010). I agree that eventually one of those paths will materialize. Before any bifurcation can be observed, however, the eurozone will enter deep into the phase of political uncertainty where non-cooperation dominates. Muddling through is the name of the game.

In the Zone of Political Uncertainty

The eurozone entered a zone of instability and multiple equilibria when the aftershock of the 2007 crisis hit its shores. Since then, uncertainty has increased and markets have become driven by expectations and economic narratives that perfectly reflect the reduced level of trust in established practices and rules. The lack of consistent and decisive political crisis management has added to the uncertainty and helped put financial markets – not the most suitable adjudicators of economic risk management - into the driver's seat. The interplay between various subsets of crises moved the eurozone into a state of 'bad equilibrium' that will be difficult to overcome. The strong and seemingly increasing interdependencies between the various stages of the crisis cycle trap troubled economies, and actually the entire eurozone, in a situation with three possible outcomes.

First, continuing with the muddling through approach that needs, from time to time, small but pompous economic policy injections in order to avoid the worst case scenario, even though the quality of such a 'bad equilibrium' will suffer over time. The slow decay of the eurozone is then the future. Second, 'Grexit', Spexit', or for that matter 'Gexit' (German exit) may be seen as the individual first best option, and this would be the sudden death of the eurozone, at least in the form we know it. A third possibility is the 'magical' simultaneous launch of a banking union, a fiscal union as well as a political union. This seems to be the preferred option of the German government, or at least critical parts of it, and is getting support at eurozone summits. Let me briefly discuss those options by starting with the latter.

1) The hope that the 'three Us' – banking union, fiscal union, and political union – may ultimately solve the eurozone crisis, is rooted in the conviction that money is historically (as well as theoretically) connected to the nation-state. This view definitely has a significant amount of merit but cannot contribute much at this moment to fix the serious problems. Even if one is more optimistic in regards to the survival chances of the eurozone than the International Monetary Fund (headed by Christine Lagarde, who already in June 2012 gave the euro not more than three months to figure out an appropriate path to overcome the crisis), it is clear that the 'three Us' are long-term projects that also come with many implementation risks. I see such a solution as magic because all three variants of union would require fundamental transfers of sovereignty away from the nation-state, and/or the willingness of national governments to agree: to mutualize national debts, to make the ECB to an unrestricted lender of last resort, and to give the European Parliament, as well as the Commission, overriding rights over national parliaments. Despite the EU's history of using crises as movers towards deeper integration, it seems that the probability of such an outcome is very low. Unlike previous crises, the sovereign debt default crises are getting a far broader and deeper active (as well as passive) involvement of national political audiences – and these audiences increasingly seem to lose confidence in the euro and even in the project of European integration. Such a change in attitude even makes it difficult for Europhile politicians to actively advertise deeper integration as a method of overcoming the current crisis. Euroskepticism elevates political hurdles for an encompassing strategy even higher. Moreover, the legal hurdles may be insurmountable. In Germany, the Constitutional Court has already begun to define new legal interpretations that make the mutualization of debt, and forms of banking as well as financial unions into a politically difficult or even impossible undertaking. Those hurdles make the 'three Us' more of a vision than an actual crisis management tool that can be of use today. It is exactly this contradiction in time horizons of crisis management needs and crisis management tools that disqualifies the 'three Us' as a feasible strategy to successfully address the crisis at this time.

2) It is a sure bet that any disorderly exit of one or more eurozone member economies would generate disruptive and negative effects for the deserting economy, the eurozone, as well as the global economy. Bank runs and the closure of access to international credit markets may be the two most prominent features of such an option, and given the interconnectivity of eurozone economies, as well as the overall degree of nervousness of global financial markets, such a strategy has the potential to kick-start a global crisis. Things may be less dramatic in the case of an orderly exit of one or more economies. Greece is currently the most probable candidate to leave the eurozone, and this may happen sooner rather than later. Greece is not the only candidate, though, as others may see an exit as the best option available to overcome their bad equilibria. It has been argued that – given the ability to exit in an orderly fashion – the economic incentives in (aggregated) terms of growth effects, borrowing costs, and balance sheet effects to exit the

eurozone are strongest for Italy and Ireland, whereas the incentive to leave is lowest for Germany (Woo and Vamvakidis 2012).[11] As the EU seems unable to move out of its 'bad equilibrium' and thus to overcome uncooperative strategies on the part of main players, the probability that one government is opting for an orderly exit increases with each increase in yields.[12] Italy is indeed a prominent exit candidate, and Italy's political players have already indicated their willingness to make Italy leave the eurozone. Since 1988 (!) and only with a few short crisis-related interruptions various Italian governments posted primary surpluses, and thus did, for example, better than Germany in this respect; however, since Italy came into cross wires of financial markets, their primary surpluses were given away in order to finance the increased risk premiums. Continuing efforts by the Monti government to increase the primary surplus over time are not targeted towards an absolute reduction of the debt level, but only prepare the pool to finance the yield asked for by financial markets. Leaving the eurozone and returning to its own currency has the potential to break this circuit, even though it would come with net economic and social costs in the short-run. The case is slightly different for Spain, mainly due to its far lower absolute public debts. However, overall (public plus private) Spanish debts are even higher than Italy's. Its shattered banking sector is closely connected to the burst of the real estate bubble. The massive austerity program of the new Spanish conservative government not only prolongs the economic decline and drives the rise of unemployment to record levels but also meets increasingly with social protest. This protest has the potential to mobilize anti-EU sentiments, and a desperate government may see the chance to break the vicious cycle by exiting the eurozone. If Italy (or Spain, for that matter) decides to leave, this would trigger an avalanche effect, and probably turn a planned orderly exit into a disorderly exit. Still, assumed that a stampede can be avoided exit may seems to become the more attractive the less cooperative attitudes prevail in the European Council.

3) Muddling through and hoping that the markets will eventually buckle seems to be the hope of the current policy approach. The strategy to move forward in small steps without offering a full turn-around may continue to prevent a full breakup of the eurozone. This strategy may include making Greece leave by way of refusing

---

11   A study by McKinsey Germany (2012) comes to similar conclusions. The study tries to quantify the economic effects of membership in the eurozone and comes to the conclusion that the benefits in 2010 amounted to euro 332 billion (3.6% of the GDP of the eurozone). Half of the benefits were accrued by Germany. Those figures indicate the 'economic value' of the euro and stresses simultaneously why Germany should have a strong interest in keeping the eurozone intact. Then Sachverständigenrat zur Begutachtung der gesamtwirtschaftlichen Entwicklung embarks in its special study from July 2012 on a different route by calculating the actual claims of Germany against eurozone member economies to around euro 3 trillion. This figure can be read as a defensive pro-argument to rescue the eurozone.

12   The study by Wood and Vamvakidis employs a game theory approach and argues that uncooperative outcomes (Nash equilibrium) dominate the situation.

a third rescue program due to insufficient efforts by Greek governments and by the refusal of the ECB to buy additional Greek government bonds. The route is already prepared. In case the IMF retires from the troika, this would no longer allow governments of the Netherlands and also Finland to continue their support for Greece. Chancellor Merkel would have enormous problems getting a majority in the Parliament for a third rescue package as her coalition partner made clear that support is running out. Unlike in the first two years of the crisis, a Greek exit may not be the end of the euro but only a change in the composition of the eurozone. Such a change comes with risks and costs.[13] Still, two developments work in favour of the muddling through approach which entails the exit of Greece. First, Greece's exit would result in a further depreciation of the exchange rate of the euro, as international investors will fear contagion.[14] If the ECB and the European Council are able to make proper use of the existing crisis management tools, they can manage the depreciation to their advantage. A *controlled depreciation* would significantly improve international price competitiveness and give the export sector, even in a relatively depressed global economy, a push.[15] A weaker euro exchange rate against the US dollar, but also the renminbi, would strongly improve the survival chances of the euro but only to the disadvantage of other currency areas – and they may see such revival as a 'currency war'. Second, and somewhat contradictory to the previous argument, the probably still unresolved debt situation in the US may redirect the attention of financial markets across the Atlantic and provide the eurozone with a period of tranquility. At the moment, the US benefits from sailing under the wind of the eurozone crisis, but this will change when the political impasse plays out at the end of the year and the automatic budget cuts begin. Muddling through would not solve the eurozone crisis, but would add time resources to the political system. Still, in order for this to work out the European Council, and more so the ECB, would have to continue their crisis management efforts by bank recapitalization programs, via direct equity injections from the ESM, and by pan-European deposit guarantee schemes, as well as by the proper funding of the ESM.

At the time of writing I calculate the following probability values for each option: (i) 'three Us': 5%; (ii) exit of two or more members: 20%–30%; exit of Greece: 70% (iii): muddling through: 70%. The low probability value for (i) has to do with the simple fact that magic is in scarce supply. Even though European politicians under the leadership of Chancellor Merkel will continue talking about a closer political union, such a project will – if at all – not come quickly, and in

---

13   See next section.

14   Such a depreciation against key currencies can go hand in hand with an appreciation of the euro against a new drachma – in any case, a new Greek currency will be weak and anyway probably only see small turnovers at global foreign exchange markets.

15   Controlled depreciation is a difficult business and would imply an active exchange rate management on the side of the ECB plus a well-orchestrated voice common voice by national governments.

the hypothetical case that it does come it may arrive with other 'meanings' than experts of today would expect. In fact, the German interpretation of the 'three Us' differs fundamentally from the concepts provided by some (mainly Anglo-Saxon) economists. The latter imply the mutualization of debt, direct capital injections to banks, turning the ECB into a true lender of last resort, when phrases like 'banking union', or for that matter 'political union' come up. The German understanding of the 'three Us' comes with even closer fiscal controls, debt brakes and high fines in case of violations and a much smaller dose of sovereignty transfer than is required. In reality these differences are not important at all, as the current political and legal situation in core EU economies rejects the feasibility of any of those plans. This is particularly true for Germany where the Constitutional Court has in the past made decisions that restrict room for leeway by the federal government, and it is to be expected that the upcoming decision on the ESM and the Fiscal Compact will stay along this line of argument. Eurobonds of all forms and other mutualization tools will be banned. In other words, any quick fixes to the crisis will have to be designed and planned outside the 'three Us'. This leaves us with the two other options presented above. This is also where the zone of political uncertainty begins.

Much has been speculated about the potential exit of Greece and its implications for the eurozone, and for the global economy as such. It seems to me very obvious that Greece will be the first candidate to leave, as the country is not able to even come close to delivering the conditionalities that came with the rescue programs as well as the haircut. Each program so far has resulted in even worse macroeconomic outcomes, and the various governments have bad records in terms of delivery. The reasons for the under-performance are manifold. There are definitely serious structural administrative issues on all levels; there are political and social fights that prevent even ambitious administrations from delivering; and there may be deliberate attempts not to deliver and to simultaneously promise creditors that everything is back on track. Whatever the reasons are, it should be accepted that Greece is not in an economic, political, and social situation to fulfill the requirements of the troika. So far, various Greek governments have relatively easily avoided getting cut off from external financial injections by making use of the self-imposed trap of European governments that an exit of Greece may result in disorderly contagion. The time may have come, though, that the eurozone bodies as well as its core members are willing to let Greece leave in order for it to deal with its underlying problems, outside the restricting corset of the eurozone. Such an exit decision by the Greek coalition government could be indirectly enforced by refusing further payments of tranches due to Greece's low level of implementation and commitment. A sudden stop of external financial inflows would move the Greek government to the brink of default, and probably start a new round of violent social protests. In such a situation the Greek coalition government would probably move actively forward and announce overnight its intention to leave the eurozone.

Such a decision would also drastically shift power relations inside the eurozone, as at least two of the most vulnerable member economies would then be seen by financial market actors as the next exit candidates, namely Italy and Spain. The current emergency funds as well as the newly launched ESM are by far not big enough to deal with the debt of those two economies. The European Council would have to move far beyond its crisis management practices and either allow and 'order' the ECB to use its unlimited firepower and thus to directly buy government bonds without the detour of secondary markets. The Italian and Spanish governments could make use of the threat of a quick break-up of the eurozone in case main lender economies oppose such actions. Assuming that Germany has the most to lose in the event of a break-up it seems reasonable to conclude that such a chain of events would break the German dominance in the European Council. If we further follow the analysis by Woo and Vamvakidis (2012) and conclude that Italy would gain most from an exit from the eurozone, the Monti government could leverage on this asymmetry and eventually force the Merkel coalition into a significant about face in its crisis management philosophy.

However, this may not be the end of the game. Germany may already be anticipating that such a chain of events could be triggered by a Greek exit, and be preparing her own exit. Instead of marching into the 'Greek trap,' with the support of an increasing number of the electorate, Germany could opt out, maybe attracting a small number of like-minded economies, and return to the Deutschmark (and a smaller-sized fixed exchange rate regime within Europe). The economic costs for such a move would be high and damaging, but at least it would avoid giving in to pressure from fellow member states. Whatever the chosen route, the economic and political costs for the eurozone and its members would be significant.

At present the majority of European politicians seem to think that exit costs would be prohibitively high. Given the legal and political hurdles necessary for a 'big solution', it is safe to assume that the tendency to muddle through is widely seen as the second best option. This option includes small compromises, probably the orderly exit of Greece, and the continuation of the practice of bribing financial market actors to go along with muddling through. Under the mantra of financial stability and the 'too-big-to-fail-approach' many policies of the recent past have already benefitted mostly financial market actors, and this can be read as a bow to those markets in a plea for patience, and the willingness to follow the muddling through route. Muddling through is not without risks, mainly from uncontrollable economic and political contagion. The worsening growth performance of the eurozone, which has officially entered a phase of recession, further hinders the strategy. Negative economic growth, i.e. the shrinking of nominal GDP and the tendency towards deflation, are not ideal conditions under which to deal with fragile banking industries; nor are they conditions that help to win the trust of the electorate for the implementation of ambitious austerity programs. Bad equilibria have built-in self-reinforcing mechanisms, and it needs only a few sparks to deteriorate its quality.[16]

What Else?

Muddling through of course will eventually weaken the Euro as an international reserve currency and motivate financial actors to leave the euro as deposit of value – and will eventually generate a drastic depreciation of the euro. So far, the turbulence in the eurozone has not been dramatically reflected in the exchange rate of the euro against main currencies. This is about to change. International investors have so far not fled the euro but data for the last quarter of 2011 indicates that investors' decisions are dominated by safe haven syndromes (ECB 2012). In some respects it is astonishing that the euro has not totally lost its status as international reserve currency, in particular its role as an internationally recognized store of value (see ECB 2012). Muddling through may avoid a *jump depreciation* of the euro, as global investors may still cling to the hope that European politicians are ultimately willing to save the euro by introducing new policy tools, providing more funds and by officially encouraging the ECB to make use of its (unlimited) firepower. External help may also come along. The best candidate is the economic development in the US, where at the end of 2012 automatic state expenditure cuts will come into effect in the case that the political system stays put. This may direct the attention of international financial markets towards the US and damage the reputation of the US dollar as the key safe haven currency. Accordingly this would make investment decisions even more difficult as the number of safe and deep financial markets that offer value-stable currencies is already shrinking. This would not rescue the euro but may decelerate flight out of the euro.

It goes without saying that the economic, political and social situation in the eurozone is extremely fluid. Small events may trigger an avalanche which would have effects far beyond the crisis management capacity of the main economic policy actors. If this analysis is correct in arguing that the 'three Us' strategy is a worthless vision in terms of an efficient crisis management strategy, then we are indeed nearing a bifurcation where a break-up is becoming more and more

---

16   How long can such a bad equilibrium last? Answers differ. In any case, I am not as optimistic as Streeck (2012: 67) who seems to assume that muddling through will go on for decades: 'The Sachzwänge of the international markets – actually the historically unprecedented empowerment of the profit and security needs of financial-asset owners – is forging an integration that has never been willed by political-democratic means and is today probably wanted less than ever. The legal forms within which this takes place are secondary: whatever happens, the European Central Bank will buy endless quantities of bonds that private investors no longer want; and Frankfurt, Brussels, Berlin, maybe also Paris, will "clamp down" (Angela Merkel) on the households of debtor nations for decades, with or without treaty change'.

a politically viable option. It should be clear by now that what may be seen as politically rational at a point of time will come with a large number of (destructive) unintended consequences which may extend far beyond the eurozone.

Does this mean that the eurozone needs to be rescued at any rate (or price)? One straightforward answer makes the point that you cannot unscramble scrambled eggs, and thus there is no alternative than to rescue the currency union. However, this is a misleading analogy as indeed the euro can be dissolved and each member can potentially return to its previous currency. The question that remains is what price will renationalized economies have to pay? If the individual costs of leaving the eurozone are lower than the costs of staying, members with net negative costs have a strong incentive to leave. As argued above, the process will not stop here but will immediately start a political and economic dynamic that has the potential to undermine the initial individual cost-benefit calculation. What may have been seen at first as a calculable political decision may turn out to be an incalculable political and economic risk. However, political actors only learn about these risks after the fact – and by then crisis management is all about taming contagion. In a situation of incalculable costs the preferable option should be to act 'conservatively' and to engage in cooperative joint efforts to save the common currency, rather than going it alone. Nominally, this is the foundation of the current dominating crisis management strategy. Paradoxically, it is exactly the current type of crisis management that encourages individual governments to consider exiting. In order to make such an option politically and economically unattractive there needs to be a drastic reorientation of the crisis management strategy. Generally speaking, members with strong positive net benefits should be willing to share some of these benefits in order to rebalance the negative balance of others.[17] 'Burden sharing' should be seen as a broad concept that can take various forms. According to the current crisis management plan, highly indebted economies make strong efforts to improve their price competitiveness by reducing unit labour costs, mainly by shrinking nominal wages. Given that price competitiveness is a relative concept, creditor economies of the eurozone can support those efforts by simultaneously increasing their unit labour costs, mainly by rising (real) wages above the growth rate of hourly productivity. Unlike in the long period of the build-up of macroeconomic asymmetries in the eurozone, the gap in terms of competitiveness has not widened in the last three years. However, creditor economies are far from contributing their part

---

17   The current debate about burden sharing is dominated by the misleading view that it is up to Germany to save the eurozone. This hubris is widely shared in Germany itself, probably as an expression of pride about the relatively stable state of the German economy. There is no doubt that Germany would be vastly overstretched to carry most of the rescue burden. As soon as burden sharing takes a broader notion it is no longer all about Germany but about surplus economies in general. Many supranational institutions in the meantime recommend that economies with enough fiscal space should make proper use of this space to the benefit of the eurozone.

(De Grauwe 2012).[18] The same holds for the IMF suggestion that economies with sufficient fiscal space should make ample use of this space in order to provide the level of effective demand that would lift the eurozone out of its hole. Such proposals are generally labelled as Keynesian in character, and thus already disqualify as adequate tools. Yet, the idea to make use of fiscal space is based on simple accounting logic. In a situation where the private sector is forced to deleverage, and does so successfully as all empirical data show, the other macroeconomic sectors, i.e. government and current account, must go into deficit, and respectively generate or increase a current account surplus. In regards to the creditor economies of the eurozone, this would imply increasing their government deficits and accepting decreasing current account surpluses by means of increasing import demand. The debt redemption fund suggested by the German Economic Advisory Committee is another short-term tool that has the potential to calm markets and to provide the foundation for long-term solutions.[19] Opting for such an instrument would probably change the calculations of all actors, and also return some trust to the joint political efforts of eurozone governments. Such a debt mutualization policy currently meets the resistance of key eurozone governments, not least the Merkel coalition, and also of broad sectors of the public in net benefit economies.

The negative sentiment towards 'burden sharing' has a lot to do with the fixation of the debate on Greece, and more so with the fixation of sovereign debt default crises as public debt crises.[20] It is up to politicians as well as the civil society to change the narrative and to provide for the insight that even though burden sharing is no free lunch it is worth engaging in the exercise. Attention should be turned to the much larger pile of private debt and thus to the role of an unregulated and overly liberalized financial industry that turned entrepreneurial capitalism into a rent-seeking system. Such a narrative should stress the economic and social benefits of a reformed eurozone that tames private financial profligacy as well as institutionally implants public fiscal responsibility for socio-economically sustainable development. Transforming financialization is a huge political, social and economic project but worth the while given the destructive effects of a financial regime that has lost guidance and value over time. Still, it runs into the same time horizon disparity problem as the 'three Us' strategy.

---

18   The relative improvement is much driven by wage cost reductions and not by above-the-average increases in hourly productivity. There is still a very long way to go for productivity convergence of key sectors to arrive (Sondermann 2012).

19   Bofinger, Buch, Feld, Franz and Schmidt (2012) provide a condensed version of the plan. The Advisory Committee also came up with a legal evaluation that came to the result that such a fund does not collide with the Basic Law, and hence the Merkel coalition's argument that such a proposal would be illegal has no legal grounding.

20   What kind of *idée fixe* this has become has been recently demonstrated by Gros (2012) who made the point that whatever the negative effects of austerity may be for economic growth, it needs retrenchment of the public sector after years of fiscal profligacy.

For the moment, the only economic policy actor of the eurozone that has the ability to extinguish the fire is the ECB. At the minimum, the ECB should be allowed to directly buy significant amounts of government bonds of economies that have already shown that they are willing and able to fulfill conditionalities.[21] When Mario Draghi stated at the end of July 2012 that the ECB would do 'whatever it takes' to save the euro, this message was widely interpreted to mean that the ECB would not only return to its Long-Term Refinancing Operations (LTRO) policy, but would eventually make use of its unlimited lending capacity without simultaneously restricting this policy (Wyplosz 2012). In the dramatic situation of summer 2012 this was a courageous message, however returning to LTRO implies that the ECB still would use private financial institutions as transmission units. This transmission channel has turned out to be insufficient, as many banks used the facility to improve their own balance sheets rather than refinance troubled governments. Then again, Draghi may only have tested the water for his discussion with the members of the Council, and in particular with the head of the German Bundesbank who is probably the strongest opponent of the lender of last resort role for the ECB. Still, even a clearer policy stance of the ECB may not be sufficient as the eurozone is confronted with a serious and potentially existence-threatening banking crisis. Many years ago when Garber analysed what would happen if there was a sudden loss in trust in the euro and a potential exit of a member state; he pointed out that the institutional mechanisms of the euro, namely the TARGET mechanisms, leave room for the possibility of financing capital flight from one eurozone jurisdiction to another (Garber 1998, 2010). That is exactly what happened in the last two years or so, when capital left crisis-prone economies like Greece and Spain and turned to safe euro-havens such as Germany and the Netherlands.[22] This ongoing capital flight further undermines the integration of European financial markets. As a matter of fact, today the degree of integration is at its lowest since the launch of the euro as the polarization between weak and strong banks gets stronger. Thus it would make economic sense that the successor to the EFSF should get a banking license that would allow the ESM to directly refinance with the ECB, and hence immediately increase the size of the rescue fund.[23] Injecting trust and confidence is key to successfully addressing the critical

---

21   The ECB was active in this respect but act under political suspicion of national governments as well as under the verdict that direct financing of government debt (monetization) is not allowed. There are nevertheless strong indications that ECB purchases of government bonds are calming down markets, not least as they can get rid of 'bad assets'. The downside of those purchases is that the ECB has no instrument that would connect bond purchase actions with parallel 'punishment' of bondholders. For the latter the ECB action is a cheap escape.

22   It is reported that in the first five months of 2012 about euro 163 billion left Spain, mainly to safe destinations inside the eurozone.

23   Like many suggested policy tools this instrument, too, is highly contested. ECB President Mario Draghi rejects the proposal to give the ESM a banking license, and so does German Chancellor Merkel. Edward Novotny, the Austrian member in the Governing

situation of the eurozone, and reassuring financial market actors that governments are willing and able to handle the erosion of the eurozone is crucial.

Paradoxically, this task can currently be better performed by a democratically uncontrolled authority as the ECB than by national governments and the EU. Not only because the latter tend to procrastinate and follow often narrowly defined national interests, but also because the eurozone *per se* is constructed as an elitist and technocratic project where democratic control mechanisms were not foreseen. Changing the rules of the game in the current situation seems a no-win proposal. That the ECB has become the most critical savior of the eurozone reflects the flaws in the institutional architecture of the euro. In the current situation of increasing challenges this weakness has become a political strength, if only to avoid an economic and political catastrophe in Europe. Yet, this strength should be only of temporary character and needs to be re-balanced by a truly democratic makeover of the architecture of the euro.

The wave of financialization has made economic policy-making a much more difficult business that ever before. The political decision to unleash financial markets during the preparation phase of the common currency added a powerful force to the European power matrix. Securing the trust and confidence of investors in order to safeguard the profits of this industry has become the paramount objective for economic policy, despite the efforts to re-regulate and to partially tax some financial transactions. Democratic control has been subordinated to financial stability, and it is mainly the ECB that has the tools and resources to return to financial stability. One can predict that financial markets will be the winners of the new game. True, so far they could make excellent use of their implicit threat power and bias rescue operations to their favour, not least due to the inefficient and indecisive actions of official crisis management. The longer this type of crisis management continues, the stronger the position of financial market actors. In this situation, a revamped ECB could become a critical game-changer. If the ECB were permitted to act like any other key central bank and truly become a lender of last resort, the power matrix would be drastically altered, as the main threat would evaporate.[24] Such a decisive ECB action does not mean that the crisis would be solved. It would only mean that no new gas is fueling the fire – a necessary condition to begin the task of reconstruction.

Council of the ECB, is much more open for such an addition, and seems to be willing to mobilize for such an enlargement of the tool kit (see *Financial Times*, July 25, 2012).

24   The crisis provides an enormous opportunity for governments to tame financial markets. Rather than solely recapitalizing troubled banks a newly launched EU-wide regulatory banking authority has the chance to compose conditionalities, acquire direct shares and hence control, as well as has the ability to close whole financial units, and all this without jeopardizing assets.

References

Aglietta, M. (2012), 'The European Vortex,' *New Left Review* 75, 15–36.

Ahearne, A. and G. Wolff (2012), 'The Debt Challenge,' *Bruegel Working Paper* 2012/02.

Committee on the Global Financial System (2010), 'Long-term Issues in International Banking,' *CGFS Papers* No. 41, Basel.

De Grauwe, P. and Y. Ji (2012), 'Mispricing of Sovereign Risk and Multiple Equilibria in the Eurozone,' *CEPS Working Document*, No. 361.

Doluca, H., Hübner, M., Rumpf, D. and B. Weigert (2012), 'The European Redemption Pact: An Illustrative Guide,' German Council of Economic Experts, *Working Paper* 2.

ECB (2012), 'The International Role of the Euro,' Frankfurt.

Eichengreen, B. (2012), 'Europe's Divided Visionaries,' Project Syndicate.

Garber, P.M. (1998), 'Notes on the Role of Target in a Stage III Crisis,' *Working Paper* 6619, NBER.

Garber, P.M. (2010), 'The Mechanics of Intra Euro Capital Flight,' Economics Special Report Deutsche Bank.

Gros, D. (2012), 'Austerity is unavoidable after a bout of profligacy,' VoxEU.org (accessed 19 July 2012).

Hübner, K. (2012), 'German Crisis Management and Leadership – From Ignorance to Procrastination to Action,' *Asia Europe Journal* 9, 159–77.

Lane, P. and G. Milesi-Ferretti (2008), 'The Drivers of Financial Globalization,' *IIS Discussion Paper* No. 238.

McKinsey, Germany (2012), 'The Future of the Euro. An Economic Perspective on the Eurozone Crisis,' Frankfurt.

Merler, S. and J. Pisani-Ferry (2012a), 'Sudden Stops in the Euro Area,' *Policy Contribution* 2012/06, Bruegel.

Merler, S. and J. Pisani-Ferry (2012b), 'Hazardous Tango: Sovereign-bank Interdependence and Financial Stability in the Euro Area,' *Bruegel Working Paper* 05.

Reinhart, C. and K. Rogoff (2009), *This Time is Different. Eight Centuries of Financial Folly.* Princeton: Princeton University Press.

Ruscher, E. and G.B. Wolff (2012), 'Corporate Balance Sheet: Stylized Facts, Causes and Consequences,' *Working Paper* 2012/03, Bruegel.

Streek, W. (2012), 'Markets and Peoples. Democratic Capitalism and European Integration,' *New Left Review* 73, 63–71.

Wolf, M. (2012), 'Getting Out of Debt by Adding Debt,' *Financial Times*, 25 July 2012.

Wolff, G. and E. Ruscher (2012), 'Corporate Balance Sheet Adjustment: Stylized Facts, Causes and Consequences,' *Brugel Working Paper* 07.

Woo, D. and A. Vamvakidis (2012), 'Game Theory and Euro Breakup Risk Premium', Bank of America Merrill Lynch, FX and Rates, 10 July 2012.

Chapter 3

The Eurozone Crisis and the Fiscal Treaty: Implications for the Social Dimension and Democracy

Robert Finbow

Introduction

The recent eurozone crisis demonstrates the complex challenges of democratic governance in this unique, evolving regional system. The crisis has stressed the European Union (EU) as never before and has led to regime changes in two member states, with non-elected leaders temporarily anointed to reassure investors and secure the future of the common currency. In addition, the EU negotiated a new fiscal treaty which would reinforce requirements for joint budgetary planning and empower the Union to scrutinize national policies and programmes more comprehensively. Resources for bailouts have been amassed through the European Stability Mechanism (ESM) and a fiscal discipline pact now goes beyond the eurozone to cover 25 EU members. While the final shape of such initiatives remains to be determined, the new system strengthens an agenda of fiscal austerity and bureaucratic constraint which could weaken national democratic practice and undermine the social dimension to integration, already imperilled by liberalizing EU treaties.

This chapter will examine how EU fiscal policy affects democratic governance as Brussels and national states respond to the eurozone crisis. Using secondary sources, stakeholder briefs and EU documents, it will consider the implications for European democracy – at the national and transnational levels – and the future of a social dimension in the eurozone and the larger union. It will provide a preliminary comment on the state of democracy in a Union in which national states cannot consult their populace or deviate from central bank and bureaucracy directives for fear of destabilizing Europe's currency and economy. There is a complex disjuncture with the move towards great power at a European level, where democracy remains underdeveloped, while requiring more constraint of policy by national governments which has consequences for the nature of democratic practice in future.

The compatibility of 'technocratic rule' with democracy will be considered and the implications of fiscal reforms for the EU's democratic character will be assessed. Can the 'output legitimacy' of rational EU-level decision-making compensate for the weakness of popular input as power is delegated to non-elected, transnational institutions? (Thatcher and Sweet 2001: 19). So far, the measures adopted have not rectified imbalances in the eurozone while imposing transnationally-mandated austerity which constrains public policy and arguably undermines national democratic accountability. The evolving circumstances surrounding fiscal management demonstrate the complexity of democratic input, as national elections and referenda alongside continued economic uncertainty create ever changing circumstances for negotiation of workable fiscal arrangements. Given this evolving context, this chapter is of necessity preliminary.

The Nature of the Crisis

When European states boosted stimulus spending after the 2008 crisis, the European Union warned countries like France, Ireland, Spain and Greece, to reduce deficits in order to avoid unsustainable debt to GDP ratios (Schuknecht 2011). During 2010, the EU set austerity conditions on bailouts for Greek, Portuguese and Irish governments and banks, but these did not improve the Euro's stability (Belke and Polleit 2011). Regulators criticized Greek accounting methods, since deficits were four times above Stability and Growth Pact (SGP) recommendations (Alogoskoufis 2012) Greece was pressed into more austerity, despite recessionary conditions. Concern spread that other countries would replicate its descent into deficits, high borrowing costs, and spiralling debt (Feinman 2011). Eurozone finance ministers established a European Stability Mechanism, initially at €500 billion, to provide financial support to eurozone states (Pisani-Ferry et al. 2012). The troika of the European Commission, European Central Bank (ECB) and International Monetary Fund (IMF) imposed conditions before providing further funds. Greek Prime Minister George Papandreou eventually balked at the unpopular measures and called for a referendum. European leaders challenged this democratic initiative for fears it could diminish credit ratings for vulnerable states like Italy and weaken stock markets. Under pressure, Greek Parliamentarians backed an unelected Prime Minister, Lucas Papademos, former head of the Greek Central Bank, who agreed to further austerity.

The EU boosted funds in the ESM and got private banks to absorb losses and raise capital to prevent the spread of crisis. Italy's problems forced the replacement of Prime Minister Silvio Berlusconi with another unelected government headed by Mario Monti, a former European commissioner and an economist, as the imposition of austerity became a new norm. As one cynic suggested 'the European debt crisis has been almost as damaging for democracy as it has been for the economies of the eurozone. In Greece and Italy, democratic legitimacy is clearly regarded as an unaffordable luxury' (Skelton 2011). As the Greece's fiscal deficiencies worsened, EU officials scrambled for a fiscal 'firewall' to prevent contagion to other states.

While Greece's domestic problems of uncollected taxes and overspending gained headlines, structural elements in the eurozone make it difficult to restore stability to national finances. The 'fundamental contradictions inherent in a "one-size fits all" monetary policy for a group of countries without a fiscal union, without effective mechanisms for enforcing fiscal discipline on sovereign countries, with only limited effective labour mobility and with increasingly disparate economic conditions, have been laid bare' (Feinman 2011: 1). Economies like Greece, Spain, Portugal, and Italy face 'severe, unsustainable imbalances in real effective exchange rates and external debt levels that are higher than in most previous emerging market crises' (Maudlin 2012). The euro acts like the gold standard, forcing peripheral economies to accept adjustment costs as they lack currency flexibility and devaluation possibilities which could ease fiscal crisis and restore competitiveness. This inability for countries in recession to devalue their currencies renders exports less competitive, hurting employment and increasing demand for social security and unemployment support. This weakens revenues and boosts expenditures, increasing indebtedness (Peterson 2012: 2). Reduced competitiveness erodes these countries' trade and current account balances.

As long as these countries remain in the eurozone and forfeit an independent monetary policy this problem cannot be cured without increased demand from core states or ECB purchases of bonds to reduce interest rate spreads. However financial agencies, governments and lenders insisted on more austerity as the 'solution' which worsened recession, condemning these states 'to contraction or low growth' (Maudlin 2012). European policy has imposed austerity despite national recessions. This could undermine stabilization in economic policy and force these states into spiralling recessions. The implementation of a centrally monitored fiscal pact with enforcement mechanisms, threatens to impose such policies irrespective of national circumstances and perspectives, as determined by democratic political practice.

New Fiscal Instruments

As the crisis unfolded, bureaucratic and business interests sought new governance instruments to prevent the destabilization of the eurozone. Business Europe advocated that EU voting 'should be strengthened to make it tougher for the Council to overrule the Commission's recommendations regarding deficits'. Business called for 'greater ambition and commitment from Member States in their National Reform Programmes' and 'a transfer of significant budgetary authority from the national to the European level' to ensure national 'public finance positions are in genuine adherence with the Maastricht criteria' (Business Europe 2011: 2–3). The Commission must exert convergence pressures so that corporate-friendly criteria take precedence over other policy priorities and 'above all the Commission needs to get serious in ensuring that all legislation is firstly subject to comprehensive competitiveness checks to ensure maximum impact on growth and jobs, and secondly, incorporated into national law within a short and strictly defined timeframe' (Business Europe 2011: 3).

Similar measures found their way into the fiscal pact, which 'endowed the Stability and Growth Pact with effective enforcement mechanisms for euro-area Member States' (European Commission 2012a: 4). The heads of state committed to 'enhanced governance to foster fiscal discipline and deeper integration in the internal market as well as stronger growth, enhanced competitiveness and social cohesion' and pledged 'significantly stronger coordination of economic policies' (European Council 2011). Despite objections by the UK and the Czech Republic, which precluded a treaty amendment, the Council sought a new legal method to implement the fiscal arrangement; the avoidance of a formal treaty process allowed for rapid adoption with less political debate and public scrutiny.

The Treaty on Stability, Coordination and Governance (SCG) committed all parties 'to maintain sound and sustainable public finances and to prevent a government deficit becoming excessive,' using 'a balanced budget rule and an automatic mechanism to take corrective action'. Members would ensure that deficits were no higher than 3% of GDP and that public debt did not exceed 60% of GDP. Legislation and directives would strengthen the 'economic and budgetary surveillance of Member States experiencing' financial instability, via monitoring, assessment of draft budgets and reversing of excessive deficits (EU Treaty 2012: 1–2). The treaty strengthens the SGP with enforcement mechanisms based on neo-liberal monetarist principles, with a binding 'Balanced Budget Rule' in national law or constitutionals subject to the jurisdiction of the EU Court of Justice which could 'impose the payment of a lump sum or penalty on a Member State of the European Union having failed to comply with one of its judgments' once alerted by the Commission or any member state. Once 'the debt brake has come into full operation' each country must 'run their budgets in surplus or balance, and ... keep their structural deficit (that is, the amount of borrowing required to maintain their day to day operations – hospitals, schools and so on) below 0.5% of GDP". The EU preferred that states limit debt in their constitutions, but since 'this may require referenda' in some states 'a constitutional debt brake is not obligatory' but a 'debt brake must ... be binding on the national budgetary process' (O'Brien 2012).

The SCG is accompanied by the European Stability Mechanism (ESM) to rationalize previous ad hoc financial bailouts. The ESM is a Luxembourg-based institution, available to Euro states and non-euro EU members, to provide 'financial assistance under strict conditions' if essential 'to ensure the financial stability of the euro area as a whole' eurozone states which receive funds 'must implement a macro-economic adjustment programme and a rigorous analysis of public-debt sustainability, and foresee IMF participation in liaison with the ECB [European Central Bank]' (DG ECFIN 2012b). The ESM has substantial revenues to supply assistance and will varied tools to assist states whose fiscal imbalances could destabilize the Euro; the ESM may 'grant loans to its members, provide precautionary financial assistance, purchase bonds of beneficiary member states on primary and secondary markets and provide loans for recapitalization of financial institutions' (European Council 2012a).

The ESM treaty incorporates detailed clauses specifying the creditor protection allotted to the ESM alongside the IMF and national states which may also serve as lenders to other eurozone members. The ESM and SCG seek policy convergence backed by financial sanction: 'Assistance will be provided under strict economic policy conditionality' only if recipients ratify the SCG 'and implement the balanced budget rule as specified in that treaty within ... one year after entry into force' (European Council 2012b: 2).

All parties to the Treaty agree that major economic policy 'will be discussed ex-ante and, where appropriate, coordinated' with the involvement of 'the institutions of the European Union' (EU Treaty 2012: 9) Governance of the eurozone is formalized with biannual heads of state summits to which parliamentary leaders 'may' be invited (EU Treaty 2012: 9). In its press release on the treaty the Council made clear that summits would promote 'the coordination and convergence of member states' economic policies' (European Council 2012: 2). Hence financial incentives, legal systems, even constitutions would be integrated into a transnational enforcement system which would constrain what democratically elected governments could do in future. The SCG ensures that budgets are to be kept in surplus, irrespective of demands from social forces or recessionary conditions which might make temporary deficits necessary. If states exceed deficit and debt to GDP ratios, a 'correction mechanism' will apply, and states will impose austerity to return to proper ratios. Limited room is permitted in 'exceptional circumstances', outside a state's control such as economic downturn, but only if 'the temporary deviation of the Contracting Party concerned does not endanger fiscal sustainability in the medium term' (EU Treaty 2012: 6). If a state does exceed debt guidelines, it 'shall put in place a budgetary and economic partnership programme including a detailed description of the structural reforms which must be put in place and implemented to ensure an effective and durable correction of their excessive deficits .... Their submission to the European Commission and the Council for endorsement and their monitoring' is to occur within SGP mechanisms (EU Treaty 2012: 7).

Disingenuously, the treaty asserts that this will not negate 'the specific role of the social partners, as it is recognized in the laws or national systems of each of the Contracting Parties' (EU Treaty 2012: 5). How social concerns will be heard given policy constraints in the new treaties is not specified. As Fox suggests, 'the challenges [these treaties] pose to the principle of democratic accountability are disquieting. The further empowerment of unelected European Commission officials, combined with the emergence of technocratic, national unity administrations in Italy and Greece, point to an assumption that in this time of economic crisis it is "expertocracy" not representative democracy that holds the key to the future' (Fox 2012: 465).

Bailouts, Democracy and Autonomy

The idea that there is a democratic deficit at the heart of EU institutions is hardly novel. The widening and deepening of the union has seen the growth of executive power at the expense of national parliaments. 'The design of the EU means that policy-making at the European level is dominated by executive actors: national ministers in the Council, and government appointees in the Commission. This, by itself, is not a problem. However, the actions of these executive agents at the European level are beyond the control of national parliaments' (Follesdal and Hix 2006: 534–5). As well, the European parliament has been too weak to render these actors accountable in the complex framework of European institutions; the lack of effective European-wide elections focussed on European issues, and the distance at which the EU sits in relation to citizens in member states limits its ability to emerge as a coequal branch to the Council or Commission. The EU is free to adopt policies which diverge from preferences of citizens in many if not most member states. Leftist scholars argue that structural and institutional biases in the European system results in 'policy drift' with EU decisions emerging to the right of national preferences. 'Concentrated interests such as business interests and multinational firms have a greater incentive to organize at the European level than diffuse interests, such as consumer groups or trade unions, and the EU policy process is pluralist rather than corporatist. These features skew EU policy outcomes more towards the interests of the owners of capital than is the case for policy compromises at the domestic level in Europe' (Follesdal and Hix 2006: 537).

Critics feared the rushed decisions in the wake of the crisis could weaken democratic practice. Despite the importance of parliamentary control of taxation and spending powers to notions of popular sovereignty, the treaty transfers decisions to transnational bureaucrats, enforceable by a European court, which could determine if adequate fiscal adjustment is undertaken in delinquent cases. The pact is frequently described as 'austerity forever' and unlike most treaties contains no provisions for withdrawal or abrogation or democratic oversight (Oberndorfer 2012). The Commission pledged that the European and national parliaments would convene a conference of representatives from parliamentary committees to debate budgetary policy. Given the weakness of legislatures it is unclear if this would allow flexibility from liberalizing constraints. As the *Economist* opined,

> [I]f the new euro-plus fiscal union adopts its planned restrictions on taxation and spending, you could easily imagine a future general election in which one party's manifesto, full of Keynesian stimulus policies or tax-cuts, is run through a think-tank's calculators and discovered to be euro-incompatible, while a rival party's plan fits the criteria handed down from Brussels. At which point, it will surely be argued, it is pointless to vote for the first party, because the fiscal union will stop them from doing what they promise (*The Economist* 2011).

There were explicit statements from treaty supporters illustrating the brake on domestic policy choice. Commission Vice President Olli Rehn stated that the Greek bailout is 'based on rigorous conditionality which is strengthened by reinforced monitoring of the implementation of the programme through enhanced and permanent presence of the Commission's task force on the ground, supported by experts provided by member States'. The goal was a permanent reorientation of Greek policy which cannot sustain a large public sector funded by cheap debt but should instead promote private foreign and domestic investment to promote growth and create jobs. Investment must be encouraged 'through an efficient and fair tax system, effective public administration, more favourable business climate, the full use of available structural funds and by allowing unit labour costs to adjust' (Rehn 2012). This necessitates a reduction of choices for decision makers, a smaller public sector and a flexible labour market where worker compensation falls to whatever level Union and global pressures demand. The head of the Euro group, Jean-Claude Juncker threatened that 'the EU would withdraw its financial aid for Greece if the "extremist" parties gained ground in Greek elections' (Delastik 2012). Chancellor Merkel declared 'The Fiscal Pact is about inserting debt brakes permanently in the national legal systems. They shall possess a binding and eternal validity!' (Oberndorfer 2012).

Some suggest that this has been the final blow to any pretence that the EU is compatible with national, sovereign democratic practices:

> Rule by technocrats has replaced rule by the people – with unelected, economically orthodox international bodies like the European Commission and the IMF working with unelected technocrats now heading up national governments to implement tough austerity measures that have never received public backing. The democratic deficit at the heart of Europe has become a democratic chasm (Skelton 2011).

On the other hand, the intricacy of the European model creates complexities, and disagreements arise respecting the criteria for assessing democratic practice. Analysts differ, using 'indirect legitimacy' via national democracies delegation of power to EU institutions; 'parliamentary legitimacy' via the role of legislatures at the national and European level; 'technocratic legitimacy' via the solution of key problems by European level actors; and 'procedural legitimacy' via creation of accepted processes for collective action (Wimmel 2009: 183–4). Clearly EU actors pushing the fiscal pact prefer technocratic and procedural legitimacy in indirectly delegated institutions to a popular mandate via referenda or parliamentary elections. Authors like Moravcsik defend the legitimacy of indirect democratic processes like the ECB, the Council, Commission and Court as equivalent to domestic institutions in established democracies, which are not generally regarded as illegitimate (Moravcsik 2009: 340).

Collignon has pointed out the difference between 'government *for* the people' via 'output-legitimacy' which legitimizes technocratic governments if focussed on the general welfare, which citizens retroactively approve; versus government '*by* and through the people' or 'input-legitimacy' via votes in elections where a majority gives government authority to 'implement collective choices in accordance with their will and preferences'. He goes on to say that 'the technocratic argument for European integration is based on a patriarchal philosophy of output legitimacy: great leaders know best, and the people should be grateful for what they get' (Collignon 2012). If democracy requires input *and* output legitimacy, the recent evolution of the European Union, especially the SGP and the SCG fiscal pact, fail to meet these criteria. There is a clear absence, as well, of democratic legitimacy to central institutions, including the European Parliament which, despite some changes after Lisbon, has not acquired the powers and stature to become a legitimate democratic institution balancing the mysterious workings of the Council, Court and Commission; as tension between central authority and states mounts over the costs of bailouts and austerity programmes 'there is no democratic accountability mechanism that commands legitimacy across the continent to mediate the consequences of this tension as it arises' (Fox 2012: 466). In addition, while formalizing a role for national parliaments to comment on Commission proposals as they are considered, the requirements for agreement among a third of legislatures before the Commission needs to heed their concerns (and then only on matters of subsidiarity) clearly limits the balancing role of national states on policy development.

The problem in the long run is most acute in those countries bearing the brunt of adjustment. Fox argues that: 'prioritising the saving of the European single currency imposes a policy straitjacket on member states giving them limited scope for flexibility; consequently, there are none of the usual carrots to incentivise public support for the measures adopted' (Fox 2012: 464). It remains uncertain whether the public will continue to support such measures if austerity continues to bite deeply in the future. Individual political actors may seek to remove their states from the embrace of EU centralization but at high economic costs. Yet the Greek government secured a parliamentary majority to back reforms, and the Italian regime likewise secured support from legislators, and Irish voters did ratify the fiscal pact in a referendum. For the union to flourish, democratic renewal would require more input legitimacy at the European level, which would require greater empowerment of the parliament, perhaps enabled but as yet unrealized after Lisbon; to preserve the benefits of 'a more efficient and centralized European economic management, ... we must tame the tiger by submitting such government to proper democratic control' (Collignon 2012).

The Social Dimension and the Fiscal Pact

In the neo-liberal climate of the 1980s and 1990s, the European Union put forward an alternative model, with emphasis on social cohesion and dialogue. Collaboration among social constituencies, enterprises and state and union officials in decision-making sought an intermediate course between waning socialist models and Anglo-Saxon states' unfettered capitalism. Europe would enhance social cohesion and 'stimulate growth in knowledge based economies', through the Tripartite Social Summits for Growth and Employment (Schmidt 2009: 7). While globalization undermined states' ability to regulate their economies and engage in social adjustments, the 'complete subjugation of politics to market imperatives can be avoided ... through institutional adjustments on the national level, supplemented by the creation of supranational institutions' supportive of a distinct European Social Model (Schmidt 2009: 9). However the social model evolved from enforceable hard law to soft law coordination mechanisms which failed to live up to their promise. Slow growth in Europe and expansion of the Union to poorer states undermined any ability to use economic gains to promote cohesion.

Critical groups link liberalization with unbalanced business access to EU policy formulation. Lisbon is considered the embodiment of liberalization, with its emphasis on competitiveness in response to globalization and the rise of rival regional trade blocs and newly emerging economies; 'the inherent trade-offs between better jobs vs. flexibilisation of labour markets, and higher social inclusion vs. cuts in social security systems were never intended to be negotiated in a – democratic – political arena' as corporate preferences for retrenchment were prioritized (Vander Stichele 2006: 9). Lisbon emphasized service sectors, economic, social and environmental advances. Yet the definition of competitiveness is neo-liberal; 'the term "competitiveness", originally defined by the OECD as a nation's ability to increase real-wages while remaining competitive on international markets, received a new, if not contrary meaning in Lisbon as it became synonymous for the reduction of wages as an instrument to preserve the competitiveness and high-profitability of European business' (Vander Stichele et al. 2006: 8–9). Despite slow growth, EU decision-makers narrowed Lisbon, to a 'growth and jobs' model 'that reads like a cost-reduction programme for industry. Social and environmental goals which had been, on paper at least, part of the Lisbon agenda were dropped' to 'boost European economy and subsequently deliver on the other policy objectives' (Vander Stichele et al. 2006: 9). This narrowing paralleled corporate concerns with the drag of such social and environmental components of the treaty on profits.

For critical groups, the new SGC and ESM further these liberalization efforts. The Corporate Europe Observatory (CEO) noted the influence of lobbyists in Business Europe, whose pressure 'exerted substantial influence on the Treaty, urging a more authoritarian form of neoliberal governance of member state economies by Brussels, leaving less scope for manoeuver and effective democratic control of fiscal policy' (2012). The European Trade Union Confederation (ETUC) criticized the fiscal pact for its lack of balance, noting that 'this Treaty might reassure Kanzlerin Merkel's political friends, but not the millions of unemployed, poor or precarious workers in Europe who are waiting for decisive support from EU institutions. .... Austerity is killing growth and jobs. What we really need is a social compact to give a fresh impetus to the European Union and restore the confidence of its workers and citizens' (ETUC 2012b). Such groups note that the mechanisms in the SGC focus 'more swift action against countries with budget deficits, and ... the so called "debt brake" – strong enforcement of rules to keep deficits down and the debt from growing' a form of 'automatic austerity' (CEO 2012a) which entrench conservative state budgets in future. The provisions on 'structural deficits' suggest that strong retrenchment measures could be imposed on most states. Council documents target pensions, health care and similar expenditures including recommendations that older workers to remain employed longer to collect benefits, or curtailing health provision as the means to reduce deficits and debt. 'The Commission's recommendations to member states which have an excessive deficit procedure – that's currently it's 23 (!) of the 27 member states – are clear that cutting social expenditure is the right way to bring down any structural deficit' (CEO 2012a).

Unions feared that the incorporation of austerity measures would not only fail to improve the situation or reassure markets, but would worsen recession and limit employment. The ETUC argued that 'the process of negotiation ignored the democratic scrutiny that should normally characterise any reform of the Union ... by not giving the full role to the European Parliament.' (ETUC 2012a). The crisis required 'sustainable investments for growth ... fair taxation policies, a financial transaction tax, combating tax fraud and tax evasion, a partial pooling of the debt, adequate intervention of the ECB, and strong control over the financial sector'. Instead the pact was designed to attack 'industrial relations systems and put downward pressure on collectively agreed wage levels; to weaken social protection and the right to strike and privatise public services'; 'cumulated over the years, [it] will dismantle a social model which is unique in the world' (ETUC 2012a). UNI Europa declared the pact 'anti-social, anti-democratic and anti-European' (IBOA 2012).

The ability of transnational social movements to counter these trends is limited, given diverse circumstances in donor and debtor states, and weak incorporation of popular input in EU institutions. The social dialogue is widely regarded as window-dressing for liberalization, as social actors complain of the futility of 'consultation'. Social constituencies fear that the pact will pressure member states to cut welfare spending, increase privatization and seek flexible labour markets, with wage reductions, lay-offs, and decreased living standards. It will hasten the transfer of income and wealth to capital, and increase the power of unelected judicial and bureaucratic entities at the expense of democratic practice – a deepening of transnational constitutionalism which makes popular influence ever more marginal (O'Brien 2012). Strange argues that the constitutional argument is overblown – especially given the SGP's failure to reduce spending (Strange 2012: 261). Should it survive the current uncertainty, the fiscal treaty would increase automatic application of deficit and debt ratios and promote fiscal homogenization. This could further the power of the transnational at the expense of national, differentiated, socially-responsive policies.

Balancing National Democracy and Europe-wide Needs

The crisis and response raised questions respecting the balance of power between European and national authorities, and the ability to balance democratic input with good economic governance in the increasingly intertwined eurozone. Fox argues that

> If democracy means anything in practice it must surely mean the right of citizens to decide their own political and economic destiny through their elected representatives and to 'kick the rascals out' should they be dissatisfied with them. The proposed reforms of European economic governance thus raise vitally important questions about what role national parliaments can and should play in this process in the future (Fox 2012: 463).

Even before the crisis and hardening of austerity rules, Collignon warned that national governments, accountable to domestic electorates, may undertake budget policy which runs against the SGP, which seeks to apply 'the hard coordination rule: keep structural deficits in balance'. This 'is a technocratic rule to which democratic governments have subscribed, but there is no mechanism to deal with the problem of preference change. Inevitably this must lead to the de-legitimization of European policies' (Collignon 2003: 241–2). The current crisis provides and important test of this imbalance.

In elections in May 2012 in France and Greece, voters rejected the austerity basis for the fiscal pact. At first it seemed that the 'irresistible force of German austerity has clashed with the immovable object of Greek popular resistance' (Elliot 2012). However, the Greek results were soon reversed and Ireland approved the pact in a referendum. The French election proved more important to the future of fiscal collaboration, with the socialist government of Francoise Hollande advocating stimulus – in direct contrast to the German approach – including lowered retirement age, higher taxes on wealth, inheritance and dividends, an increased minimum wage, and measures to make it harder for employers to fire workers. Hollande advocated use of the 'European Stability Mechanism to purchase indebted nations' bonds in a way to counter rising yields' (Donahue 2012). He suggested policies to 'deepen' Europe as a fiscal union, including 'a financial transactions tax and joint debt issuance, including Eurobonds, euro bills and a debt redemption fund' (Hollande in EurActiv 2012).

After an indecisive vote, in which anti-austerity opposition parties gained ground, the Greek population narrowly confirmed a pro-austerity government lead by Samaras. A 'tenuous coalition' emerged between the socialist Pasok party, the moderate Democratic Left party and Samaras' New Democracy. The government committed to austerity, but with support from France, Spain, and Italy Samaras sought changes to promote growth in a Greek economy which had endured recession for years. Changes included extension of the fiscal adjustment period to 2016, so that targets can be met without additional cuts to salaries and pensions, cancellation of changes to private sector collective bargaining, reversals of public sector layoffs and capping tax payer's repayments for overdue obligations at 25% of income (Kitsantonis 2012). Greece had undertaken cuts equalling 1.5% of national output, labour market reforms to increase flexibility, a new tax on property, reduction in the minimum wage, pension cuts, elimination of rent subsidies and 30,000 civil servants placed on partial pay, which generated significant opposition and undermined middle class purchasing power further diminishing economic prospects. Fears that such measures could prompt the loss of power by pro-austerity parties motivated some eurozone partners to accept adjustments. These included infrastructure and modernization projects from European Union structural funds 'to ease the pain of a deeper-than-expected recession' with GDP decrease of up to 7% expected (*Economist* 2012). However, the future remained unclear as German politicians expressed frustrations with Greece's continued inability to meet austerity targets, leaving open the possibility of a Greek default and exit from the euro (Reuters 2012).

The European Summit of June 2012 demonstrated the effects of this democratic push-back. Under pressure from Spain and Italy, who threatened to reject a summit declaration, Germany partially conceded to changes sought by Hollande. Germany accepted short-term measures to reduce Italy and Spain's borrowing costs; the ESM would be allowed to recapitalize banks directly rather than through governments, so loan conditions cannot be forced on governments. This would allow for support for the banking sector in future without imposing greater debt or conditionality on member states, separating private and public sector debt. In return, members accepted that the ECB would become a supervising authority with member states ceding more control of banking to the ECB (Beyond Brussels 2012b). The characteristics of a more robust banking union, including the precise role of the ECB remain unclear, and there remains the question of continent-wide fiscal policy to avert future crises.

Germany also acceded to a 'growth pact' including contributions from structural funds, the European Investment Bank, and project bids from private partners in infrastructure projects to offset recessionary pressures in some states. However, this included little new commitment of resources, unlike past stimulus packages. Moreover, Germany resisted the creation of euro-bonds which could more permanently lower borrowing costs for peripheral states. The ECB expressed a willingness to buy enough bonds of fiscally troubled states to reduce their borrowing costs, though there would be a limit to such purchases given the scope of the crisis. These concessions were not enough for some, with the Dutch opposition indicating their rejection of the 3% deficit rule with a threat to ignore treaty requirements if elected. While German politicians agreed to the pact, it was challenged in the Constitutional Court by social groups and opposition members, which could delay or thwart implementation (Bloomberg 2012). The eventual outcome of this balancing of fiscal imperatives, technocratic initiatives and democratic input remains uncertain as this chapter goes to press.

Conclusions

The recent electoral outcomes and consequent adjustments to the new fiscal framework indicate that national-level democratic practice has not become irrelevant. However, the solution to the crisis cannot be a simple return to national-level policies, given the intertwined fates of members of the Union and eurozone in the stability of the common currency. Collignon suggests that,

> Nation state democracy in the European Union is the tyranny of national majorities that are a minority in Europe. What is needed is democracy by, for and through all of Europe's citizens. European policies need to be authorized by all citizens, not just by some fraction. When policy decisions by one member state affect citizens in all other member states as well, it is no solution to let only a small part of them vote (Collignon 2011).

EU leaders seem content to accept that procedural and output legitimacy are sufficient to justify a portrayal of the EU as democratic. This fits with Moravcsik's (2008) view that the EU's democratic legitimacy is derived not from responsiveness to national publics but rather from concrete results for the population overall. There is a sense that 'What the EU achieves through integrating markets – or even eliminating passport controls – underscores the benefits of its "delegated democracy"' (Tassinari 2011). Schmidt argues that the emergence of the EU as a 'regional state' engaged in making 'policy without politics' has altered the nature of national democracy, which now involves 'politics without policy' as domestic partisan politics loses importance and leaders and citizens lose influence; national politicians must more effectively articulate new legitimizing ideas which do not involve policy-making to offset disillusionment and populist radicalization (Schmidt 2005: 769). Such approaches assume that European integration and economic liberalization are positive and benefit of the majority by increasing peace, prosperity, stability, mobility and global influence for all Europeans.

The recent crisis demonstrates that liberalized systems have produced very uneven results, that some states and their citizens bear the brunt of stabilizing the system as a whole. In this climate it is unclear that citizens will continue to regard indirect, delegated decision-making as equivalent or preferable to national democracy. Moreover the crisis and response has sharpened tensions among members of the union, between donor states and their affected financial institutions and recipient countries and their beleaguered austerity-deprived citizens. There is a risk that popular resistance and push back will make effective policies to reduce deficits and debt more problematic as people tire of the burdens, leading to the danger of nationalist, even nativist, backlash against technocratic solutions imposed on increasingly unwilling publics. Scharpf suggests that 'political resignation, alienation and cynicism, combined with growing hostility against "Frankfurt" and "Brussels", and a growing perception of zero-sum conflict between the donors and the recipients of the "rescue-cum-retrenchment" programmes, may create the conditions for anti-European political mobilization from the extremes of the political spectrum. In the worst case, therefore, attempts to save the Euro through the policies presently enacted may either fail on their own terms, or they may not only undermine democracy in EU member states but endanger European integration itself' (Scharpf 2011). Volatile public opinion in Germany and other donors and social strife in Greece and elsewhere support this. Imposition of austerity via the new fiscal instruments may only hasten destabilization and deligitimization if not matched with efforts to control borrowing costs, stimulate recovery and promote social cohesion.

Is there a way to reconcile eurozone wide policy with national democratic practices? The *White Paper on European Governance* (European Commission 2001) outlines how European governance includes varied rules, processes, and behaviours which determine how powers are implemented at the European level, and emphasizes core principles like 'openness, participation, accountability, effectiveness, and coherence' (Gatto 2006: 487). As it has evolved in the light of the crisis, EU governance has aimed for greater 'effectiveness and coherence' (from an incoherent, ineffective situation) at the expense of 'openness, participation and accountability'. Some observers fear it will require the breakup of the Union and eurozone to permit peripheral states to revive democratic practices. As pressures within the common currency work against the sustainability of these smaller economies, the route to sovereignty comes, for these critics, from decoupling. The centralized imposition of policy for which there is no democratic sanction or reversal is not justified or durable. As Fritz-Vannahme points out, '[i]t is surely detrimental to the democratic cause to give people the impression that policymaking consists of nothing more than a set of decisions to which there is no other alternative' (Fritz-Vannahme 2012: 1).

Yet others suggest the European project needs elevation to a 'United States of Europe' reconfigured sufficiently so that the political and economic space are again coterminous, and a democratically-empowered public through representative institutions can effectively influence and transform policy priorities. At time of writing central institutions like the ECB seem to have finally realized that a sustainable monetary and fiscal policy requires adjustments – such as European-wide bond purchases to limit interest rate pressures on the affected states – to offset pressure for fragmentation of the eurozone. Whether further political integration will follow to ensure more democratic input on monetary and fiscal measures at the European level or generate interregional fiscal transfers in future remains doubtful. The current circumstances illustrate that while the European Commission and ECB are gaining authority, backed by the European Court of Justice, the popular legislative input at the European level – a proto-bicameralism with the Parliament and Council serving as the representative core – remains underdeveloped. The constitutional elements for an effective popular role and workable separation of powers remain largely absent amidst resistance to political integration. It is unclear whether proposals to elevate the EC President by making this office head of the European Council and turning the European Parliament into a genuine continental legislature – to permit democratically accountable European fiscal policy – would gain approval from enough member states to become reality.

European decision makers must rediscover the spirit of the White Paper: 'Democratic institutions and the representatives of the people, at both national and European levels, can and must try to connect Europe with its citizens. This is the starting condition for more effective and relevant policies' (European Commission 2001: 3). Fox argues that democratic renewal may only be obtained if national parliaments are brought on board, for instance, by recalling the '"assises" (or Conference of the Parliaments) to debate the future direction of democratic accountability in the European Union' to redesign institutions to reconcile democratic and fiscal imperatives (Fox 2012: 464). Hagemann (2012) suggests the need for transparency as the fiscal pact evolves 'as well as greater parliamentary participation in debates over Europe's economic future'. By increasing constraints on elected governments, boosting the power of central, bureaucratic, financial institutions and orchestrating the switch from democratic to technocratic governance in two states, the fiscal reforms could move the EU away from these goals. It remains to be seen how the democratic pushback will play out or if fiscal stability will be fostered, which could permit meaningful dialogue on the democratic nature and social dimension of the European project in future decades.

References

Alogoskoufis, G. (2012), 'Greece's Sovereign Debt Crisis: Retrospect and Prospect' GreeSE Paper No.54, Hellenic Observatory Papers on Greece and Southeast Europe. London School of Economics. Available at www2.lse.ac.uk/europeanInstitute/research/.../GreeSE-No54.pdf (accessed 9 April 2012).

Belke, A. and T. Polleit (2011), 'How Much Fiscal Backing Must the ECB Have? On the Political and Financial Dependence of a Central Bank'. Available at http://pubchoicesoc.org/papers_2012/Belke_Polleit.pdf (accessed 9 April 2012).

Brkić, L. and K. Kotarski (2010), 'Managing Crisis in the Eurozone' *Politička misao* 47(5), 7–26. Available at http://hrcak.srce.hr/file/101608 (accessed 8 April 2012).

BusinessEurope (2011), Council of Presidents, 'Declaration on Economic Governance', Warsaw, 2 December. Available at http://vbo-feb.be/media/uploads/public/_custom/press/Declaration_Economic_Governance_final_-_05_12_2011.pdf (accessed 1 April 2012).

Collignon, S. (2003), 'Is Europe Going Far Enough? Reflections on the Stability and Growth Pact, the Lisbon Strategy and the EU's Economic Governance'. *European Political Economy Review* 1(2) (Autumn), 222–47.

Collignon, S. (2011), 'European Catharsis'. *Social Europe Journal* (November). Available at http://www.social-europe.eu/2011/11/european-catharsis/ (accessed 8 April 2012).

Corporate Europe Observatory (CEO) (2012), 'Inspired by Big Business: The EU Austerity Treaty' Brussels 8 March. Available at http://www.corporateeurope. org/news/inspired-big-business-eu-austerity-treaty#footnote2_16e6up4 (accessed 1 April 2012).

Corporate Europe Observatory (CEO) (2012a), 'Automatic Austerity: 10 Things You Need to Know about "The Fiscal Compact"'. Available at http:// www.corporateeurope.org/sites/default/files/publications/Automatic%20 Austerity%20-%2010%20things%20you%20need%20to%20know.pdf (accessed 27 August 2012).

Delastik, G. (2012), 'Juncker Doesn't Have Say on Athens Government'. 29 February.

Devuyst, Y. (2008), 'The European Union's Institutional Balance after the Treaty of Lisbon: "Community Method" and "Democratic Deficit" Reassessed' *Georgetown Journal of International Law* 39(2), 247–325.

DG ECFIN (2012), European Commission, Economic and Financial Affairs EU Economic Governance 'Stability and Convergence Programmes'. Available at http://ec.europa.eu/economy_finance/economic_governance/sgp/ convergence/index_en.htm (accessed 2 April 2012).

DG ECFIN (2012a), European Commission, Economic and Financial Affairs EU Economic Governance 'Excessive Deficit Procedures'. Available at http:// ec.europa.eu/economy_finance/economic_governance/sgp/deficit/index_ en.htm (accessed 2 April 2012).

Donahue, P. (2012), 'Merkel Balks at Sovereign Debt Purchases to Beat Crisis'. *Bloomberg News* 21 June 2012. Available at http://mobile.bloomberg. com/news/2012-06-20/merkel-pushes-back-on-direct-bond-purchasing-to- overcome-crisis (accessed 11 July 2012).

Economist (2011), 'Britain and the EU the Moment, Behind Closed Doors, that David Cameron Lost his EU Argument Last Night'. Bagehot's Blog Dec 9th. Available at http://www.economist.com/blogs/bagehot/2011/12/britain-and- eu-1 (accessed 27 March 2012).

Economist (2012), Relief, but Little Hope. 23 June. Available at http://www. economist.com/node/21557383/print (accessed 22 July 2012).

Elliot, L. (2012), 'Eurozone Crisis: Democracy Trumps Austerity but Will the Euro Survive?' *The Guardian* 7 May. Available at http://www.guardian.co.uk/ business/2012/may/07/eurozone-crisis-democracy-trumps-austerity-euro/ print (accessed 22 May 2012).

To Ethnos (In Greek). Translated synopsis available at http://www.eurotopics.net/ en/home/debatten/links-2010-05-euroangst/ (accessed 3 April 2012).

ETUC (2012a), Declaration on the 'Treaty on Stability, Coordination and Governance in the Economic and Monetary Union'. Adopted by the ETUC Steering Committee on 25 January. Available at http://www.etuc.org/IMG/pdf/EN-Declaration-on-the-new-treaty_FINAL.pdf (accessed 27 March 2012).

ETUC (2012b), 'Council Fails to Deal with Sustainable Growth and Jobs'. 31 January. Available at http://etuc.org/a/9605 (accessed 1 April 2012).

EurActiv (2012), 'Hollande Meets Monti in Move to Counter Merkel'. *EurActiv* 15 June 2012. Available at http://www.euractiv.com/euro-finance/hollande-meets-monti-emancipates-news-513325 (accessed 18 July 2012).

European Commission (2012), 'Treaty on Stability, Coordination and Governance in the Economic and Monetary Union'. Available at http://www.european-council.europa.eu/media/579087/treaty.pdf (accessed 27 March 2012).

European Commission (2012a), 'Specifications on the Implementation of the Stability and Growth Pact and Guidelines on the Format and Content of Stability and Convergence Programmes'. Available at http://ec.europa.eu/economy_finance/economic_governance/sgp/pdf/coc/code_of_conduct_en.pdf (accessed 27 March 2012).

European Commission (2001), 'European Governance: A White Paper'. COM (2001) 428 final. Available at http://eur-lex.europa.eu/LexUriserv/site/en/com/2001/com2001_0428en01.pdf (accessed 25 March 2012).

European Council (2011), 'Statement by the Euro Area Heads of State or Government'. Brussels, 9 December. Available at http://www.consilium.europa.eu/uedocs/cms_data/docs/pressdata/en/ec/126658.pdf (accessed 1 April 2012).

European Council (2012), 'Fiscal Compact Signed: Strengthened Fiscal Discipline and Convergence in the Euro Area'. Brussels, 2 March 2012. Available at http://www.consilium.europa.eu/uedocs/cms_data/docs/pressdata/en/ec/128454.pdf (accessed 8 April 2012).

European Council (2012a), 'European Stability Mechanism Treaty Signed'. 2 February 2012. Available at http://consilium.europa.eu/homepage/showfocus?lang=en&focusID=79757 (accessed 8 April 2012).

European Council (2012b), 'Factsheet: Treaty Establishing the European Stability Mechanism'. 2 February. Available at http://www.consilium.europa.eu/uedocs/cms_data/docs/pressdata/en/ecofin/127788.pdf (accessed 8 April 2012).

Feinman, J.N. (2011), 'A Closer Look: Europe in Crisis'. Deustche Bank Advisors, Frankfurt. Available at https://www.dbadvisors.com/content/_media/DAM470_CloserLook1011.pdf (accessed 9 April 2012).

Follesdal, A. and S. Hix (2006), 'Why There is a Democratic Deficit in the EU: A Response to Majone and Moravcsik', *Journal of Common Market Studies* 44, 533–62.

Fox, R. (2012), 'Europe, Democracy and the Economic Crisis: Is It Time to Reconstitute the "Assises"?' *Parliamentary Affairs* 65, 463–9, doi:10.1093/pa/gss003.

Fritz-Vannahme, J. (2012), 'Long Live the United States of Europe'. *Spotlight Europe* March 2012. Available at http://aei.pitt.edu/id/eprint/34186 (accessed 7 April 2012).

Gatto, A. (2006), 'Governance in the European Union: A Legal Perspective'. *Columbia Journal of European Law* 12 (Spring), 487–516.

Hagemann, S. (2012), 'The Political and Economic Crisis in Europe Has Meant a Step Back for the EU's Major Institutions'. Available at http://blogs.lse.ac.uk/politicsandpolicy/2012/01/09/eu-crisis-institutions/ (accessed 22 May 2012).

IBOA – The Finance Union (2012), 'EU Unions' No to EU Stability Treaty'. 30 January. Available at http://www.iboa.ie/media/keyissues/2012/01/30/eu-unions-no-to-eu-stability-treaty/ (accessed 27 March 2012).

Keohane, R.O., Macedo, S. and A. Moravcsik (2009), 'Democracy-Enhancing Multilateralism'. *International Organization*, 63, 1–31 doi:10.1017/S0020818309090018.

Kitsantonis, N. (2012), 'Greek Coalition Outlines Plan to Renegotiate Loan Deal'. *New York Times*, 24 June. Available at http://www.nytimes.com/2012/06/24/world/europe/greek-coalition-outlines-plan-to-renegotiate-loan-deal.html (accessed 22 July 2012).

Mauldin, J. (2012), 'A Primer on the Euro Breakup'. 27 February 2012. Available at http://www.johnmauldin.com/images/uploads/pdf/mwo022712.pdf (accessed 26 March 2012).

Moravcsik, A. (2008), 'The Myth of Europe's "Democratic Deficit"'. *Intereconomics: Journal of European Economic Policy* (November–December 2008), 331–4. doi: 10.1007/s10272-008-0266-7.

O'Brien, P. (2012), 'The European Fiscal Treaty: Constitutionalising "The Road to Serfdom"?' Constitutional Law Group Blog 24 February. Available at http://ukconstitutionallaw.org/2012/02/24/patrick-obrien-the-european-fiscal-treaty-constitutionalising-the-road-to-serfdom/ (accessed 27 March 2012).

o Broin, P. (2012), *The Euro Crisis: The Fiscal Treaty – An Initial Analysis.* Dublin, Institute of International and European Affairs. Available at http://www.iiea.com/documents/the-euro-crisis-the-fiscal-treaty--an-initial-analysis (accessed 27 March 2012).

Oberndorfer, L. (2012), 'The Fiscal Compact Bypasses Democracy and the Rule of Law New Treaty Next Step in Neoliberal Crisis Management'. Transnational Institute. Available at http://www.tni.org/article/fiscal-compact-bypasses-democracy-and-rule-law#_ftn10 (accessed 2 April 2012).

Peterson, T. (2012), 'Stability has a Price'. *Spotlight Europe.* 2 March 2012. Available at http://www.isn.ethz.ch/isn/Digital-Library/Publications/Detail/?lng=en&id=139403 (accessed 30 July 2012).

Pisani-Ferry, J., Sapir, A. and G.B. Wolff (2012), 'The Messy Rebuilding of Europe'. Bruegel Policy Brief January 2012, March 2012. Available at http://aei.pitt.edu/34445/1/%28English%29.pdf (accessed 9 April 2012).

Rehn, O. (2012), 'Statement by Vice-President Rehn at the Eurogroup'. European Commission, Economic and Financial Affairs. Available at http://ec.europa. eu/economy_finance/articles/eurogroup_ecofin/2012-02-21-rehn-statement-eurogroup_en.htm (accessed 2 April 2012).

Reuters (2012), 'Senior Merkel Ally Sends Stark Warning to Greece' (13 March 2012). Available at http://www.reuters.com/article/2012/08/13/us-germany-greece-idUSBRE87C09H20120813 (accessed 17 August 2012).

Scharpf, F.W. (2011), 'Monetary Union, Fiscal Crisis and the Preemption of Democracy'. Paper presented at the LEQS Annual Lecture 'Saving the Euro – at the expense of democracy in Europe?' LSE 'Europe in Question' Discussion Paper Series (LEQS). Available at http://papers.ssrn.com/sol3/Delivery. cfm/SSRN_ID1852316_code1425528.pdf?abstractid=1852316&mirid=1 (accessed 3 April 2012).

Schmidt, V.A. (2005), 'Democracy in Europe: The Impact of European Integration'. *Perspectives on Politics* 3(4), 761–79.

Schmidt, I. (2009), New Institutions, Old Ideas: The Passing Moment of the European Social Model. *Studies in Political Economy* 84 (Autumn), 7–28.

Schuknecht, L., Moutot, P., Rother, P. and J. Stark (2011), 'The Stability and Growth Pact: Crisis and Reform'. ECB Occasional Paper No. 129. Available at http://ssrn.com/abstract=1791598 (accessed 9 April 2012).

Skelton, D. (2011), 'Government of the Technocrats, by the Technocrats, for the Technocrats'. *New Statesman.* 16 November. Available at http://www. newstatesman.com/blogs/the-staggers/2011/11/european-greece-technocrats (accessed 3 April 2012).

Strange, G. (2012), 'The Euro, EU Social Democracy, and International Monetary Power: A Critique of New Constitutionalism'. *Globalizations* 9(2), 257–72.

Tassinari, F. (2011), 'In Times of Crisis, Europeans Aren't Big On Democracy'. *Business Insider.* 15 November. Available at http://articles.businessinsider. com/2011-11-14/europe/30396603_1_european-central-bank-eurozone-democratic-deficit (accessed 8 April 2012).

Thatcher, M. and A. Sweet (2002), 'Theory and Practice of Delegation to Non-Majoritarian Institutions'. *West European Politics* 1(25), 1–22.

Vander Stichele, M., Bizzarri, K. and L. Plank (2006), 'Corporate Power over EU Trade Policy: Good for Business, Bad for the World'. Brussels: Seattle to Brussels Network. Available at http://www.s2bnetwork.org/download/ Corporate_power_over_EU_Trade_policy (accessed 15 June 2011).

Weisbach, A. and K. Matussek (2012), 'Germany's ESM Role, EU Fiscal Pact Challenged in Court'. Bloomberg News 30 June. Available at http://www. bloomberg.com/news/2012-06-30/germany-s-esm-role-eu-fiscal-pact-challenged-in-court.html (accessed 16 August 2012).

Wimmel, A. (2009), 'Theorizing the Democratic Legitimacy of European Governance: A Labyrinth with No Exit?' *European Integration* 31(2), 181–99.

Chapter 4
Britain and Monetary Union

Alasdair Blair

Introduction

Barely a day goes by without some reference in the media to the European Union (EU), of which the eurozone crisis that erupted in 2009 has become the dominant thread. In Britain this discussion has been reflected in the country's position outside of the eurozone. To this end, the eurozone's turmoil has led to Eurosceptic columnists in the likes of the *Daily Mail* and *Daily Telegraph* triumphantly reporting on Britain's position outside of the eurozone and at the same time offering a degree of pleasure in the possibility of its demise. For some commentators, the crisis has also offered the possibility of Britain being able to positively distance itself further from European integration. But the problem with these approaches is that they fail to take into consideration the pragmatic issues associated with Britain's linkage to the eurozone bloc. These issues are themselves complicated by the Eurosceptic viewpoints held by Conservative MPs. The aim of this chapter is to examine British policy towards monetary union. In doing so, it addresses a number of issues. The first is to chart Britain's engagement with the objective of monetary union. The second is to explain British non-participation. The third is to examine the implications of these issues for the future direction of Britain's European foreign policy. Before discussing these questions it is necessary to set the scene in terms of the general context of Britain's relationship with the EU.

British Sovereignty and Europe

In the 40 years that Britain has been a member of the EU, a constant feature of its membership has been its portrayal as a disconnected member state (Aspinwall 2004; George 1998; Gowland and Turner 2000; Wall 2008; Wallace 1997). Such viewpoints have been crafted out of the reality that Britain came late to the European table, gaining membership in the then European Economic Community (EEC) on 1 January 1973. Britain's route to membership had been a humbling one, going from a position of an imperial to regional power in barely two decades after the end of World War II. Economics had dictated the necessity of British membership of the Community, with the anticipated benefits of the European Free Trade Association (EFTA) giving little in the way of comfort to Britain's economy. For all intents and purposes, membership of the Community was viewed as a last resort for the future of Britain. Yet this economic weakness would, in part, be Britain's undoing in its first and second application, allowing the French President Charles de Gaulle to cast his veto in 1963 and 1967 (Uri 1968). De Gaulle was conscious that Britain would have challenged French predominance of the Community and would have brought other interests – most notably the Commonwealth and the transatlantic relationship – to bear on the Community's policies. Once de Gaulle left office on 28 April 1969, the 'irremovable obstacle' to Britain's membership was removed and as a result the membership door was opened by his successor Georges Pompidou, not least because of the pressure exerted by the West German Chancellor, Willy Brandt (O'Neill 2000: 341).

Before the terms of Britain's membership were settled, Pompidou insisted that agreement be reached on the financing of the Community budget, most notably the Common Agricultural Policy (CAP). The resulting April 1970 agreement provided the Community with its own resources through a combination of duties on imports into the Community and up to 1% of a member state's Value Added Tax (VAT). Such an agreement was at the expense of placing greater burden on countries such as Britain which, because of its small agricultural sector, gained little in return from its contributions. Yet because there was no alternative for Britain but to be a member of the Community, the Heath government accepted this state of affairs when it joined on 1 January 1973 (Kitzinger 1973; Lord 1993). A direct implication of Britain's new found status as a net contributor influenced the Heath government to secure additional financial support for Britain through the creation of a regional policy. However, a lingering feeling of injustice, as well as the desire to keep the 'clashing balls of the Labour Party' apart, led Harold Wilson to seek a renegotiation of Britain's terms of membership in 1974 and hold a referendum on the renegotiated terms in 1975 which resulted in a two-to-one vote in favour of membership (Henderson 1994: 72).

Subsequent developments confirmed that the referendum vote failed to cement Britain's place as a committed European. Of the reasons for this, a key point to note is that whereas Britain went somewhat drudgingly into the Community, other member states pursued membership in far more enthusiastic terms. This ranged from establishing peace and security in the post-1945 period to gaining legitimacy after military rule. But more importantly, in the vast majority of member states there has until recent times been a consensus among the public and political parties as to the benefit of membership. By contrast, this cannot be said of Britain.

The significance of these events cannot be underestimated in ascertaining the reasons why Britain has been regarded as an awkward partner and why in over 40 years of membership it has not shared the same enthusiasm as other member states have had for closer European integration. In unpacking the reasons for this, one of the most basic points to note is that governments in the majority of the EU member states have been able to publicly demonstrate to their electorate the benefits of EU membership. At one extreme, France has benefited the most from CAP payments. Alternatively, others have gained significant benefits from structural and cohesion funding, with governments in Portugal, Spain, Italy, and newer member states such as Hungary and Poland being able to point to noteworthy infrastructure projects financed by the EU. Such has been the significance of this financial support that it has had a notable impact on the gross domestic product (GDP) in many EU member states, which in turn has positively influenced public opinion. By contrast, successive British governments have both been less able to point to these sorts of benefits and have at the same time faced a more hostile domestic media that has highlighted the levels of support that the EU has provided to other member states. This has in turn resulted in British governments tending to emphasize the negative impact were Britain not to be a member state rather than the positive benefits of membership.

These factors have themselves been greatly conditioned by the fact that with the exception of Edward Heath, Britain has been served by a succession of Prime Ministers who have not made a positive case for membership; even when governments have had the electoral capacity for this task – as the Blair government had after 1997 – there has been a reluctance to pursue such a policy (Scott 2004: 190). This strategy has largely been shaped by a concern about the potential domestic backlash. As Sir Stephen Wall (a former head of the Cabinet Office European Secretariat) has commented, 'successive British governments were to be nervous of press, parliamentary, and public scepticism about Europe, and to frame their policy responses accordingly' (Wall 2008: 4). In other words, Britain has suffered from the absence of an outright commitment towards the EU either from the echelons of the power elite in government or from other key decision-makers such as the media and business, which is a state of affairs that for all intents and purposes is not to be found in other member states.

This has in turn influenced the tendency of British governments to publicly set out key negotiating 'red lines' in advance of EU meetings and to pronounce victory upon their conclusion. Margaret Thatcher regarded the single market programme that was an integral part of the Single European Act (SEA) to be a success for British business. But she also regarded it to be the limit of European integration, a position which crucially did not equate with the views of other European leaders who considered that European integration should expand into policy areas that had traditionally rested under the control of the member states. This included the objective of monetary union which is included in the Preamble and Article 20 of the SEA. Thatcher found the idea of monetary union particularly unpalatable and this resulted in titanic clashes between her and other European leaders, as well as between herself and members of her own political party over the future direction of European integration. John Major sought to position Britain at the 'at the heart of Europe' and reportedly came back from the December 1991 Maastricht European Council proclaiming '"Game, Set and Match" for Britain' (Major 1991, 1999: 579; Hogg and Hill 1995: 157, fn. 7). The history of Britain's difficult relationship with European integration prompted Prime Minister Tony Blair in 1998 to request a review of Britain's overall approach to the EU. The outcome of this review was a 'step change' programme that emphasized the necessity for Britain to advance a more positive negotiating position on European issues. Tony Blair would go on to sign the Amsterdam and Nice Treaties, arguing that that 'Britain's future is inextricably linked with Europe' (Blair, T. 2001). Gordon Brown attempted to solve the global financial crisis and turned his attention away from Europe. David Cameron would introduce a referendum lock on the transfer of power to the EU in July 2011, but would be unable to use enforce the veto that he supposedly used at the December 2011 European Council on a new fiscal treaty.

For each of these leaders a common theme has been the way in which European integration has dogged their period in office, where the general pattern has been for governments to shift from a position supportive of European integration at the start of their period in office to ending in one of hostility. This could even be applied to Thatcher whose appointment as Prime Minister was greeted as a positive development by other European leaders. Yet by the end of her period in office she would be able to reflect 'I was turned out because I said to Europe No, No, No. That No, No, No has turned to Yes, Yes, Yes' (Blair, A. 1999: 7). Her successor, John Major, at first attempted to offer a positive European foreign policy. This, however, quickly became a hostage to fortune as his period in office became dominated by political infighting. He would go on to famously describe three of his Cabinet colleagues as 'bastards' in comments that were accidentally recorded after a television interview in July 1993, while the latter years of the Major premiership were dominated by a policy of non-cooperation with the EU. Just as with Major, Blair sought to offer a fresh approach to Britain's relations with Europe, but in the end proved unable to chart a constructive policy. Blair prevaricated on the possibility of Britain entering the euro, submitting to Treasury influence and being unable to shake off the view that the government's policy towards Europe was 'full of stunts but not strategy' (Blair, T. 2010: 532). Gordon Brown's European policy was saddled by his decade-long tenure as Chancellor when he was at best lukewarm towards European integration, a position that did not change as Prime Minister with him most notably turning up late for the signature of the Lisbon Treaty (Barber 2007). In opposition David Cameron took Conservative Members of the European Parliament (MEP) out of the European Peoples Party (EPP) grouping, thereby reducing Conservative Party relations with other European political parties to an all-time low. In government he has charted a set of policies that have been influenced by a considerable body of backbench Eurosceptic MPs.

These positions have reflected the warning given in a speech by the then leader of the Labour Party, Hugh Gaitskell, to Prime Minister Harold Macmillan at the October 1962 Labour Party conference, that Britain's participation in the European Community would mean 'the end of Britain as an independent European state, the end of a thousand years of history' (Charlton 1983: 274). This concern has become a more complex situation for British governments to manage as the EU has progressed towards deeper levels of integration from the mid-1980s onwards with the introduction of the SEA. Subsequent developments would see integration progress into social policy, interior policy, foreign and security policy, and most notably monetary policy. These developments not only threatened British sovereignty, but they challenged to the core the view held by successive

British governments that the European integration process should be controlled by the member states. It was this concern that influenced Prime Minister Margaret Thatcher's speech at the College of Europe in Bruges in September 1988, when she stressed that 'we have not successfully rolled back the frontiers of the state to see them re-imposed at a European level, with a European super-state exercising dominance from Brussels' (Thatcher 1997: 315–25). The speech became a lightning rod for the Eurosceptic audience in Britain and served as a totem pole that they could pin their colours to.

This came to the fore in 1989 with the publication of the Delors Report that advocated the creation of a single currency. For some member states, the creation of a single currency represented a means of strengthening what were often regarded as weak currencies. This was certainly true of Italy. However, for Britain and some other member states, this represented an unacceptable move to the creation of a federal Europe and the downgrading of the influence of national governments. In the House of Commons on 30 October 1990, Prime Minister Thatcher famously said 'no, no, no' to the Delors proposal. This would be subsequently captured in *The Sun* newspaper's 1 November 1990 headline, which read 'Up Yours Delors'. This brilliant and in many ways ludicrous piece of journalism conveyed a crucial and profound message about the Eurosceptic tide that was engulfing British politics.

Britain and Monetary Union

Given that Britain's hesitancy to join the European Community had, among other reasons, been shaped by a concern about the impact on national sovereignty, it was unsurprising that it was less than enthusiastic towards proposals for monetary cooperation. The first of these had come forward before Britain actually joined the Community, with the then six member states reaching agreement at the December 1969 Hague European Council that Economic and Monetary Union (EMU) would be recognized as an official goal of European integration. Yet the turbulent international financial conditions of the 1970s finished off this goal and it would not be until the end of the 1970s that member states and EU institutions began to turn their attention once more to monetary cooperation. This would be reflected in the creation of the European Monetary System (EMS) in 1979 of which the Exchange Rate Mechanism (ERM) was designed to bring about the coordination of member states economic policies (Jenkins 1991: 463). Britain, however, chose not to join the ERM, with the government's position at the time being that they did not want to be committed to maintaining the value of sterling within a fixed system. This was because the view in Whitehall was that sterling was subject to a different set of external pressures to that of other member states, for example its sensitivity to oil price fluctuations and the significance of trading networks with non-EC countries such as the Commonwealth. There was also a concern that participation in the ERM would result in sterling being dominated by the

Deutschmark. Finally, it is also worth pointing out that the government had been taken by surprise by the desire of other member states to pursue the EMS initiative (Dyson and Featherstone 1999: 540).

Although Britain's absence from the ERM provided the government (which, rather than the Bank of England, was the key determinant of monetary policy) with flexibility to determine monetary policy, government policy drew criticism from business circles who were concerned that a lack of exchange rate stability was hampering their economic growth. As early as 1981 there were visible signs of tension within government as to whether Britain would be better off within the ERM, of which Chancellor of the Exchequer Nigel Lawson was a key advocate (Lawson 1992: 111–13). It would be another four years before the issue of British membership of the ERM received serious debate (Dyson and Featherstone 1999: 544–8; Lawson 1992: 484–5).

By 1987 the issue of ERM membership had created an open sore within Cabinet, with Lawson undertaking a policy of sterling shadowing the Deutschmark within a DM3 ceiling between early 1987 and spring of 1988 as part of his efforts to make the case for entry (Thompson 1996: 86–95). Such a policy created much heated debate within Cabinet as the decision to shadow was for all intents and purposes a unilateral action by Lawson. John Major would later reflect that 'it was clear to all that Nigel was no longer working in harness with Margaret; by shadowing the Deutschmark and pressing, repeatedly, for our entry to the ERM, he was setting out his own stall in competition with his prime minister' (Major 1999: 132). The attractiveness of ERM membership was also bolstered by the fact that the system was proving to be relatively stable in the late 1980s in delivering low-inflationary economic growth. Stability was influenced by the growing political commitment to monetary union which saw a committee being formed in the wake of the June 1988 Hanover European Council, under the chairmanship of Commission President Jacques Delors, to investigate the means by which a monetary union could be established.

Just as Britain had been slow to recognize the impetus behind the creation of the EMS, it was equally behind the curve on the monetary union discussions that commenced in 1988. In Thatcher's eyes policies such as the SEA could be ring-fenced so that they would not result in pressures for integration in other policy areas. This view was not shared by France and Germany who argued that the internal market could only be fulfilled by the creation of a European Central Bank and a common currency. In the face of these differing viewpoints, the Delors Committee was regarded as a compromise way forward. For Thatcher, the Committee was a means of 'pushing the proposal for EMU into the long grass', with the view being that 'the whole implication at the beginning was that this was not a serious runner' (Blair, A. 2002: 119–20). To this end, the government was relatively relaxed about the possible outcomes from the Delors Committee, with the view in Downing Street being that the President of the German Bundesbank, Karl-Otto Pöhl, would not been in favour of its abolition as this would obviously dilute his own power (and that of the Bundesbank). To this end, Thatcher thought that an Anglo-German alliance could be established to halt any progress towards monetary union (Lawson 1992: 902).

This was somewhat fanciful thinking, given Britain's general isolation within the Community and the fact that Britain and Germany had not established a close relationship under Thatcher and Kohl's leadership. Moreover, the German government was in favour of monetary union. Thatcher's cause was additionally not helped by the lack of symmetry between herself and the Governor of the Bank of England, Robin Leigh-Pemberton, who believed that the remit of the Delors Committee was not to 'answer whether, but rather the question of how' EMU could be achieved (Blair, A. 2002: 122). In Thatcher's eyes, Leigh-Permberton had gone 'native' by adopting a position that was entirely out of sympathy with the government's line (Thompson 1999: 128–30). A consequence of this was rather than reducing the pace of integration, the Committee actually accelerated matters by charting a three-stage course for the creation of a monetary union (Dyson and Featherstone 1999: 606–10; Lawson 1992: 904).

More than anything else, the Delors Report brought to a head the implications of Britain's non-participation in the ERM as it symbolized the government's lack of engagement on matters relating to monetary union. Such was their concern about these matters that Howe and Lawson threatened Thatcher with resignation unless Britain gave a commitment to enter the ERM prior to the June 1989 Madrid European Council (Howe 1994: 580; Lawson 1992: 932). At the Madrid meeting Thatcher established the conditions that would make membership possible, albeit without setting a date for membership. Thatcher's change of tack on ERM entry would see her return from Madrid to undertake a bloody Cabinet reshuffle that would result in Howe being replaced as Foreign Secretary by John Major. Three months later, Lawson's disagreements with Thatcher came to a head and resulted in his resignation on 26 October 1989, with Major taking over as Chancellor. But while Thatcher hoped that Major would be less dogmatic than Howe and Lawson had been, by the summer of 1990 he was publicly making it clear the importance of British membership of the ERM (Blair, A. 2002: 108). Major was particularly concerned that a two-tier Europe could develop, with Britain isolated (Thatcher 1993: 724). Thatcher maintained her opposition until Britain eventually entered the ERM on 5 October 1990.

Apart from its role in reducing inflation, ERM entry was regarded by Major and Howe as a key method of ensuring that Britain would be able to have a full voice in the intergovernmental conference (IGC) negotiations on monetary union that were scheduled to commence in Rome in December 1990. This very fear of isolation resulted in the government advancing a proposal in 1989 to create a 'hard ECU' which in London's eyes had the benefits of a single currency while at the same time allowing member states to retain control over their national currency. And while the proposal had many admirers as it had all the benefits of a single currency – such as creating economic convergence and assisting with delivering low inflation – while it failed to drum up sufficient support among the member states who only wanted a single currency. This was hardly surprising given that

Thatcher's 'deepest hostility was to a single currency and the political implications of surrendering monetary authority' (Major 1999: 154). Thatcher's intransigence on Europe would eventually lead to her downfall and see her replaced as Prime Minister by John Major on 28 November.

Given that Britain was faced with a Franco-German juggernaut in favour of monetary union, the government's strategy during the IGC negotiations was to ensure that a single currency would not be imposed on Britain. Although Britain's preference was for a general exemption clause so that it was not singled out as a special case, this position was not shared by France and Germany who did not want a situation to materialize where other countries could decide not to participate in the single currency (Blair, A. 2002: 143). A consequence of this was that Britain obtained an opt-out from monetary union when the IGC negotiations were concluded at the December 1991 Maastricht European Council (a position that would subsequently be shared with Denmark). It would not be an underestimate to say that Britain's contribution to the monetary union negotiations was minimal, a situation that was shaped by the government's foot-dragging in this policy area. The government's position was heavily influenced by domestic political considerations, with there being little appetite for monetary union among members of the Cabinet, backbench Parliamentarians and the public at large.

It was with more than a sense of relief that Major returned from the Maastricht European Council with what he regarded to be a good deal for Britain (Blair, A. 1999: 210–15; Young 1998: 433). Major would later reflect that 'in Cabinet all was sweetness and light ... It was the modern equivalent of a Roman triumph' (Major 1999: 288). This sense of success quickly proved to be short-lived as the combination of a reduced parliamentary majority after the April 1992 General Election and the difficulties that ensued with the ratification of the Maastricht Treaty in Denmark and France whipped up a Eurosceptic backlash among Conservative MPs. Uncertainty over the ratification of the Maastricht Treaty created a crisis of confidence in the ERM which led to Britain's exit from the system on 16 September 1992 which thereafter became commonly referred to as 'Black Wednesday'. Britain's ERM exit had taken place after the government had twice sought to defend the value of sterling from speculative attacks by raising interest rates from 10% to 12% and subsequently to 15%. This action proved futile in the face of currency speculators who regarded sterling as being over-valued and in so doing the government had spent in the region of £3 billion of its official reserves in a valiant attempt to defend sterling. This action would add further fuel to the Eurosceptic cause and while sterling's exit from the ERM allowed devaluation in its value, which benefited business competitiveness, the period after September 1992 witnessed significant division within the government on the European issue and cemented Britain's position on the sidelines of Europe (Major 1999: 312–41; Lamont 1999: 246–66). As Major would later reflect, 'we entered the ERM to general applause, and left it to general abuse' (Major 1999: 340). The ERM exit increased the tone of scepticism within the Conservative Party concerning the ratification of the Treaty on European Union. As Dyson and

Featherstone point out, 'the September 1992 crisis in the ERM emboldened the Eurosceptics, cast a shadow over claims that Britain was at the "heart of Europe", necessitated a redirection of government economic policy and seriously damaged its electoral fortunes' (Dyson and Featherstone 1999: 73–4).

The events of Black Wednesday cast a long shadow over the remainder of John Major's premiership. This would materialize in significant difficulties over the ratification of the Maastricht Treaty which in the end could only be secured by Major holding a vote of confidence in his government on 23 July 1993. And while this halted the Eurosceptic tide against the Maastricht Treaty – as a 'no' vote would have brought about a general election which would have resulted in many Conservative MPs losing their seats in the face of a predicted Labour victory – it did not stop the overall influence that Eurosceptic MPs were having on government policy. Major's position as Prime Minister was increasingly hanging on a knife-edge, as by-election defeats had meant that more and more he had to pander to the interests of backbench Eurosceptics to secure a government majority. He eventually sought to tackle this situation by holding a leadership election on 4 July 1995 (Lamont 1999: 434–47; Major 1999: 608–47). For Major, this was an attempt to impose some form of authority on the Conservative Party by challenging critics to 'put up, or shut up' (Major 1999: 612). Yet the election failed to deliver this expected outcome, with Major's victory not silencing the Eurosceptic influence which resulted in the government coming to a decision in April 1996 that the Conservative Party would commit itself to have a referendum on the question of monetary union. This decision had been influenced by Major's desire to silence criticism from Eurosceptic MPs and Sir James Goldmith's Referendum Party. Major hoped that the referendum commitment would reduce divisions of opinion within the Conservative Party on the subject of monetary union. However, just as previous initiatives to achieve party unity had proved fruitless, so too did the referendum commitment. As the 1997 general election drew closer, discipline within the Conservative Party worsened. In the end, despite Major's early endeavours to place Britain at the 'heart of Europe', the country had drifted further away from Europe, with government policy largely being dictated by a Eurosceptic position.

With the backdrop of a divided government, it was inevitable that the Labour Party would win the May 1997 general election. In a foretaste of future policy, the Labour Party had committed itself in its manifesto to a rather schizophrenic policy towards the EU, whereby it sought both to take a leading role in the EU and at the same time to hold a referendum on the single currency (Bulmer 2008: 599). For the Labour Party, such a strategy was designed to defuse any potential criticism of its European policy. Despite this defensive approach, the early months of the Labour government would see a concerted effort to offer a positive approach to the EU. However, beneath such public overtures there were noticeable divisions within government, with Foreign Secretary Robin Cook's defence of the benefits of euro membership being in contrast to the more cautious approach of Brown (Rawnsley 2001: 386). A central feature of Labour's approach was the setting out in October 1997 of five economic tests that would have to be met for Britain to join the single currency. Although the government had committed itself to enter EMU if the economic conditions were right, it did so with the precondition that any decision on membership would need authorization from the Cabinet, the Parliament and by means of a popular referendum. To this end, it was evident that the economic tests were subservient to broader political considerations and as such in themselves could not provide a clear picture of the direction of policy (Rollo 2002).

Labour Government's Five Economic Tests for EMU

1. Sustainable convergence between Britain and the economies of the single currency.
2. The new currency system should have enough flexibility to be able to cope with economic change.
3. Membership of the single currency should have a favourable impact on investment.
4. The financial service industry of Britain, especially the City of London, must benefit from the single currency.
5. The single currency must have a positive impact on employment within Britain.

Although the establishment of economic conditions upon which membership would be based offered a more positive approach, an emphasis on economic conditions mirrored the policy of preceding Conservative governments. The prominence attached to economic factors for membership was representative of the stance taken by Thatcher towards participation in the ERM, whereby the government would join when the 'time was right'. The net effect of the setting of such economic tests was an appreciation that making a decision to join the single currency would be an unrealistic objective during the lifetime of the 1997 Parliament. As far as the economic tests of membership were concerned, the question as to whether there was sufficient convergence between the British economy and those on the continent was not a new issue. One of the main issues against British membership of the ERM in the mid-1980s was the lack of convergence between Britain's economic cycle and those on the continent.

Holding to a line that economic factors would be the determinant factor in establishing Britain's case for membership of the single currency did, however, become an increasingly difficult task in the latter years of the 1997–2001 Parliament. The desire of Prime Minister Blair to play a front line role in the EU, evidenced by being a key player in the creation of a stronger European foreign policy, meant that participation in the euro was a central aspect of Britain's renaissance as a proactive and positive member of the EU (Bulmer 2000). The Prime Minister did, nevertheless, take care not to be too forthright on the subject, though on the occasion of the publication of the national changeover plan in February 1999 he announced that 'We have stated today as a matter of government policy that in principle Britain should join a single European currency. That principle is real. The practical preparation we have set out are real' (*The Guardian* 1999). Blair's delivery of this upbeat assessment was in contrast to the Chancellor who was ever more sceptical on the merits of the single currency.

The outcome was that the Chancellor's more cautious approach increasingly seemed to be at odds with the viewpoints of other more pro-European members of the Cabinet. This particularly applied to his relations with Robin Cook at the FCO and Stephen Byers at the DTI. While both Cook and Byers considered that the government should advocate a more positive approach in regard to the single currency, the latter was more concerned about the practical implications that the government's uncertainty on the euro was having on British jobs rather than the wider issue of British engagement within the EU (Rawnsley 2001: 386–7). Yet, as far as the Chancellor was concerned, the wisdom of a cautious approach was greatly influenced by the extent to which the Conservative Party was prepared to use the single currency as a political tool. For the Chancellor, who was also in charge of the 2001 Labour general election campaign, there appeared to be no sense in creating undue tension on the subject in the run up to the election. Indeed, the Chancellor could argue that Labour's landslide victory in the 2001 campaign and the Conservative's over emphasis that was attached to the euro, vindicated this strategy. It is therefore evident that the single currency was a key point of division between Blair and Brown. Whereas the Prime Minister had become convinced as to the importance of Britain's membership of the single currency, the Chancellor had become more sceptical, not least because Brown feared that membership of the single currency would reduce his control over the economy (Rawnsley 2001: 497).

In the wake of the June 2001 general election victory, Tony Blair undertook a sweeping reshuffle of ministerial posts within government. Of the changes that were made, the FCO had a complete changeover of ministerial staff, with the replacement of Robin Cook by Jack Straw being the most notable element of the reshuffle (Rawnsley 2001: 507). The significance of this change of Foreign Secretary was that it represented a desire by Tony Blair to advance a more cautious approach to the euro and one which followed a lead from Downing Street and the Treasury rather than the more pro-European instincts of the FCO. At the same time Blair also sought to bolster his own position by strengthening his ministerial team at the Cabinet Office (Rawnsley 2001: 507–8). It was also noticeable that Cook's change of post to Leader of the House of Commons was the same position taken up by Sir Geoffrey Howe when Thatcher moved him out of the FCO. And just like Thatcher, Prime Minister Blair offered a 'sweetener' to ease the transition, this being the continued use of the Foreign Secretary's official London residence. The government reshuffle was also noticeable for the replacement of the Europhile Stephen Byers by Patricia Hewitt at the Department of Trade and Industry (DTI).

The importance of these ministerial changes was that they resulted in the removal of two of the most pro-European Cabinet Ministers from key posts that had a significant input to the construction of Britain's position on monetary union. In the first instance, this was a means of shoring-up the role of the Prime Minister on the question of euro membership at the expense of the FCO. Secondly, whereas Cook might have regarded Labour's landslide general election majority as a signal for advancing a more positive approach to the euro, the change in Foreign Secretary was a means of Blair ensuring that a more cautious tone was advanced by the more naturally Eurosceptic Jack Straw. Finally, this meant that although Tony Blair had previously announced that a re-elected Labour government would decide within two years whether to hold a referendum or not, the Prime Minister was not going to attempt to bounce the electorate into a decision at an early stage. Such a viewpoint was mindful of the failure of Denmark to obtain a 'yes' vote on the euro in a referendum in 2000, and the 'no' vote recorded by Ireland in its 2001 referendum on the December 2000 Nice Treaty. Thus in the wake of its historic election victory, the Labour government was clearly conscious that even if it fully supported the euro, there would be strong likelihood that an early referendum on the question would not be endorsed by the electorate. The net effect of this was that the government moved to a publicly more cautious approach towards the single currency that would not shift for the remainder of its period in office as worsening economic conditions ended the possibility of Britain adopting the euro.

In reflecting on these events it is evident that the euro lessened in significance as an area of Labour government policy after the 2001 general election and the issue of euro membership only receives a fleeting mention in Blair's memoirs, with some two pages being devoted to the subject (Blair, T. 2010: 536–7). In making his defence of the government's position, Blair notes that he 'took care not to go beyond what was reasonable for British opinion' (2010: 536) and that 'the economic case was at best ambiguous; and certainly not beyond doubt' (2010: 537). However, the fact of the matter was that war in Afghanistan and Iraq became a significant distraction for government policy-making and in the wake of the 2005 general election victory Blair's ability to lead on policy developments was weakened by the view that he would be leaving office (Darling 2011: 11). By the time that Gordon Brown succeeded Blair as Prime Minister on 27 June 2007 it was clear that government policy-making had drifted and that Britain's participation in the single currency was nowhere on the government's radar. It was a situation that was further compounded by the unwillingness of the government to tie itself into the fiscal policy rules of joining the euro at a time when it had, over a number of years, massively increased domestic expenditure in key areas of education and health in order to remedy decades of under-investment. This concern that British interests were somewhat divergent from the policy demands of the euro would subsequently be emphasized by the economic crisis that unfolded the following year and which unleashed significant turbulence in EU economies, most notably the eurozone. Reflecting on these events, the Chancellor of the Exchequer, Alistair Darling, would later comment that 'One of the most astute decisions we ever took was to stay out of the euro' (Darling 2011: 295).

By the time a Conservative-Liberal Democrat coalition government took office after the 2010 general election, the unfolding eurozone crisis was the dominant concern in the governments of all member states. Britain was no exception, with the government undertaking a so-called policy of austerity that resulted in it unleashing some of the most radical reforms in a generation. At a European level, the construction of Britain's policy towards the EU was greatly influenced by the fact that the 2010 election had resulted in a sizeable number of Eurosceptic Conservative MPs gaining office. This would in turn result in the government facing a series of rebellions on the issue of Europe and would shape government policy on its willingness (or lack of it) to support broader European financial stabilization mechanisms. This would result in the government indirectly supporting the eurozone through increasing IMF funds rather than a direct policy as a means of trying to head off Eurosceptic critics. As a sign of what was to come later, in September 2011 five new Conservative MPs produced a book '*After the Coalition*' that urged the government to repatriate such powers as farming, fisheries, financial regulation, social policy and criminal law (Kwarteng et al. 2010). A Eurosceptic tone would lead to referendum lock being introduced as a result of the European Union Bill. This would be followed up with Prime Minister Cameron's public refusal to support a new EU fiscal treaty through the use of his veto at the December 2011 Brussels European Council. But while this resulted in much congratulations from Eurosceptic Conservative backbench MPs, nearly one month later at an EU meeting on 30 January 2012 the government had altered its position so that it would no longer object to a fiscal treaty. This change of policy was representative of the see-saw nature of the coalition government's European policy that would provoke criticism of a lack of strategy, direction and long-term thinking on government policy (King 2012). Yet in contrast to the strategy of previous British governments which have been concerned about retaining British influence at the European negotiating table, Cameron's strategy appears to be somewhat the opposite by accepting British isolation (Stephens 2011).

Explaining British Non-participation

Taking the above points into consideration, it is possible to identify five key factors that have determined British policy towards monetary union.

1. A failure to understand the political commitment towards monetary union
In chronicling Britain's policy towards monetary union, a common theme that emerges from this debate is the extent to which successive governments have underestimated the political willingness in other member states to pursue monetary integration. Margaret Thatcher underestimated the significance of the reference to monetary union in the SEA and failed to appreciate the significance of the Delors Committee by which time monetary union was firmly on the agenda at the European level (Wall 2012). This theme of not fully comprehending the

significance of monetary union has continued in the years that have followed, with the move to establish a European Financial Stability Fund leading to the recent agreement in January 2012 on a new Treaty on Stability, Coordination and Governance in the Economic and Monetary Union, which was finalized by all EU member states with the exception of Britain and the Czech Republic. The implication of the most recent of these developments is that they signal a move towards political governance. These developments in turn are likely to sideline Britain's position within the EU.

2. The dominance of the Treasury

As far as matters relating to monetary policy are concerned, it is evident that they have generally not been subject to the same degree of cross-departmental consultation as other EU policies, with the Treasury being the dominant department. The strength of the Chancellor is, of course, greatly determined by the personality and relative power and influence of the person who occupies the office. To this end, the high status that Nigel Lawson had within the Conservative Party and the government meant that Prime Minister Margaret Thatcher could not just ignore her Chancellor, though towards the end of the 1980s she did become increasingly reliant on Alan Walters (her economic advisor). John Major equally could not simply ignore the pro-European views of Kenneth Clarke because of his standing within government. The Chancellor, and more broadly the Treasury, is consequently able to exercise influence by essentially blocking proposals that it is unhappy with. This 'veto' power has similarly been mirrored in Gordon Brown's refusal to be pressurized on the question of Britain's membership of EMU.

3. A lack of political consensus

Despite the establishment of Conservative and Liberal Democrat coalition government, the Westminster model of British politics has traditionally been dominated by a two-party system that has rewarded governments with workable electoral majorities as a result of the first-past-the-post nature of the electoral system. A consequence of this has been the absence of cross-party positions on matters relating to European integration. This has often resulted in matters relating to European integration becoming 'politicized' which in turn has led to political parties using EU policies as a battleground at the domestic level (Forster and Blair 2002: 126). But at the same time, EU policies have themselves become matters of extreme intra-party conflict, with Prime Ministers having to face the reality of backbench MPs being prepared to vote against government policy. This is a situation that has worsened in recent years as MPs have become more rebellious within Parliament by voting against party policy. For example, in October 2011 David Cameron faced the largest European rebellion of the post-war era when 81 Conservative MPs voted against government policy in favour of a referendum on Britain's membership of the EU (Cowley and Stuart 2012).

4. Public opinion and the media

It is hardly surprising that given the absence of a cross-party consensus on Europe that many people in Britain have a sceptical attitude towards the EU. Polls regularly indicate that the British public are one of the least positive about the EU. This is a situation which is itself shaped by a national media that is dominated by a debate that is heavily shaped by a Eurosceptic discourse. Linked to this is the fact that the public at large have tended to display a low level of knowledge and awareness about European issues. This in turn has materialized in statistics which demonstrate the public tend to have a negative attitude towards European integration and view that the economic costs of membership outweigh the benefits. But a key problem with these issues is the fact that political parties have failed to undertake a mature debate on European integration, with the result being extremely low levels of European identification among the public as a result of the fact that the case for Europe has rarely been made.

5. Economic cycle

One of the factors that influenced Britain's initial reluctance to engage in the ERM was a concern that Britain's economy operated a different economic cycle to that of other Community member states. Relevant factors included Britain's exposure to oil price fluctuations and trading links with the likes of Commonwealth countries. When Britain eventually joined the ERM, the conditions of membership proved to be too restraining and this in turn led to Britain's exit in September 1992. The years that have followed have seen some of these factors decrease in significance, such the impact of oil price movements and trade outside of the EU, with there also being an increase in the UK's trade within the EU. Nevertheless, there has continued to be a number of structural factors that have underpinned a slightly more divergent economic cycle. This has included the significance of the UK housing market and the significant contribution of the finance sector to the UK economy, which before the financial crisis contributed about 25% of the UK's corporate taxes (Darling 2011: 7).

A Withering Relationship?

Viewed in perspective, Britain's engagement with the project to create monetary union and the policy positions adopted since the introduction of the euro have confirmed its position as sitting on the EU sidelines.

In the first instance, the euro crisis has brought to the fore the divisions that exist between those member states that are part of the eurozone and those that are not. Given the introduction of a fiscal treaty and the moves towards eurozone governance, it is evident that going forward this will create a fundamentally different relationship between the UK and other member states. One potential likelihood of this is the emergence of greater tension between the UK and other member states.

Second, given the fact that the response to the eurozone crisis has largely been driven by heads of state and government, this has acted as a public demonstration of their commitment to the eurozone's survival.

Finally, the above events have brought to the fore the importance of a stronger sense of public connection with the EU. Britain has suffered from the combination of an absence of elites making a proactive and collective case that advocates the significance of EU membership. It is also evident that decisions have for the most part been taken by government elites who have rarely made an effort to connect with the public. This lack of public engagement with European integration is problematic at a pan-European level, where an ever more integrated EU is taking place without much in the way of public debate (Habermas 2012). To this end, decisions are being taken by political leaders without anything in the way of consultation with their public. In this context, European integration is potentially moving into an unsustainable situation where it is being driven by an elite that is politically out of touch with its electorate.

References

Aspinwall, M. (2004), *Rethinking Britain and Europe. Plurality Elections, Party Management and British Policy on European Integration*. Manchester: Manchester University Press.

Barber, T. (2007), 'Brown's Late Signing of EU Treaty Attacked'. *Financial Times*, 13 December.

Blair, A. (1999), *Dealing with Europe: Britain and the Negotiation of the Maastricht Treaty*. Aldershot: Ashgate.

Blair, A. (2002), *Saving the Pound: Britain's Road to Monetary Union*. Harlow: Prentice Hall.

Blair, T. (1996), *New Britain: My Vision of a Young Country*. London: Fourth Estate.

Blair, T. (2001), 'Britain's Role in Europe', speech to the European Research Institute, University of Birmingham, 23 November. Available at http://www.number-10.gov.uk/output/Page1673.asp (accessed 28 August 2012).

Blair, T. (2010), *A Journey*. London: Hutchinson.

Bulmer, S. (2008), 'New Labour, New European Policy? Blair, Brown and Utilitarian Supranationalism'. *Parliamentary Affairs* 61(4), 597–620.

Bulmer, S. (2000), 'The Europeanisation of British Central Government', in R.A.W. Rhodes, *Transforming British Government, Volume 1: Changing Institutions*. Basingstoke: Macmillan, 46–62.

Charlton, M. (1983), *The Price of Victory*. London: BBC.

Cowley, P. and M. Stuart (2012), 'The Cambusters: The Conservative European Union Referendum Rebellion of October 2011'. *The Political Quarterly* 83(2), 402–6.

Darling, A. (2011), *Back from the Brink*. London: Atlantic Books.

Dyson, K. and K. Featherstone (1999), *The Road to Maastricht: Negotiating Economic and Monetary Union*. Oxford: Oxford University Press.

Forster, A. and A. Blair (2002), *The Making of Britain's European Foreign Policy*. London: Longman.

George, S. (1998), *An Awkward Partner*, 3rd edn. Oxford: Oxford University Press.

Gowland, D. and A. Turner (2000), *Reluctant Europeans: Britain and European Integration 1945–1998*. London: Longman.

Habermas, J. (2012), *The Crisis of the European Union*, translated by Ciaran Cronin. London: Polity Press.

Henderson, N. (1994), *Mandarin: The Diaries of an Ambassador 1969–1982*. London, Weidenfeld and Nicolson.

Hogg, S. and J. Hill (1995), *Too Close to Call: Power and Politics – John Major in No. 10*. London: Little, Brown and Company.

Howe, G. (1994), *Conflict of Loyalty*. Basingstoke: Macmillan.

Hughes, K. and E. Smith (1998), 'New Labour – New Europe'. *International Affairs* 74(1), 93–103.

Jenkins, R. (1991), *A Life at the Centre*. Basingstoke: Macmillan.

King, A. (2012), 'It is the Dilettante Prime Minister Got a Grip'. *Financial Times*. 10 April, 13.

Kitzinger, U. (1973), *Diplomacy and Persuasion: How Britain Joined the Common Market*. London, Thames and Hudson Ltd.

Kwarteng, D., Patel, P., Raab, D., Skidmore, C. and E. Truss (2010), *After the Coalition: A Conservative Agenda for Britain*. London: Biteback.

Lamont, N. (1999), *In Office*. London: Little, Brown and Company.

Lawson, N. (1992), *The View From No. 11*. London: Bantam Press.

Lord, C. (1993), *British Entry to the European Community under the Heath Government 1970–1974*. Aldershot: Dartmouth Publishing Company.

Major, J. (1991), *The Evolution of Europe*. Speech to the Konrad Adenauer Foundation. 11 March, London: Conservative Political Centre.

Major, J. (1999), *The Autobiography*. London: Harper Collins.

O'Neill, C. (2000), *Britain's Entry into the European Community: Report on the Negotiations of 1970–1972*. Edited by Sir David Hannay, London: Frank Cass.

Rawnsley, A. (2001), *Servants of the People: The Inside Story of New Labour*. London: Penguin.

Rollo, J. (2002), 'In or Out: The Choice for Britain', *Journal of Public Policy* 22(2), 217–29.

Scott, D. (2004), *Off Whitehall: A View from Downing Street by Tony Blair's Adviser*, London: I.B. Taurus.

Stephens, P. (2011), 'Cameron Makes a Dash for the Sidelines', *Financial Times* 8 February, 13.

Thatcher, M. (1993), *The Downing Street Years*, London: HarperCollins.

Thatcher, M. (1997), *The Collected Speeches*, London: HarperCollins.

The Guardian (1999), 'Blair: "We can no longer pretend the euro does not exist"', *The Guardian*. 23 February. Available at http://www.guardian.co.uk/business/1999/feb/23/emu.theeuro2 (accessed 31 August 2012).

Thompson, H. (1996), *The British Conservative Government and the European Exchange Rate Mechanism. 1979–1994.* London: Pinter.

Uri, P. (ed.) (1968), *From Commonwealth to Common Marke.* Harmondswoth, Penguin in association with the Atlantic Institute.

Wall, S. (2008), *A Stranger in Europe: Britain and the EU from Thatcher to Blair.* Oxford: Oxford University Press.

Wall, S. (2012), 'Britain and Europe'. *The Political Quarterly* 83(2), 325–33.

Wallace, H. (1997), 'At Odds with Europe'. *Political Studies* 45(4), 677–88.

Young, H. (1998), *This Blessed Plot: Britain and Europe from Churchill to Blair.* London: Papermac.

PART III
Other Policy Developments and Challenges

Chapter 5

The Common Agricultural Policy:
The Right Path versus Blind Alleys

Jacek Chotkowski and Benon Gaziński

Introduction

Institutional economics, one of the branches of economic theory, defines institutions as certain rules governing people's actions and behaviour in economic and social life. It is the shape of these institutions that determines costs of concluding contracts and operating the entire economic system, consequently influencing the effectiveness of the whole economy. In general, norms and patterns of human activities can be divided into 'formal' and 'customary' categories. Customary norms originate from traditionally established standards of behaviour, as well as ethical, moral and religious principles. They can undergo modifications, but only over a long time, usually spanning a few generations (Williamson 1985). In a shorter time perspective of just a few years, economic activity, including agriculture, can only be improved and enhanced by perfecting institutions classified as formal. Such institutions include legal norms (regulations) that must be abided by (in contrast to customary norms), administrative (bureaucratic) procedures as well as actions undertaken by all formally existing institutions. In the EU member states, the rules of the Common Agricultural Policy have become important elements in the development of farming and rural areas (Wilkin 2011).

Since its foundations were laid out in the 1957 Treaty of Rome, the Common Agricultural Policy (CAP) has undergone evolutionary changes. These changes improved the effectiveness of expending considerable financial means from the EU budget on agriculture, and generated quite satisfying results in other areas, such as environmental conservation and the prevention of poverty in agricultural communities. However, there are significant shortcomings of the CAP that have not yet been overcome, for example poor orientation towards formally set goals, providing richer farmers with extra bonuses, more support given to intensive farming rather than to more eco-friendly farming technologies, excessive absorption of natural resources, and infringement of fair competition principles. Additionally, the CAP is excessively complicated, and therefore hardly comprehensible, as well as extremely bureaucratic, requiring an expensive management and control system. Thus, while discussing CAP guidelines for the next financial framework of 2014–2020, the need to simply the policy is frequently emphasized.

The purpose of this chapter is to analyse the up-to-date reforms and discussions on the difficult issue of simplification of the Common Agricultural Policy. Against the background of its creation and the history of previous reforms, the drawbacks of the present legal and administrative system have been characterized. The authors demonstrate why it is necessary to change the philosophy governing the CAP and suggest directions that future reforms should follow.

The Common Agricultural Policy: Formation, Principles and Early Changes

History and General Principles

Heralded in with the Treaty of Rome in 1957, the Common Agricultural Policy is among the oldest EU policies. Its special importance is confirmed by high budgetary outlays, which exceeded 75% in the record years prior to the reforms and, despite numerous efforts, continue to amount to around 40% of the total budget. This is why the CAP has fuelled many controversies, both among the EU countries and during trade negotiations, first the General Agreement on Tariffs and Trade (GATT) Rounds and now the World Trade Organization talks.

In spite of being written over 50 years ago, the general objectives of the Common Agricultural Policy have remained the same as declared in Article 39 of the Treaty of Rome, in the following five points:

1. to increase agricultural productivity by promoting technological progress and by ensuring (…) the optimum utilization of the factors of production, in particular labour;
2. to ensure the fair standard of living for the agricultural community;
3. to stabilize markets;
4. to assure the availability of supplies;
5. to ensure the supplies reach consumers at reasonable prices (Gaziński 2002).

The above principles can be seen as a reflection of the then existing conditions in agriculture. The memories of the war were still vivid as was the fear of food shortages (in many countries, not only the occupied ones, food was rationed during and after World War II). Farms were small and rural areas were poor and technologically backward, which was demonstrated by a high percentage of people employed in agriculture and a considerably large contribution of agriculture to the national product. Besides, the six countries which founded the European Community were not self-sufficient and food was treated as kind of 'strategic weapon'.

It is clear that when the foundations for the Common Agricultural Policy were established, its objectives focused on questions related to food production and supply. Moreover, the goals defined in Art. 39.2 and Art. 39.5 are contradictory

– a compromise is achieved by the market regulatory mechanism. Otherwise, predictably, policies benefit some market players over others. Indeed it soon became clear that agricultural producers benefited from the policy whereas food consumers' gains were illusory. It is also noteworthy, especially from today's perspective, that the initial five objectives did not mention the natural environment or food quality.

These objectives, however, helped to work out guidelines for running the Common Agricultural Policy in the EEC (Ackrill 2000), which are as general as the objectives from which they were derived. The three pillars of the CAP are:

1. the common market
2. preferences for the Community,
3. financial solidarity.

The first one was a real breakthrough – food products could be transported freely between member countries. The second pillar, in practice, meant protecting the EC borders from cheaper imports. Financial solidarity, in turn, indicated the costs of maintaining the system; all member states share the costs according to the budgetary requirements, and all countries which meet the community support criteria take advantage of the system. In practice, some states are net payers to the system while others are its beneficiaries (Tracy 1998).

Those general principles of the Common Agricultural Policy (implemented in 1962–1968) were accompanied by detailed, very specific solutions. High intervention prices, as well as changeable levies (which in time, by the power of international agreements, were converted into customs), and export subsidies were among the most important instruments.

In practice, high intervention prices, designed as an instrument for market stabilization, rapidly replaced market prices. Stable intervention prices additionally stimulated the growth of production, especially that they were separated from the global market by levies imposed on imported products and calculated as a difference between a changeable global price and the threshold price, usually established on a higher level than the corresponding intervention price. Such a system quickly generated chronic surpluses, so a broader use of export subsidies became unavoidable. The CAP system has become ever more complicated because different products generated a wide range of solutions; for example 21 common market organizations were distinguished (Drago and Gaziński 1998b).

Experiences of the First Cycle of Reforms

Although the first reforms of the Common Agricultural Policy were suggested by its 'architect', Sicco Mansholt, as early as the late 1960s, it took well over 10 years before any modifications were implemented. The delay was due to strong opposition from agricultural communities, who feared that changes would be detrimental. In 1984 dairy production became limited when dairy quotas were allocated to farms (Grant 1997).

In the late 1980s and early 1990s, another series of GATT negotiations, known as the Uruguay Round, were carried out. During the talks, the question of agriculture proved to be a very delicate matter. The EU countries opposed a group of several states known as the Cairns Group, which included the United States, Canada, New Zealand and a few other countries, among which the presence of Hungary – at that time an EU candidate – was conspicuous.

The GATT negotiations coincided with another round of CAP reforms, known as the MacSharry reforms, after the name of the then European Commissioner for Agriculture, Ray MacSharry. It was not a coincidence that European Community members incorporated several of the discussed compromises into their reform package (Kay 1998). The most significant change was a considerable reduction of intervention prices, the main culprit of accumulating excessive food supplies; likewise, export subsidies were limited. The loss of farmers' revenue was set off by a system of direct payments. The amount of direct payments depended on the so-called reference yield, and not on the actual yields recorded by the farm. This was a big step towards separating subsidies from production and agricultural prices (Swinbank and Tanner 1996).

In a 1997 document, Agenda 2000, the European Commission reviewed the results of the MacSharry reforms a few years after its implementation, in the context of the upcoming financial framework of 2000–2006 and the expected EU enlargement encompassing countries from Central and Eastern Europe (at that time, the EU declared that new member states would not be eligible to receive direct payments, but following a series of negotiations, this scheme was abandoned) (Drago and Gaziński 2000a). The principles underlying Agenda 2000 were accepted during a 1999 Berlin summit. It was then decided that another review of the CAP would take place in the middle of the new multiannual financial framework.

Changes in Recent Years. What Will Happen after 2013?

In 2003, the CAP was neither reviewed (as announced a few years before) nor altered. The decision was made to continue decreasing intervention prices and consequently increasing direct payments. The more widespread use of direct payments was accompanied by certain differences in how such payments were calculated between countries or even regions. Direct payments played an increasingly important role as a tool for the redistribution of revenues and not as a direct market intervention instrument. Thus, questions were raised whether there should be an upper limit established on direct payments per farm and if so, what criteria should be applied?

Direct payments became subjected to the so-called modulation, a type of taxation which is deducted from the sum of calculated direct payments given to an EU member state if the latter exceeds the set threshold value (at present,

5,000 euro per farm). These funds, however, are at the disposal of each country provided they are allocated to the development of rural areas.

The eligibility of each farmer to receive direct payments is ever more closely conditioned by a number of requirements pertaining to the conservation of the natural environment, the quality of farm produce, compliance with the rules of hygiene and animal welfare as well as good agronomic practice, together known as cross-compliance.

The reforms are similar to the ones initiated by MacSharry, gradually encompassing new markets, thus broadening the range of payments not connected to the level of production achieved on a given farm, known as decoupling. The Single Payment Scheme (SPS) is becoming more popular, and in the future it is expected that the methods for calculating subsidies under the SPS will become simpler and more uniform. This means that to some extent the farmer has now more freedom in decision making; the farmer is not just a producer of agricultural products, but also 'a guardian' of such public goods as the rural landscape or the natural environment (Sorrentino, Henke and Severini 2011).

Gradually, the CAP has expanded from solely an area of agriculture into a policy for the development of rural areas, considered to be the CAP's Pillar II. This process of expansion began in the mid-1970s and has accelerated in recent years. The new challenges currently facing the Common Agricultural Policy include:

- protection of species biodiversity,
- water resources management,
- prevention of climatic changes,
- generation of energy from alternative resources,
- supporting innovativeness,
- restructuring the dairy industry (in view of proposed abandoning dairy quotas in 2015).

In the future, to a larger extent than today, farmers will have to face the demands of flexible market prices. They can counteract this development in a few ways, e.g. by making contracts with food processing and trading companies more common, by developing new ways of selling directly, or – like farmers in Canada – by taking out insurance policies to protect themselves from income loss (Burny 2011).

The Common Agricultural Policy costs billions of euro but when divided by the entire EU population, the cost is just slightly over 100 euro per capita. At present, there is a debate as to the form the CAP will take in 2014-2020, in the next budgetary period.[1] A decision undertaken at a forum of the ministers for agriculture of all the EU states is not expected earlier than the end of 2012 and soon afterwards, new regulations will have to be approved.

---

1   It is suggested to maintain the budget expenditure on a level similar to the one in the preceding seven-year period, i.e. 371.7 billion euro (cf. Bugnot 2011).

The Bureaucratized CAP – Why it Should Be Simplified

The complicated rules and practices governing the CAP are mainly due to the adopted management model which relies on an excessively developed bureaucratic system. The simplicity and clarity of adopted solutions are not encouraged by the fact that each decision is a compromise, which is supposed to satisfy the diverse and often conflicting interests of each of the 27 member states. Consequently, implementation of the EU legislation encounters growing obstacles, as the CAP beneficiaries perceive it as a burden, and the development of agriculture and rural areas do not proceed as smoothly as expected. With the CAP being so bureaucratic, agricultural and rural communities find it almost impossible to comprehend the policy's development-oriented goals; in fact, most of the CAP information policy, including training sessions, deals with several overwhelming administrative procedures. The essential matters come second (Cetner and Żok 2011), and the connection between the complicated system of managing the CAP and the policy's overall objectives is much harder to notice (Forum Inicjatyw Rozwojowych EFRWP 2010). Thus, all the previous CAP reforms have attempted to simplify its rules and procedures. In contrast, the cross-compliance principle, adopted by the reform of 2003, was accompanied by a series of additional requirements, which imposed a new burden on the CAP beneficiaries as well as on management and implementation institutions. A broader discussion on the simplification of the CAP began in 2004, stimulated by the initiative to simplify and improve the quality of legislation as a way of strengthening competitiveness of the EU economy under the framework of the renewed Lisbon strategy.

Among the major aims of the CAP simplifications are:

- decreasing transaction costs for all agricultural market participants (diminishing administrative costs and public expenditures),
- improving the competitiveness of the agricultural sector,
- enhancing the transparency and clarity of the CAP regulations, thus making it more acceptable to farmers, consumers and tax-payers (SEAEPR/FAPA 2006).

The European Commission issued several memoranda in which it formulated the principles that should underlie the reformed common agricultural policy:

- reduce the number of the CAP regulations and describe them more clearly,
- lessen the bureaucratic burden and formal administrative procedures,
- avoid labour duplication, for example by maximizing the incentives to use IT tools,
- simplify trade norms and geographical indications,

- base the control system on risk analysis and adopt a more flexible approach to engage member countries in planning inspections; penalties imposed on farms should be commensurate with the scale of infringements; requirements and responsibilities should be defined more precisely,
- improve communication with the CAP beneficiaries and the general public (European Commission 2010; European Commission 2009).

The European Commission claims that hundreds of millions of euro could be saved if the administrative burden on the agricultural sector was reduced by about a quarter. Savings could be achieved, for example, by lifting the requirement to obtain export and import permits for many products, abolishing unnecessary trade norms, simplifying the support system and support application forms, repealing or consolidating some legal acts (including obsolete ones), and limiting the number of control activities. Also planned is conducting training for officials on farms (the Harvest Experience programme) so that they could gain better understanding of the everyday life of farmers and create better laws and more successful policies (European Commission 2009).

The strongest stimulus for the CAP simplification is the fact that agriculture will have to face new challenges. The CAP will pursue its current goals, such as ensuring safe (healthy) and good quality food at reasonable prices, improving the standard of living in agricultural and rural communities, protecting the natural environment and assuring animal welfare, improving the competitive advantage of EU agricultural products on the global market, supporting sustainable development, and stabilizing agricultural and food markets (Van der Zee 1997). In addition, it will also have to address new challenges such as climatic changes (through soil amelioration, irrigation, and insurance policies), use of renewable energy, the need to maintain biodiversity and protect the rural landscape as well as unpredictable demand for agricultural products (Józwiak 2011).

The role of the bureaucracy and officials manifests itself in the EU social and economic policy. EU officials are appointed to execute decisions of democratically elected organs of power, and not to substitute for them. Excessive bureaucracy does not only entail higher budgetary expenditure. The much worse outcome is that it creates barriers to the development of entrepreneurship. The bureaucratic approach means that formal acts, certificates or permits take priority over essential goals of the social and economic activity, which leads to generating additional costs, both in the economy and in other spheres of life.

Constraining the excessive role of bureaucracy is difficult albeit possible. Rather than by a revolutionary change, it may be achieved through a consistent long-run policy, which will gradually modify the philosophy behind the administration of public matters and growth. Denmark is an example of a country which has attained considerable success in reducing such a burden.

The excessive role of the bureaucracy is particularly burdensome to farmers and countryside residents who take advantage of various forms of support from the EU budget. Although farmers in the 'new' EU member states have quickly learned how to fulfill formal requirements associated with the CAP, they can also benefit from constraining the dictatorship of officials, which will additionally stimulate the spirit of enterprise.

The implementation of the Common Agricultural Policy is associated with an extremely developed legal system and numerous procedures. The CAP legislation is so complicated and bureaucratic that access to support funds can be rather difficult and costly, especially to smaller farms. Farmers frequently complain that Paying Agencies request too many documents and are too bureaucratic. For example, it is not enough to build a well-managed pig shed. The farmer is also required to describe, in great detail, the entire construction in writing. Agencies are strict about deadlines set for expending the funds, but it is obvious that certain deviations are unavoidable after an application for support (including the costs breakdown) is submitted. Cases have been reported that local Paying Agencies have demanded more documents from farmers, and applied stricter procedures, than imposed by the EU regulations. Procedures and formal requirements regarding the submission, execution and auditing of support funds obtained from the CAP should therefore be made simpler and more stable.

Prospects for the Simplification of the CAP in 2014–2020

In October 2011 the proposal for a reformed CAP post-2013 was presented, and contains ten key recommendations to make the CAP simpler and more efficient. In order to avoid excessive administrative burden, the European Commission suggests the simplification of several mechanisms, including the inspection system. Support to small farmers should be made simpler by introducing lump sum payments of 500–1,000s euro per farm. Small farmers will also be encouraged to pass their land to those who want to enlarge their farms (AgroNews 2011). However, the reform seems to create excessive and unnecessary requirements that farmers would have to fulfill, namely three environmental measures (crop diversification – crop rotation, maintenance of permanent pastures, and dedicating 7% of the farm's area to creating ecological niches). Moreover, the planned reform lacks sufficiently clear signals indicating further simplification of the CAP.

The simplification of the CAP must make the policy clear and understandable to the average recipient. This will also make the policy more efficient. The change, however, requires that the approach (philosophy) should be modified and that detailed regulations as well as bureaucratic control measures be replaced by mutual trust and partnerships between institutions and beneficiaries. What needs to be avoided is a situation where beneficiaries 'feel like criminals when trying to battle with the various administrative documents and regulations' (European Parliament 2011). The simplification and reduction of the number of legal regulations and administrative procedures would make them understandable and more transparent.[2] The impact of the proposed regulations would be assessed more precisely through consultations with all interested parties.

Technical simplification would involve a review of the legal framework, administrative procedures and management mechanisms. The purpose of the revision would be to repeal many unnecessary regulations. Apart from abolition of some legal acts, the consolidation, codification and transformation are some other technical simplification measures (SEAPPR/FAPA 2006). Additionally, technical simplification requires:

- a change in the legal approach – to make the legal process more coherent; directives replaced by with regulations,
- the simplification of procedures and requirements pertaining to documentation,
- acquiring the information required by the CAP from the data gathered on a given farm,
- collecting information, e.g. on farm animals, in electronic databases,
- delivering documents in the electronic form.

The expected outcomes are: more efficient circulation of documents, lower costs (according to the estimates by the European Commission, saving up to 400 million euro) and avoiding the duplication of work.

Law simplification entails fewer and more stable legal acts, which, however, shall require very strict compliance. Legal regulations, as opposed to customary norms, are mandatory and must be abided by. Unfortunately, the EU legal framework has many flaws. Regulations are written in a language hardly comprehensible to a layman. For legal acts to be understood and interpreted, law experts have to be employed. Ambiguity can lead to controversies and disputes, often brought to court. All this adds to the costs of operating companies. Lawyers seem to be the only group of professionals that profit from the current situation.

---

2   The following are some examples of detailed solutions suggested to simplify the CAP:
- simplifying agricultural product labelling regulations,
- reducing the number of products (markets) that require import and export permits (international trade),
- reducing the number and obligatory character of trade and quality standards with respect to food safety parameters, while broadening the scale of self-certification in the sector,
- limiting the requirement of formal notification about new domestic support of the state to agriculture (especially in crisis and natural disaster situations) and development of rural areas (replacing formal notification with information addressed to the European Commission),
- as long as possible (except some products, like tobacco or potato starch), incorporating specific regulations into the Single Payment Scheme,
- establishing lump sum payments for smallest farms.

Similar to the struggle with the bureaucratic plague, law simplification and transparency could be achieved through a consistent long-term plan. Political good will must be accompanied by some social pressure, including this one from the mass media. The large number of scattered legal documents favours frequent changes. Far too often we learn that an issue is regulated by a certain act with a number of amendments. This problem would be solved by issuing a complete version of a legal act (known as a consolidated text), especially when there are more than 10 amendments.

Law simplification entails a clear, more comprehensible language, a limited number of regulations that are less detailed and more stable. An excessive number of legal regulations reduce the authority of law because not all matters should be controlled by legislation. The regulations dealing with the curvature of bananas or cucumbers, now repealed, have become anecdotal. However, the current legislation governing agriculture is still too detailed. It would be, therefore, a step in the right direction to abolish certain legal regulations.

Tax laws are an important component of the system. Business representatives advocate in favour of the lowest possible taxes, claiming that this will stimulate economic development and the creation of new business. Thus, taxation laws should be stable and transparent so as not to raise any doubts to the exact meaning of their provisions. Unfortunately, the taxation system leaves much to be desired in this regard. Ambiguous interpretations increase costs incurred by enterprises and in drastic cases may lead to bankruptcy.

The excessive intervention of phytosanitary inspection hinders production growth at small food processing plants; this includes manufacturers of traditional regional products. There is no justification for imposing identical sanitary rules on a small fruit juice producer who uses traditional technologies and employs just a few persons, and on large food processing plants, thus burdening small producers with relatively higher costs. The same applies to small meat processing plants, which process pork obtained from the traditional breeds of swine and using home-grown feed. Sometimes forgotten is that in the free market competition plays a key role in maintaining the quality of products. Moreover, inspection institutions which control sanitary and quality norms should not uncritically contribute to such outbreaks of panic as provoked by avian flu.

Expanding the area of economic freedom aids the development of entrepreneurship and the establishment of new companies. The number of business activities that are regulated by granting concessions should not be too high, and the legal as well as financial regulations or administrative solutions, including work safety, should not turn into a barrier killing the spirit of enterprise. One of the measures to test whether a state is open to business is the number of days from the first day that a prospective entrepreneur submits a business registration application to the day on which the formalities are complete and a new company is born.

Polish Agriculture within the CAP Framework

The enlargement of the European Union did not confirm most of the fears felt by farmers in both the candidate countries (EU-10) and old member states (EU-15).[3] In the period preceding accession, Poland's trade balance for agricultural and food products with the EU changed – for the first time for many years – from a negative to a positive balance. Quite quickly, Poland has become the largest exporter of food products in this part of the EU and continues to maintain its position.[4] From Poland's accession in 2004, to 2010, the value of the positive export and import balance in the agricultural and food processing sectors more than tripled (Table 5.1). The positive effects that Poland's EU membership have had on its agriculture and rural areas have been emphasized by many authors (Figiel 2009; Guba and Purgał 2009; Kameduła-Tomaszewska 2012; Kowalski 2009).

Table 5.1   Polish agricultural trade during the period 2003–2010

Item	2003	2004	2005	2006	2007	2008	2009	2010
Polish foreign trade balance (billion EUR)	-8.5	-11.4	-9.8	-12.9	-18.6	-26.2	-9.3	-13.5
Share of agricultural trade in total export (%)	8.4	8.7	9.9	9.7	9.9	9.9	11.7	11.3
Share of agricultural trade in total import (%)	5.9	6.1	6.8	6.4	6.8	7.0	8.6	8.2
Value of agricultural export (billion EUR)	4.0	5.2	7.0	8.5	9.9	11.4	11.4	13.3
Share of EU countries in Polish export (%)	65.2	71.9	73.9	76.5	80.5	80.7	80.7	78.9
Balance of Polish agricultural trade (billion EUR)	0.45	0.85	1.65	2.08	1.97	1.33	2.20	2.57
Agricultural trade balance with EU countries (billion EUR)	0.44	1.03	1.80	2.48	2.65	2.19	2.8	3.19

Source: Own calculations based on the data of Central Statistical Office, Warsaw and other sources.

---

3   Prior to Poland's access to the EU, one of the authors carried out over a hundred of lectures and workshops, hence he is well familiar with such doubts. And they were not irrational – due to the protectionist policy, for example, Poland was then 'a third country' and the European Union was 'a bad neighbour' (cf. Gaziński 2001).

4   Hungary took the second place on this ranking list (cf. Gaziński 2006).

In the summer of 2010, the Agricultural Advisory Centre, Poznań Branch, conducted a survey, which helped to define several barriers, indicated by local government units, to the successful implementation of the programme 'Revival of the Countryside', including:

- frequent lack of unambiguous interpretation of regulations, different specification of formal requirements, rules and guidelines often changed 'while the ball is in play',
- competitions announced very late, leaving little time to prepare proposals, especially when application forms are complicated and comprise many attachments,
- very detailed breakdown of an investor's costs (particularly when it is obvious that once the investment project is completed, the final costs will differ from the planned budget),
- managing institutions pay too much attention to formalities, often irrelevant to the essential subject matter, like a missing date; documents cannot be verified by communal councils,
- funds secured to provide own contribution, and laid aside for many months while the application processing procedure is prolonged,
- full documentation (including technical documents), such as a legal building permit and a cost breakdown, must be prepared, incurring costs without giving any guarantee that funds for the performance of the project will be granted,
- technical difficulties in filling in forms, e.g. wrong format of cells (Cetner and Żok 2011).

Difficulties of a similar character have been indicated by directors of Paying Agencies in a survey conducted prior to one of their regular conferences, held in September 2011.[5]

Let us now consider the proposal put forth by the Polish Forum of Development Initiatives, to have just one application form for area payments for a whole seven-year budgetary term (Forum Inicjatyw Rozwojowych EFRWP 2010). Certainly, the efficiency of EU support programmes would improve if the detailed specification of measures, conditions and requirements of granting support (including model forms and required documents), along with the relevant schedule, was known at the beginning of each multiyear financial framework. Potential beneficiaries could then analyse their capacity and prepare themselves to submit applications. At present, the period between a given measure is announced but the application

---

5   Representatives of 27 paying agencies from 23 member countries responded, and indicated that the major causes of problems were: 1. too little time: decisions taken very late leave too little time for their execution, 2. unclear rules and imprecise definitions 3. the 'rules of the game' changed far too often 4 set requirements are burdensome to beneficiaries, who also complain about difficult access to information (cf. Wardal 2011).

deadline is too short. Paying Agencies as well as all other public institutions working for the benefit of agriculture and the countryside should remember that their mission is to aid the development of farming and rural areas. This sometimes involves changing the attitude of officials.

The impact of Poland's European Union membership on the agricultural and food manufacturing sectors is multidirectional and not always quantifiable. It is, however, a common notion that agriculture is among the major beneficiaries of Poland's membership to the EU, as noted by a number of researchers (Figiel 2009; Guba and Purgał 2009; Kowalski 2009), who collectively note that:

- there has been a noticeable increase in the income per person with full employment in agriculture. The increase is significantly aided by budgetary subsidies, the contribution of which is assessed to reach about 50% (the revenue in agriculture continues to be inferior to the average in the whole economy, with the income parity in agriculture of less than 60%),
- the improved financial status means a better mood among rural residents compared to the pre-accession period, a change which is additionally stimulated by investments in technical and social infrastructure in villages and an evident technological progress,
- the ecological awareness of rural residents has grown. Likewise, their understanding of the importance of the sustainable rural development has deepened,
- the CAP measures have contributed to creating a more stable food market and restraining the rate of price rises,
- by living in an EU, Poles find it easier to create civil society and encourage local communities to pursue various forms of activity (accessibility of funds under different regional development programmes has proven to be a stimulating factor).

Apart from the benefits gained by Polish farmers from the support programmes targeted at agriculture and rural areas, certain shortcomings have surfaced, which are mostly direct or indirect consequences of the CAP's well-known weaknesses. Another source of dissatisfaction is that some of the provisions accepted by negotiators during the pre-accession talks were not really favourable and fail to satisfy farmers or food manufacturers:

- many farmers would agree with the former British MEP John Corrie, who said during his visit to Poland that 'we used to be paid for what we produced on our farms, but now we are more often paid for discontinuing production' (Corrie 2009).
- the redistribution of funds from the CAP programmes is far from satisfactory. The biggest farms can be paid substantive sums, whereas the subsidies granted to small farmers (Poland has many of them) function more like 'a social security benefit' instead of being a tool for modernization

and development. As a result, the desirable process of creating larger and economically more viable farms is slowed down;

• for more than 10 years now – also prior to Poland's access to the EU, when other support programmes, mainly pre-accession ones, were performed – there has been considerable progress in the agriculture and development of rural areas. Unfortunately, the gap between the richest and the poorest regions has been growing bigger despite the theoretical assumptions;[6]

• among examples of obstacles encountered by agricultural producers due to ineffective solutions is the problem of potato starch quotas, imposed by the Accession Treaty. The processing capacity of the Polish potato industry is estimated to be within the range of 220,000–260,000 tonnes a year. However, the negotiators failed to secure a production limit that would correspond to the potential of the industry or the demand in the domestic market. The potato starch quota is a bare 145,000 tonnes (Table 5.2) (Chotkowski and Gaziński 2011). Thus, the country which is a leading European potato producer is forced to import potato starch, although the Polish potato processing plants are not used to their full capacity (Table 5.3).

Table 5.2   Major EU-15 potato starch producers

Country	Starch potato quotas (tons) 2004–2008	Acreage of potato cultivation (1,000 hectares) in 2007	Average potato harvests (mln. tons) 2004–2007	Starch potato quota as calculated per:	
				1 ha of cultivated potatoes	*1,000 tons of harvested potatoes*
Germany	656,300	273	11.5	2.4	57.0
The Netherlands	507,400	161	6.9	3.1	73.5
France	265,400	158	6.7	1.7	39.6
Denmark	168,200	38	1.5	4.4	112.1
Sweden	62,100	29	0.9	2.1	69.0
Finland	53,200	28	0.7	1.9	76.0
Austria	47,700	23	0.7	2.1	68.1
The Czech Republic	33,700	32	0.8	1.1	42.1
Poland	145,000	570	11.1	0.3	13.1

Source: Own calculations based on the data from: Hambloch, Ch., Menth, H., Stelzer, M., Schaack, D., Wilckens, A. and Graf, G. 2007. ZMP – Marktbilanz. Kartoffeln 2007. Zentrale Markt und Preisberichtstelle GmbH, Bonn, 127.

---

6   Being aware of the problem, the Polish government set up a special programme for the years 2007–2013, addressed to the five poorest provinces, known as 'The Eastern Wall' (cf. Ministry for Regional Development 2006).

The Proposed CAP Reforms from the Polish Perspective

After nearly eight years of Poland being an EU member state, we can draw on the country's experience and make certain evaluations. An excellent opportunity to voice our opinion on the future of the CAP came during the first Polish Presidency, which fell in the second half of 2011 (Ministry of Agriculture and Rural Development 2010). A multifaceted debate was conducted during that time on the legislative package put forth by the European Commission, and included the forthcoming reforms of the CAP. These questions were discussed, for example, during an informal meeting of the Council of Ministers of Agriculture and Fisheries in Wrocław, when such issues as support measures promoting EU agricultural products were raised.

Table 5.3   Balance of exports, imports and production of starch and starch products in Poland during the period 2001–2008, thousand tons

Item	2001/ 2002	2002/ 2003	2003/ 2004	2004/ 2005	2005/ 2006	2006/ 2007	2007/ 2008	2008/ 2009*
Total exports of starch products	68.5	89.8	108.4	120.4	141.4	117.6	107.5	91.4
– in these: potato flour and starch	40.9	57.5	72.9	54.4	64.0	28.5	34.7	436.6
– other starch products	27.6	32.3	35.5	66.0	77.4	89.1	72.8	5.8
Total imports of starch products	85.0	95.0	109.9	205.9	246.2	332.7	275.4	204.7
– in these: potato flour and starch	0.4	0.4	0.2	4.6	9.8	19.5	7.6	10.7
– other starch products	84.6	94.6	109.7	201.3	236.4	313.2	267.8	194.0
Balance: exports/ imports	-16.5	-5.2	-1.5	-85.5	-104.8	-215.1	-167.9	-113.3
Production of potato starch	135	165	178	158	130	79	115	130
Domestic consumption (production minus exports plus imports)	151.5	170.2	179.5	243.5	234.8	294.1	282.9	243.3

Note: *Data in last column are preliminary.
Source: Own calculations based on: Dzwonkowski, W., Szczepaniak, I., Zalewski, A., Chotkowski, J., Rembeza, J., Lewandowski, R. Rynek ziemniaka. Stan i perspektywy. Analizy rynkowe, nr 35. IERiGŻ, ARR, MRiRW, Warszawa 2009.

Table 5.4   Evaluation of some of the proposed CAP reforms from the Polish perspective

NEGATIVE OPINION	POSITIVE OPINION
General evaluation of key issues	
The disparity in payments between member countries only partially reduced	The mechanism of digressive reduction of payments to large farms and some increase in the support to small farms (flat-rate payments)
More authority vested on the European Commission and the limited role of the Council in creating Agricultural Law	Emphasized role of small farms in the European model of farming and in attaining goals connected with sustainable development and social inclusion
Direct payments	
The CAP made more complicated, for example by distinguishing the green component and allocating 30% of the state envelope to this purpose	Abandoning the division of the GAEC standards into voluntary and mandatory ones
No coupled payments in the tobacco sector	Possible stronger support to less favoured areas (LFAs)
Development of rural areas	
Heavier administrative burden in implementing the CAP's Pillar II	Maintaining the extent of Pillar II financial support mechanisms
Stricter requirements regarding agri-environmental measures	New instruments added to the Development of Rural Areas, such as risk management and income stabilization tools
Common organization of agricultural markets	
Milk and sugar quotas phased out to 2015	Intention to strengthen the position of agricultural producers in the food production chain
Liquidation of instrument which allowed quick intervention in case of disturbances on the milk protein market	Maintaining public intervention and subsidies to private storage

Source: The authors, based on the information provided by the Ministry of Agriculture and Rural Development (2012).

The proposed changes in the Common Agricultural Policy are not satisfactory from Poland's viewpoint.[7] One of the proposals voiced by Poland, also on behalf of the

---

7   This opinion was expressed very clearly by the Polish Minister of Agriculture and Rural Development, Mr Marek Sawicki, in his address to participants of the Expert and Media Conference, *Dokąd zmierza WPR? Where is CAP going to? Stam debaty publicznej, zainicjowanej przez polską Prezydencję Status of the public debate initiated by the Polish Presidency*, Ministerstwo Rolnictwa i Rozwoju Wsi Miinistry of Agriculture and Rural Development, Warszawa, 9 January 2012: 'The proposed reform is just a minor refinement but not a fundamental change … I am deeply convinced that the lesson we have learn from

other EU-12 countries, is to move to the same level of aid per hectare for all farmers in the EU, i.e. to the level set in the 'old' EU member states. Another criticism is the lack of actual, not just formal, simplification of the CAP regulations. Moreover, it is feared that suggested measures will be insufficient to substantially improve the competitiveness of European agriculture on the world market (Table 5.4).

Despite such critical opinions, the European Commission's proposals are a good starting point for further discussions in advance of making final decisions, and therefore deserve a closer look.

The Question of the Level of Payments

Two systems for establishing the entitlement to direct payments have been used so far under the CAP. One is known as the Single Payment Scheme (SPS). It is predominantly applied in the EU-15 states and links payment entitlements to eligible farmland. The other solution, called the Single Area Payment Scheme (SAPS), is applied, for example, in Poland and the other EU-12 states. Its implementation took a Paying Agency (ARMA) in Poland over three years.

The Commission suggested the unification of these rules and substituting the two solutions with the Basic Payment Scheme (BPS). However, the new scheme will more closely resemble the SPS. For the countries which until now have used the SAPS the change is fundamental. It will incur costs (changes in the Integrated Administration and Control System) and require time, the time that – in view of prolonged negotiations and delayed agreements – we may run out of.

The Commission has proposed the redistribution of funds allocated to direct payments between member states (the so-called member state envelopes) for the years 2014–2020. Unfortunately, the basis is the historical intensity of agricultural production dating back to the pre-accession period. As a result, the current disparities in the level of payments, despite the formally accepted principle of decoupling, will remain 'fossilized' – the average rate per hectare of agriculturally used land is estimated to range from *ca* 141 euro in Latvia to *ca* 669 euro in Malta (the estimated rate for Poland is 221 euro). The disparity will therefore reach over 500 euro; the difference is in relative terms, 4.74-fold (Zagórski 2012).

In conclusion, the proposed payment model post-2013 does not correspond to the current market conditions: the level of social welfare, structure of production costs, etc., at present is largely shaped by the CAP regulations. In short, ensuring similar conditions for competition between farmers from different countries leaves much to be desired.

---

the current crisis will enable us to work out solutions that will lead to a true and profound reform of the CAP, which will make European agriculture stronger and more competitive on the global market'.

The Greening of the CAP

Among all proposed changes, the question of greening could be pointed to as a particularly difficult issue. The Commission suggests that this should be a mandatory component of the systems for payments, conditional on the provision of climate and environmental good practices. The mandatory character of this component is questioned. Such requirements as crop diversity or setting aside 7% of farmland as eco-friendly and maintaining it in good agricultural condition, may prove to be both difficult and hardly useful. The way in which payments for good climate and environmental practices are set is the other controversial issue. The calculations are based on the assumption that the contribution for 'greening' will equal 30% of the total 'envelope'. This means that the differences in payments between countries will be fossilized (Ministry of Agriculture and Rural Development 2012). Once again, it is Latvia and Malta that lie at the opposing ends (*ca* 40–42 euro/ha in Latvia and 201 euro/ha in Malta; a nearly five-fold difference). It is not easy to understand why rates for greening actions should be varied. Poland is to receive 40 euro/ha (at a payment of 66 euro/ha) and Greece – 22 euro/ha (at a payment of 117 euro/ha). Therefore, it is worth considering another proposal (Zagórski 2012), which is to first separate a pool of money for greening from the general EU budget allocated to direct payments, and then redistribute it between countries using a uniform rate – *ca* 80 euro/ha annually.

Other Proposals Concerning Pillar I

Formal declarations that the CAP will be simplified have not been confirmed by the presented proposals. We should at least consider whether the option granted to small farms, such as submitting one direct payment application for the whole budgetary period, should not cover other farms as well.

Furthermore, the way the Commission proposes to support young farmers may lead to substantial differences in the level of payments received by farmers living and working in different EU states.[8]

A Few Remarks on Pillar II

It is difficult to notice any reform in this area either, as the suggested decrease in the number of measures and their division into axes is a mere change in the way these measures are registered. Most of the measures defined as 'new' ones deal with the same issues as before. They are just grouped differently.

The states which until now have benefited from the previous solutions may oppose the proposed change in the way less favoured areas are defined.

---

8   Under the proposed scheme, a young farmer in Poland who has a 100-hectare farm would receive *ca* 1,300 euro, whereas a young Czech farmer with a similar farm would receive nearly five times more – as calculated by M. Zagórski (Zagórski 2012).

In Poland (and in Germany as well) the total area of LFAs may decrease by as much as about one-third.

On the other hand, new risk management instruments, such as co-financing farmers' insurance policies, supporting mutual funds for combating plant and animal diseases and the Income Stabilization Tool, including supporting mutual funds for insuring farmers' income (Zagórski 2012), sound very interesting. However, at this point in time these proposals are general and rather vague. Their more detailed form will be presented during further discussions.

Concluding Remarks

1)   The European Commission, especially since 2005, has undertaken various actions to simplify the rules and mechanisms of the CAP. This has evolved into one of the goals of the 2014–2020 policy reform. Simplification is perceived as a necessary condition to improve the effectiveness of the expense of agricultural policy as well as the competitiveness of EU agriculture in the global market.

2)   So far, details of the proposed initiatives are not very impressive. Such an opinion is verified by beneficiaries, who feel that the requirements and procedures are becoming more complicated rather than simpler. Therefore, the attitude of officials responsible for implementation of the CAP measures needs to change. Likewise, employees in Paying Agencies, who are now interested in the passive execution of the binding laws and procedures, should rethink their approach.

3)   There should be a close collaboration, not only between ministers of agriculture and rural areas, but also with the COPA-COGECA group, mass media and other opinion-givers for the sake of attaining true simplification of the CAP. Any such actions deserve broad support.

4)   The integration of the Polish agricultural sector into EU structures caused numerous worries among interested parties. Most of the doubts have proven groundless.

5)   The total balance of the first years of Poland being an EU member state for the entire food production sector is positive; this is confirmed by the fact that Poland is now the leading exporter of food products among the EU-12 countries. EU rural development support programmes have been used successfully.

6)   Certain problems have emerged. Some difficulties originate from the provisions of the Accession Treaty; not all of them were favourable for Poland, for example the low potato starch quota. Others can be attributed to general weaknesses of the CAP and other EU programmes. Although all rural areas have been developing recently, the increasing gap between the poorest and the richest areas is a significant concern.

7)   Poland is no longer a passive 'recipient' of support programmes. The country aspires to be a leader among the Central and Eastern European Countries (CEECs), and perhaps it has already become one. This is why it is critical that the country is vocal in regard to proposed reforms to the CAP. Several more

detailed proposals were phrased during the first Polish presidency (second half of 2011). Among the key questions are the ones which aim to level the differences in payments per hectare of farmland between the EU-12 and EU-15 member states, a change which Poland advocates on behalf of all the new member states.

8)   The proposed extent of reforms in the CAP is not sufficient in light of the recent economic crisis and changes in the world economy (emerging markets, for instance the growing economic and political role of China, India and several other countries). There is less than a year left before the final decisions are made and now is the time for working towards better solutions.

References

Ackrill, R. (2000), *The Common Agricultural Policy.* Sheffield: Sheffield Academic Press.

AgroNews (2011), The CAP Reform Proposal Presented by the European Commission on 12.10.2011 and Planned for Implementation after 2013. Available at www.agronews.com.pl (accessed 13 October 2011).

Bugnot, P. (2011), *Future Legal Framework for Financing the CAP and Requirements for EU Paying Agencies*, 30th Conference of the Directors of the Paying Agencies, Sopot, September 21 to 23, 2011. Available at http://www.arr. gov.pl/index.php?option=com_content&view=article&id =1159&Itemid=590 (accessed 30 November 2011).

Burny, Ph. (2011), *Reforming the Common Agricultural Policy. Perspective of 2013 and Beyond*, in Szkice europejskie. Historia – Gospodarka – Polityka, ed. B. Gaziński, Olsztyn, 203–16.

Cetner, G. and K. Żok (2011), *Odnowa wsi w opinii jednostek samorządu terytorialnego*, 'Zagadnienia Doradztwa Rolniczego', 2, 24–48.

Chotkowski, J. and B. Gaziński (2011), 'Problem of Fair Competition on the Single EU Market – The Case of Potato Starch', *Olsztyn Journal of Economics* 6(1), 89–98.

Corrie, J. (2009), *EP to Campus. Visit to Poland (24 May – 29 May 2009)*, 'FMA Bulletin', 28, 2009, 12–13 (a French language version of the report in J. Corrie, *PE au Campus. Visite en Pologne (du 24 au 29 mai 2009)*, 'Bulletin de l'AAD', 28 2009, 12–13).

Drago, F. and B. Gaziński (1998a), Agenda 2000. *W kręgu opinii Komisji Europejskiej o przyszłym rozszerzeniu Wspólnoty*, 'Humanistyka i Przyrodoznawstwo', 4, 159–64.

Drago, F. and B. Gaziński (1998b), *Od Rzymu do Amsterdamu. 40 lat podróży. Szkice o Unii Europejskiej*, WODR, Olsztyn, 55–61.

European Commission (2009), Memorandum of 18.03.2009, COM (2009) 0128, *Uproszczenie europejskiej wspólnej polityki rolnej naszym wspólnym sukcesem.* Available at www.ec.europa.eu/agriculture/simplification/index_ en.htm (accessed 10 November 2011).

European Commission (2010), *The CAP towards 2020, Meeting the Food, Natural Resources and Territorial Challenges of the Future*, 672 final, Brussels, 18 November; Directorate General for Agriculture and Rural Development and the RDC, *Uproszczenie WPR. Zmniejszenie biurokracji*, 2010. Available at www.ec.europa.eu/agricilture (accessed 10 November 2011).

European Parliament (2010), *R. Ashworth's Report on Simplification of the CAP, Delivered on Behalf of the Committee on Agriculture and Rural Development*, Strasburg 19.04.2010 r. Available at www.europarl.europa.eu/ (accessed 10 November 2011).

Figiel, S. (2009), *Reformować, ale jak. Ocena skutków potencjalnych zmian wspólnej polityki rolnej*, 'Nowe Życie Gospodarcze', 23–4, 36–7.

Forum Inicjatyw Rozwojowych EFRWP (2010), *Wspólna Polityka Rolna po 2013 roku. Propozycje zmian*, 'Wieś i Rolnictwo', 2, 9–19.

Gaziński, B. (2001), *Polish Agriculture as Faced by European Integration*, 'Vagos Mokslo Darbai', 51(4), 38–41.

Gaziński, B. (2002), *Unia Europejska nie tylko dla początkujących*, LITTERA, Olsztyn, 136–41.

Gaziński, B. (2006), *Polskie rolnictwo w Unii Europejskiej i niektóre doświadczenia pierwszego roku członkostwa*, 'Biuletyn Instytutu Hodowli i Aklimatyzacji Roślin', 242, 3–14.

Grant, W. (1997), *The Common Agricultural Policy*. St. Martin Press, New York.

Guba, W. and P. Purgał (2009), *Wnioski z debaty*, in Międzynarodowa konferencja. 'Rolnictwo i obszary wiejskie – 5 lat po akcesji do Unii Europejskiej', MRiRW, Warszawa 28–29 April 2009, www.minrol.gov.pl (accessed 15 February 2012).

Józwiak, W. (2011), *Efektywność i innowacyjność polskich gospodarstw rolnych* 'Wieś i Rolnictwo', no. 1, 75–86.

Kameduła-Tomaszewska, R. (2012), *Polska wobec Wspólnej Polityki Rybackiej*, in Where is CAP Going to? Status of the Public Debate Initiated by the Polish Presidency. Konferencja Ekspercko-Medialna, MRiRW, CBR, Warszawa 2 January 2012, 22–9.

Kay, A. (1998), *The Reform of the Common Agricultural Policy: The Case of MacSharry Reform*. CAB International, Wallingford, Oxon, New York.

Kowalski, A. (2009), *Polski sektor żywnościowy 5 lat po akcesji*, 'Biuletyn Informacyjny ARR', 6, 21–33.

Ministry for Regional Development (2006), *Program Operacyjny: Rozwój Polski Wschodniej 2007–2013. Projekt*. Ministry for Regional Development, Warszawa.

Ministry of Agriculture and Rural Development (2010), *Agriculture and Food Economy in Poland*. Warsaw, 59–61.

Ministry of Agriculture and Rural Development (2012), *Ocena najważniejszych założeń pakietu legislacyjnego WPR 2020 z perspektywy Polski, Dokąd zmierza WPR? Where is CAP Going to? Stan debaty publicznej, zainicjowanej przez polską Prezydencję. Status of the Public Debate initiated by the Polish Presidency*, The Expert and Media Conference, Ministry of Agriculture and Rural Development, Warszawa, 9 January 2012, p. 2.

SAEPR/FAPA (2006), *Dylematy uproszczenia Wspólnej Polityki Rolnej*, FAPA, Warszawa.

Sorrentino, A., Henke, R. and S. Severini (2011), *The Common Agricultural Policy after the Fischler Reform. National Implementation, Impact Assessment and the Agenda for Future Reforms*. Burlington, VT: Ashgate.

Stanowisko uczestników II Kongresu Nauk Rolniczych wobec Reformy WPR w latach 2014–2020 (2011). Available at www.cdr.gov.pl/kongres2/ (accessed 10 November 2011).

Swinbank, A. and C. Tanner (1996), *Farm Policy and Trade Conflict. The Uruguay Round and CAP Reform*. Michigan University Press.

Tracy, M. (1998), *Government and Agriculture in Western Europe. 1890–1988*. Hemel, Hemstaed.

Van der Zee, F.A. (1997), *Political Economy Models and Agricultural Policy Formation: Empirical Applicability and Relevance for the CAP*. Wageningen Agricultural University, Wageningen.

Wardal, M. (2011), *Workshop 2. How Can Paying Agencies and the European Commission Ensure the Successful Implementation of the CAP Reform? Questionnaire Results*, 30th Conference of the Directors of the Paying Agencies, Sopot, 21–23 September 2011. Available at http://www.arr.gov. pl/index.php?option=com_content&view=article&id=1159&Itemid=590 (accessed 30 November 2011).

Wilkin, J. (2011), *Przyszłość wspólnej polityki rolnej Unii Europejskiej – próba podsumowania dyskusji*, 'Wieś i Rolnictwo', 1, 28–36.

Williamson, O.E. (1985), *The Economic Institutions of Capitalism*. New York: The Free Press.

Zagórski, M. (2012), *WPR po 2013 roku. Propozycja modyfikacji wniosków legislacyjnych Komisji Europejskiej*. EFRWP, Warszawa.

Zegar, J. (2010), *Wspólna Polityka Rolna po 2013 roku*, 'Wieś i Rolnictwo', 3, 11–25.

Chapter 6

New Challenges for EU Trade Policy-making: Why is the EU Pursuing a Comprehensive Economic and Trade Agreement with Canada?

Stefanie Rosskopf

Introduction

Following the Canada-European Union (EU) Summit in Prague in 2009, the EU and Canada started negotiations of the Comprehensive Economic and Trade Agreement (CETA). It is the EU's first attempt at negotiating such an agreement with an industrialized, developed country. As a second-generation trade agreement, the CETA is part of a series of trade agreements that the EU is seeking to negotiate with its international trading partners. If successful, the agreement could lay the foundation for similar agreements with other industrialized countries, such as the United States, Russia and Japan. As such, the CETA represents a new challenge to the EU and its trade policy-making.

Officially, the agreement is embedded in efforts to strengthen and deepen the Canada-EU relationship. Trade liberalization in goods and services, increased market access and enhanced investment provisions as well as improved trade rules, are the stated goals of the agreement (Government of Canada 2009). While it has been a longstanding objective for Canada to engage in a closer relationship with the EU, as part as an effort to reduce trade dependency on the United States (US), the underlying reasons for the EU to pursue such an agreement appear less clear. Moreover, most of the trade barriers left standing between Canada and the EU are non-tariff barriers to trade (NTBs) and are more difficult to eliminate. What is left standing, and what is subject to the negotiations as part of the CETA, are the issue areas of public procurement, agricultural export subsidies, investment and services. All four are areas highly sensitive for the EU, but also for Canada. It is not by accident that the two sides have collided over these issues as part of the World Trade Organization (WTO) negotiations in the Doha Round, bringing multilateral trade negotiations to a halt in 2008. Considering this broader context, on the surface it is hard to understand why the EU would be interested in pursuing such an ambitious agreement.

Unpacking and contextualizing EU rationales for pursuing the CETA is the subject of this chapter. As part of this endeavour, this chapter will argue that the EU is pursuing the proposed agreement because, in practical and symbolic terms, it 'fits' within the EU's overall emerging trade strategy. In support of these claims this chapter will first provide a brief synopsis of the broader history leading to the CETA negotiations. Formal, economic relations between the EU and Canada date back to the 1976 *Framework Agreement for Commercial and Economic Cooperation* and currently rest with the 2009–2012 CETA negotiations.[1] Mapping the history of economic relations between the two sides helps to lay the foundation for a subsequent discussion of how the CETA factors into EU trade policy and what the agreement means for the EU. Second, this chapter will briefly outline the main goals put forward in the 2010 EU trade policy and compare it to its 2006 predecessor. Doing so illuminates how the emphasis on trade negotiations has shifted to include public procurement, services, investment and enforcement of what is negotiated, which are all subject to negotiation under the CETA. Building on this fundamental understanding of EU trade policy, EU trade goals are cast against the actual negotiations as they arise from documents in the public domain, but also from media coverage. Third, this chapter will address the symbolic importance of the CETA as part of EU initiatives to maintain transatlantic ties more generally, but also in the sense that such an ambitious agreement is unprecedented in EU trade history.

Part I: The Road to the Canada-EU Comprehensive Economic and Trade Agreement (CETA)

Since the 1970s transatlantic integration between the EU and Canada has steadily grown more ambitious. Economic ties between the EU and Canada were formally established with the creation of the *1976 Framework Agreement for Commercial and Economic Cooperation.* As part of the Agreement, the EU and Canada declared their intentions of mutual economic and commercial cooperation, both at the international and bilateral levels. Moreover, the signing parties agreed on the creation of a Joint Cooperation Committee (JCC) to meet on an annual basis with the mandate to 'promote and keep under review the various commercial and economic cooperation activities envisaged between the Communities and Canada'

---

1   In this chapter the reference to Canada-EU economic relations not only refers to aspects of formal economic ties, but also those of established trade links. Consequently, both economic and trade relations are meant when this chapter refers to the bilateral 'economic relations' between the two sides.

(European Communities 1976).[2] The creation of the JCC formally put the status of bilateral relations under annual review. Overall, the framework agreement provided a 'contractual link [...] useful in reducing government impediments' to a closer, economic, Canada-EU relationship (Barry 2004: 40).

In 1990, the EU and Canada signed the Declaration on Transatlantic Relations, which built on the provisions made in the 1976 Framework Agreement for Commercial and Economic Cooperation and allowed for:

> bi-annual meetings, alternately on each side of the Atlantic, between the President of the Council of the European Communities, with the Commission, and the Secretary of State for External Affairs of Canada; annual consultations between the Commission and the Canadian Government (Delegation of the European Union to Canada 1990).

The declaration thereby institutionalized regular diplomatic exchanges between the EU and Canada, setting the stage for future transatlantic dialogue and making the current CETA negotiations possible. In addition to the implementation of annual EU-Canada Summits, the Declaration formally recognizes the importance of the bilateral relationship by emphasizing the common heritage and the close historical, political, cultural and economic ties, as well as mutual goals such as the promotion of market principles, the rejection of protectionism and the desire both to strengthen and to further open the multilateral trading system (Delegation of the European Union to Canada 1990; Barry 2004: 42). While the Declaration does not contain any crucial substance with respect to the set goals (i.e. trade liberalization), it marked an important milestone in the EU-Canada relationship and formally declared the symbolic importance of EU-Canada relations.

Historically speaking, the 1976 Framework Agreement and the 1990 Declaration represent the first building blocks on the way to the CETA. They were followed by the 1996 *Joint Political Declaration and Action Plan* and the 1998 *Creation of the EU-Canada Trade Initiative* (ECTI) (Delegation of the European Union to Canada (n/d); Barry 2004: 49). Their importance to moving the EU-Canada transatlantic agenda forward, however, were only marginal. Other than the standard agreement to cooperate in the future and a declared vision to develop trade links between the two economies, the two agreements did not contain anything of real substance (Barry 2004: 45–6, 48–9). The ECTI, however, did mention the intention of both

---

2   In 1976 when the *1976 Framework Agreement for Commercial and Economic Cooperation* was signed, it was the European Communities, and not the EU that was partner to the Agreement. For simplicity reasons, however, this chapter will use the signifier EU to refer to both the EU (after the signing of the Maastricht Treaty in 1992), but also its predecessor the European Economic Communities (EEC) and finally the European Community (EC). For simplicity reasons also, the EU is treated as coherent whole with respect to trade politics. Differences between the member states and the EU over trade issues will be addressed where applicable, but are not subject under investigation in this chapter.

sides to 'enhance bilateral cooperation in such areas as mutual recognition, services, government procurement, intellectual property rights [and] competition' (Barry 2004: 49). While the declared intentions fit the overall description of the CETA, as later sections of this chapter will show it was not until the 2002 EU-Canada Summit that a potential bilateral trade and investment agreement was publicly mentioned (Delegation of the European Union to Canada 2002). Consequently, at the 2004 EU-Canada Summit the two sides agreed on a joint scoping exercise capturing the main objectives of a future agreement, scheduled to begin by the end of 2004 (Delegation of the European Union to Canada (n/d)). The so-called Canada-EU Trade and Investment Enhancement Agreement (TIEA) meant to go beyond the previous goal of increased market access. In fact, it sought to include issue areas such as investment and financial services. As such, the agreement was quite ambitious and mirrored the currently proposed CETA. In 2006, however, the negotiations for the TIEA collapsed, presumably over EU intentions to gain access to Canadian services and procurement markets and the absence of the Canadian provinces from the negotiations. Consequently, the EU 'was ambivalent about pursuing further trade negotiations with Canada' (Kukucha 2011: 131). It was not until 2007 that the efforts to negotiate a trade agreement between the EU and Canada were renewed.

In 2007 Quebec Premier Jean Charest and Prime Minister Stephen Harper travelled to Paris and Berlin as part of a lobbying effort to convince key EU members to commence negotiations for a bilateral trade and investment agreement (Wells 2007). Following these efforts, at the 2007 EU-Canada Summit in Berlin both the EU and Canada announced that they had agreed to 'cooperate on a study to examine and assess the costs and benefits of a closer economic partnership' and to determine 'the existing barriers, especially non-tariff, to the flow of goods, services and capital, and estimate the potential benefits of removing such barriers' (Delegation of the European Union to Canada 2007). The result was a joint report by the European Commission and the Government of Canada, released during the 2008 EU-Canada Summit, outlining the perceived costs and benefits of any potential trade and investment agreement between the two transatlantic partners (Council of the European Union 2008).

Stemming from the report *Assessing the Costs and Benefits of a Closer EU-Canada Economic Partnership*, the perceived benefits of a trade and investment agreement between the EU and Canada are a trade expansion of 25.7 billion euro, with 18.6 billion euro coming from trade in goods and 7 billion euro from cross-border trade in services, following an elimination of all remaining tariffs. Moreover, considering the higher amount of tariffs EU goods are currently facing in Canada, the EU net gain is said to be 12.2 billion euro while that of Canada is estimated to be 6.3 billion euro. With respect to trade in services, the respective numbers read as follows: 4.8 billion euro for the EU and 2.2 billion euro for Canada. Overall, the EU is said to gain in the services sector while Canada is to gain from greater trade liberalization in industrial goods and machinery (European Commission and Government of Canada 2008: 163–8). To make sense of these projections it is important to note that at the time that this cost-benefit analysis report was published, EU goods entering the Canadian market were still facing average tariff rates of 3.5% while those of Canadian goods entering the EU leveled at 2.2% (European Commission and Government of Canada 2008: 165). The point here, however, is not to interpret or substantiate the numbers provided in the report, rather to indicate that the associated benefits of an agreement were enough to move both the EU and Canada to go a step further in issuing a request for a joint scoping exercise.

The goal of the initiated exercise was to determine the potential scope of a trade and investment agreement as well as to identify any factors which would be crucial to its success. Resulting from this initiative was the *Joint Report on the EU-Canada Scoping Exercise*, which was released during the February EU-Canada Summit in 2009, directly preceding the announcement of formal negotiations of the CETA during the May EU-Canada Summit in 2009 (European Commission (n/d), 2009; Council of the European Union 2009). The report outlines the parameters of subsequent negotiations as well as their underlying ambitions of going further than any of the previous EU or Canada trade agreements (European Commission and Government of Canada 2009; European Commission 2009). Its content has to be assessed in connection to the leaked draft text version of the Canada-EU CETA and the overall EU trade strategy, which will be the purpose of the next section of this chapter. Overall, from the 1976 Framework Agreement, the bilateral economic relationship between the EU and Canada has evolved from one stressing mutual economic and commercial cooperation to one pursuing an agreement of unparalleled ambition and depth in either the EU's or the Canadian bilateral trade agreement history.

Part II: EU Trade Strategy and the EU-Canada CETA

Throughout the evolution of EU-Canada economic relations there have been several attempts at creating formal trade and investment links. These efforts, however, have failed to produce an agreement formalizing terms of bilateral trade until the official announcement was made in 2009 to negotiate a Canada-EU economic and trade agreement. As the previous part of this chapter has demonstrated, it was Canada that essentially set the negotiations in motion. The question, then, arises why the EU has decided to pursue the agreement. The answer to this question is twofold in that the CETA 'fits' practically and symbolically within the EU's overall trade strategy. The focus of the next few paragraphs is to examine the practical importance of the CETA to the EU's emerging trade strategy, while part three of this chapter will turn to an analysis of the CETA's symbolic importance.

The main tenants of the EU's trade strategy with respect to the CETA are set in and around the 2010 and 2006 Trade Policies. The 2010 policy, *Trade, Growth and World Affairs – Trade Policy as a Core Component of the EU's 2020 Strategy*, builds on the provisions made in its 2006 predecessor *Global Europe Competing in the World – A Contribution to the EU's Growth and Jobs Strategy* (European Commission 2006, 2010a). In its 2006 trade policy the EU Trade Commission indicated the EU's commitment toward the WTO and a positive conclusion of the Doha Development Round (DDR) as a key priority. Moreover, the Trade Commission laid out a framework for economic conditions under which new bilateral Free Trade Agreements (FTAs) were to emerge. The perceived market potential and the level of protection against EU export industries (tariffs and NTBs) were identified as the two key economic criteria on the basis of which FTAs should be pursued. These 'new' bilateral FTAs were seen as a way to build on the WTO and to go a step further by laying the foundation for future multilateral trade negotiations. In particular, FTAs should be aimed toward liberalizing trade in services and investment, eliminating all remaining tariffs, import, and export restrictions, as well as working toward eliminating NTBs through greater regulatory cooperation (European Union Trade Commission 2006: 10–11). FTAs in this sense are a tool used to successfully conclude multilateral trade negotiations although a positive conclusion of the DDR is the main objective, indicating the EU's strong trust in multilateral trade negotiations, although this changes slightly with the 2010 EU trade policy.

Evident throughout the pages of *Trade, Growth and World Affairs – Trade Policy as a Core Component of the EU's 2020 Strategy*, is the need for a positive conclusion of the DDR. This notwithstanding, the language used in the 2010 trade policy communication suggests a certain degree of distrust toward the multilateral trade agenda and consequently puts a greater emphasis on bilateral FTA negotiations (European Commission 2010a: 4–5; De Gucht 2011). In its 2010 trade policy, the EU Trade Commissioner declared that 'the Doha agreement will not give answers to the newer questions that global trade rules ought to take care of' (European Union Trade Commission 2010a: 5). Consequently, what is needed are balanced, comprehensive and ambitious FTAs that meet the challenges posed to world trade in the aftermath of the 2008 global financial and economic crisis (De Gucht 2011; European Union Trade Commission 2010a: 4–5).[3] The context of the 2008 global financial and economic crisis becomes crucial in assessing the 2010 EU trade policy. It is a common theme throughout the trade policy communication document and numerous speeches made by the EU Trade Commissioner Karel De Gucht, as well as various supporting documents that were published alongside the 2010 EU trade policy communication (De Gucht 2011; European Union Trade Commission 2010a: 4–5, 2010b; European Commission 2010). One very good example to illustrate this is a speech given by Karel De Gucht in early March 2011. In this speech he portrayed improved trade rules and a more ambitious bilateral trade agenda as an exit strategy from the crisis. In this view, growth in trade is seen

---

3   See also, Giovanni Graziani, 'What is new with the new trade policy of the EU?,' in Kurt Huebner, *Europe, Canada and the Comprehensive Economic and Trade Agreement* (New York: Routledge, 2011), 561–2.

as a way to spur job growth and to maintain the existence of the welfare state by preventing a reemergence of protectionist trade policies (De Gucht 2011).

When referring back to the 16 to 17 billion euro expected EU net gain from the CETA referred to the first part of this chapter, the connection between more liberalized trade as part of a bilateral FTA, and economic and job growth makes sense (European Commission and Government of Canada, 163–8). The expected EU net gain of roughly 16 to 17 billion euro, however, has to be seen with some skepticism. No accurate predictions of what the CETA will most likely yield in terms of net gains can be made until the negotiations of the CETA have been concluded and the exact scope of the agreement has been assessed. Even then, perceived net gains could not be accurately determined until the agreement has been implemented and in operation for several years. Nevertheless, any expected net gain serves well to justify the pursuit of a FTA especially as part of an overall trade strategy aimed at more economic, sustainable and inclusive growth.

Moreover, the 2010 EU trade policy differentiates itself from its 2006 predecessor by emphasizing implementation and enforcement over actual negotiations. When speaking about the new trade policy in June 2010, Karel De Gucht made it explicit that, while still important, the EU's negotiating agenda is no longer sufficient if what is negotiated is not subsequently implemented by the EU's trading partners (European Parliament 2010; European Union 2006; European Union Trade Commission 2006). This clearly indicates a shift away from the 2006 trade policy which primarily emphasized trade negotiations, albeit not a radical one.

Rather, the 2010 EU trade policy builds on its 2006 predecessor by shifting the emphasis from negotiation to implementation and enforcement. It further builds on the 2006 trade policy by calling for deeper investment links with trade partners, more open public procurement markets for EU businesses, increased market access for EU service providers, an improvement of the enforcement mechanisms with respect to intellectual property right (IPR) protections, a guarantee of unrestricted access to raw materials and energy supplies as well as the overcoming of regulatory barriers to trade and investment (De Gucht 2011; European Parliament 2010; European Union Trade Commission 2010a: 4–5). By making these demands, the provisions made under the 2010 trade policy exceed those of its 2006 predecessor. It thereby represents a more aggressive and assertive approach to trade policy-making (*M2 Presswire* 2011). Consequently, what emerges from looking at the 2006 and 2010 trade policies is a strong trend toward creating far reaching, ambitious bilateral trade agreements.

As specified in the 2010 trade policy document, once the EU has concluded all the ongoing FTA negotiations of which the CETA is a part, as well as those that are under consideration, the EU will have Preferential Trade Agreements (PTAs) with 'the large majority of the WTO members,' covering half of EU trade (European Union Trade Commission 2010a: 5). To increase this number, the 2010 trade policy document indicates the US, China, Japan and Russia as the next possible candidates with whom to work toward greater trade and investment liberalization

(European Union Trade Commission 2010a: 5). It is within this overall picture that the ongoing CETA negotiations have to be assessed.

What should become clear at this point is that the CETA appears to be an integral component of the EU's overall trade strategy. In other words, it makes sense for the EU to pursue the agreement with Canada as part of its overall desire to use ambitious bilateral FTAs as gateways to maintaining global liberalized trade links and to liberalize trade in areas that are not yet fully liberalized, such as procurement, services and investment. As will become evident throughout the next few paragraphs, the extent to which the CETA 'fits' into the overall EU trade strategy just outlined can be assessed by looking at the negotiating agenda itself.

The CETA negotiating agenda confirms the assumption that the agreement is of practical importance to the EU's overall trade strategy. As the negotiations are largely conducted behind closed doors any inferences about the CETA and its practical importance to the EU's trade strategy rely on what is publicly available. Consequently, the extent to which it 'fits' into the overall emerging EU trade strategy can be derived by referring back to the 2009 *Joint Report on the EU-Canada Scoping Exercise* (European Commission 2009; European Commission and Government of Canada 2009) briefly discussed in the first part of this chapter. In addition, a leaked consolidated draft version of the negotiating text and a speech given by the EU Trade Commissioner Karel De Gucht in December 2010 are useful in illustrating the scope and ambitious character of the CETA (De Gucht 2010a; Trade Justice Network 2010). Doing so is central to demonstrating how the agreement 'fits' with the overall EU trade strategy.

The scope of the CETA has been officially determined by the EU and Canada as part of their 2009 *Joint Report on the EU-Canada Scoping Exercise.* As defined in this document the CETA considers any previously signed FTAs by either the EU or Canada as a stepping stone. As part of this endeavour, the agreement is to go beyond multilateral trade negotiations in eliminating all existing tariffs and in including all tariff lines, working toward eliminating agricultural export subsidies, making substantial progress in areas of NTBs, technical barriers to trade (TBTs), customs procedures, cross-border trade in services, investment, government procurement, regulatory cooperation, IPRs and dispute settlement provisions (European Commission 2009; European Commission and Government of Canada 2009). In particular, the report highlights trade in services and investment as well as government procurement as the three most important aspects of the agreement, in part designed to increase market access and the 'provision of non-discriminatory treatment of investors and investments, and to improve transparency' while including procedural obligations of both the central and sub-central governments (European Commission and Government of Canada 2009). The report also indicates that public procurement should be deepened to cover both central and sub-central markets (European Commission and Government of Canada 2009). The intended scope of the agreement as just outlined is broadly reflected in the draft consolidated text version of the CETA, which indicates all the important issue areas of procurement, services and investment on the agenda, but also goes into great length in defining the scope of the intended chapters (Graziani 2011: 63; Trade Justice Network 2010). The emphasis here is to indicate the extent to which the negotiating agenda reflects the content of the EU's emerging trade strategy.

Both the 2009 *Scoping Exercise* and the leaked consolidated draft text version indicate that the CETA is an agreement unparalleled in scope and intent. Further, both public statements and the ongoing negotiations as they emerge from press releases support the claim that the issue areas identified as most crucial in the 2010 EU trade policy and as part of the CETA scoping exercise are still on the negotiating agenda and have been since they were launched. This in turn suggests the seriousness with which the negotiations are being pursued (Department of Foreign Affairs and International Trade 2009, 2010a, 2010b, 2010c, 2010d; European Union Trade Commission 2010a; Government of Canada 2010; Council of the European Union 2010).

The practicality of the negotiations has also been indicated by the EU Trade Commissioner, Karel de Gucht. In his speech 'Strengthening the EU-Canada Ties' the Trade Commissioner states that the EU is pursuing the CETA in part to match trade liberalization with the 'realities of the modern business world' (De Gucht 2010a). Moreover, he emphasizes the ambitious nature of the agreement, especially with respect to the services and investment markets. He goes on to say that the negotiations have made progress in harmonizing trade liberalization in the less difficult areas whereby more work needs to be done with respect to the more difficult questions. Even though he does not indicate what the more difficult areas are, the speech nevertheless reflects the importance of the CETA to the EU's overall trade agenda. Using common theoretic assumptions about the mutual benefits of free trade, he makes links to the perceived benefits of the agreement to overall EU intentions to stimulate growth and investment (De Gucht 2010a). In other words, he links the proposed agreement directly to the EU's objectives of using the CETA 'as a benchmark and blueprint for what [the EU] can do in the future with countries of a similar level of development' (De Gucht 2010a). But what this statement also indicates is doubt about the way in which the CETA is useful in practice with respect to the EU's overall trade strategy.

As De Gucht points out, Canada is the only economically advanced and industrialized country with which the EU is pursuing such an agreement. Given this simple fact, the CETA negotiations are of great importance to the EU overall in that they can help it in exercising its 'trade negotiating muscles' to target some of its more prioritized trading partners. In fact, official EU portrayals of the CETA negotiations, not only single Canada out as one of the only developed countries with an advanced economy that the EU is currently negotiating an ambitious FTA with, but perceive Canada as one of the 'second tier of countries immediately following those identified as priority partners' (De Gucht 2011; European Commission 2010b: 9, 2011). The priority partners referred to are the US, China, Japan and Russia whom the EU wishes to target as part of its ambitious FTA strategy once the ongoing negotiations are concluded (European Union Trade Commission 2010a: 5).

Knowing the evidence presented thus far, several inferences can be made about the utility of the CETA to the EU's greater trade agenda. First, the CETA is practically important because it is conducive to the EU achievement of its overall stated goals of sustainable, inclusive growth. Second, the CETA is practically important because it allows the EU to come a step closer to maintaining a global and liberalized trade and investment environment. In this sense the CETA can be an end in itself, but also a means for achieving similar far reaching and ambitious FTAs with other developed countries, leading to the conclusion that the EU is using the CETA negotiations as a blueprint for other negotiations and agreements. In this sense, it becomes a tool by which the EU can practice for future negotiations that will most likely be more difficult to pursue, a claim that is even more interesting when thinking about the recent changes made to the EU's governing structures within the Lisbon Treaty.

Without the institutional changes made to the EU's governing structures, the EU would not have the capacity to negotiate the CETA, much less to enforce any of the provisions made within it. As Karel De Gucht pointed out in a speech made in October 2010, prior to the implementation of the Lisbon Treaty in 2009, the EU did not have the legal capacity to pursue some of the more sensitive issue areas such as procurement, services, investment and IPRs, which are the key issue areas of the agreement. Even though the EU member states maintain veto powers in issues of domestic implementation in some of these issue areas, the EU does have the power to negotiate ambitious FTAs such as the CETA. Without a deepening of EU integration, EU efforts in pursuing its new trade strategy would be almost impossible (De Gucht 2010b). The extent to which this claim is justified is a matter of debate, but for the purpose of this chapter discussion it suffices to say that the Lisbon Treaty has entrusted the EU with important trade policy powers that allow it to pursue the CETA as part of its overall trade strategy, making institutional changes another reason for the EU's interest in the these negotiations.

Part III: The Symbolic Importance of the CETA to the EU's Overall Trade Strategy

The CETA symbolically 'fits' within the EU's overall emerging trade strategy for two reasons. First, it provides the EU with an opportunity to maintain close transatlantic ties to North America. Second, it is an agreement unprecedented in EU trade history. These two reasons are ultimately intertwined. Canada-EU economic relations go back to the pre-World War I (WWI) era and largely relied on trade between Canada and the United Kingdom (UK). As Michael Hart points out, trade links between Canada and the UK were very well developed in a manner similar to those of the US and the UK. The two world wars, however, interrupted these links, and since then, trade and integration primarily occurred on each side of the Atlantic separate from each other. In other words, while Europe was rebuilding its industries and embarking on the journey toward European integration, Canada became more closely integrated with the US. This began with the Auto pact of 1965, then with the Canada-US Free Trade Agreement (CUFTA) in 1989 and finally the North American Free Trade Agreement (NAFTA) in 1994 (Hart 2000: 4). Also pointed out by Hart, is that trade between Europe and Canada steadily decreased in the period following World War II (WWII). He notes that,

> Between 1949 and 1999 Europe's share in total Canadian merchandise exports declined from 28.4 per cent to 5.1 per cent, while the US share grew from 50.9 per cent to 85.8 per cent. Canadian imports from Europe declined from 13.1 per cent to 8.7 per cent, while imports from the United States over this period grew from 70.4 per cent to 76.3 per cent (Hart 2000: 2).

The declining trade volume suggests that either side of the Atlantic has been increasingly looking inward as opposed to looking across the Atlantic. Hart uses these numbers to suggest that a potential FTA between the EU and Canada is nothing more than an attempt to hold on to something that no longer exists. In other words, it is more symbolic than practically feasible (Hart 2000: 5). While this argument makes sense, there is no way to predict the way the CETA will increase trade volumes once it comes into operation. Declining trade alone is no reason to dismiss a FTA as merely symbolic in nature. Rather, what determines the agreement's symbolic nature is what it ultimately represents.

The CETA represents a way in which the EU targets North America as whole. It is symbolic with respect to the EU's trade strategy in that it is an agreement different from others signed with either Canada or the US, but also to the extent that it is the first of the EU's ambitious FTAs to be negotiated with an industrialized and developed country. EU relations with Canada have largely mirrored those of the EU and the US. For example, the EU issued a transatlantic declaration with Canada on 22 November 1990, only one day before doing the same with the US; in 1995 the EU signed a Joint Action Plan with the US and a year later one with Canada; then in May 1998 the EU signed a Transatlantic Economic Partnership Agreement (TEP) with the US only to do the same with Canada in December of the same year, yielding the EU-Canada Trade Initiative (ECTI) (Delegation of the European Union to the United States; Delegation of the European Union to Canada (n/d)). Most of these were purely symbolic in nature as they reflected mere agreements to cooperate on important issues and in that they created a framework for further cooperation. In essence they sent signals of intended cooperation and formalized the diplomatic relationship between the EU and the US on the one hand, and the EU and Canada on the other (Barry 2004: 37–50). As such they provided so-called 'contractual links' between the EU and Canada as well as between the EU and the US, leading to the conclusion that the EU is more interested in North America as a whole, in part perhaps because of the historical legacy binding Europe and North America together, but also in part because of its overall ambitions with respect to its emerging trade policy. The CETA is one more step in this direction, as its positive conclusion would potentially lead to a similar agreement with the US.

The trend that has emerged with respect to the way the EU has been approaching both Canada and the US thus far, suggests that once the EU has achieved an agreement with one of its transatlantic partners, a similar agreement with the other will follow. The transatlantic declarations, joint action plans and trade cooperation initiatives have created this precedent with respect to EU transatlantic relations. Moreover, in its 2011 *Trade and Investment Barriers Report*, the EU explicitly states that the US is a future target for closer investment and trade cooperation, similar to the scope of what the EU is currently negotiating with Canada, in terms of the CETA (European Union Trade Commission 2011: 1, 10). Canada is the first developed country with which the EU is pursing such an ambitious FTA, making it a symbolic enterprise for the mere 'novelty' of its negotiation (European Union Trade Commission 2010b: 9). If the negotiations are successful, and the EU consequently pursues a similar agreement with the US, the trade agreement can be seen as symbolic in the sense that it led the way toward a more ambitious trade and investment relationship between the EU and North America as a whole, in part designed to increase existing transatlantic ties. At this point, though, this is a matter of mere speculation. Nevertheless, if this is indeed what is going to happen, the CETA can be said to 'fit' symbolically into the EU's overall trade strategy as emerging from its 2006 and 2010 trade policies.

Conclusion

The EU is pursuing the Canada-EU CETA because it 'fits' practically and symbolically within the EU's overall emerging trade strategy. Underlying the answer to the question of why the EU is pursing the agreement is a variety of different reasons that make up the CETA's practical and symbolic importance to the EU's trade strategy. First, the CETA, in essence, is in line with the logical progression by which EU-Canada relations have developed over time. Even though some of the earlier agreements signed were largely symbolic, they created the framework from which CETA can now be pursued. Second, the CETA is a very comprehensive and ambitious bilateral FTA that exemplifies the scope of the new type of FTAs which the EU wishes to pursue as part of its new trade strategy aimed at maintaining a global liberalized trade environment. As this chapter has shown, the CETA fits the description of the EU's newly envisioned FTAs quite well. This is especially true in regard to procurement, investment, and services, areas in which the agreement goes well beyond any of the previously signed EU FTAs. Moreover, the CETA is estimated to provide the EU with a net gain of roughly 25 billion euro, giving extra weight to the contributions the CETA could make to overall EU objectives of using these more ambitious FTAs as avenues by which to exit the financial and economic crisis. Third, even though the CETA exemplifies one of the EU's comprehensive and ambitious FTAs, it can also be seen as a tool to practice prior to pursuing similar FTAs with some of the EU's more prioritized trading partners. In this sense, the EU arguably is pursuing the agreement as a means to achieve other goals. Fourth, the EU is also pursuing the CETA for symbolic reasons, as it offers a way for the EU to maintain and perhaps increase its transatlantic ties. Moreover, if the negotiations are successful it will be the first signed FTA with a developed, industrialized country, as envisioned in the EU's new trade strategy. In addition, if successful, the agreement will give new direction to the EU's transatlantic relations in general.

This chapter has looked at official justifications for the CETA and how the FTA consequently 'fits' within the overall EU trade strategy. It has not been the intention of the chapter to test the assumptions and goals set out by the EU compared to the way the EU is conducting trade policy on the ground; if that were the case, numerous claims of reaching free global world trade, not only in goods and services, but also in investment and IPRs, would need to be compared to the way the EU has been behaving during multilateral trade negotiations and disputes, in particular. The EU's behavior at the international level testifies to the somewhat hypocritical undertone of the EU visions set out in the 2006 and 2010 trade policy documents. Doing so, however, will be the subject of further research.

References

Barry, D. (2004), 'Toward a Canada-EU Partnership?', in P.M. Crowley (ed.), *Crossing the Atlantic – Comparing the European Union and Canada*. Aldershot, UK; Burlington, VT: Ashgate, 35–58.

Council of the European Union (2008), *EU-Canada Summit, Quebec, 17 October 2008*. Under: *Press Releases*. Available at http://www.consilium.europa.eu/App/NewsRoom/latest.aspx?lang=1&cmsid=363 (accessed 28 March 2011).

Council of the European Union (2009), *EU-Canada Summit Declaration, Prague, 6 May 2009*. Under: *Press Releases*. Available at http://www.consilium.europa.eu/App/NewsRoom/latest.aspx?lang=1&cmsid=363 (accessed 28 March 2011).

Council of the European Union (2010), *EU-Canada Summit Press Statement*. Under: *Press Releases*. 5 May. Available at http://www.consilium.europa.eu/Newsroom (accessed 10 April 2011).

De Gucht, K. (2010a), *Strengthening the EU-Canada Ties*. Speech, Chamber of Commerce Canada-Belgium-Luxembourg: Brussels, 9 December.

De Gucht, K. (2010b), *The Implications of the Lisbon Treaty for EU Trade Policy*. Speech, S & D Seminar on Trade Policy, Oporto, 8 October.

De Gucht, K. (2011), *Trade after the Crisis: What is Europe's Global Role?* Speech, European Policy Centre: Brussels, 1 March.

Delegation of the European Union to Canada (n/d), *EU and Canada Overview*. Under: *EU & Canada*. Available at http://www.delcan.ec.europa.eu/en/eu_and_canada/overview/ (accessed 15 April 2011).

Delegation of the European Union to Canada (1990), *Declaration on Transatlantic Relations*. Under: *Official Documents*. Available at http://www.delcan.ec.europa.eu/en/eu_and_canada/official_documents/ (accessed 28 March 2011).

Delegation of the European Union to Canada (2002), *EU-Canada Summit, Ottawa, December 19, 2002*. Under: *Official Documents*. Available at http://www.delcan.ec.europa.eu/en/eu_and_canada/official_documents/ (accessed 28 March 2011).

Delegation of the European Union to Canada (2007), *2007 EU-Canada Summit Statement, Berlin June 4, 2007*. Under: *Official Documents*. Available at http://www.delcan.ec.europa.eu/en/eu_and_canada/official_documents/ (accessed 28 March 2011).

Delegation of the European Union to the United States of America (n/d), *Agendas, Dialogues & Summits*. Under: *EU-US Relations*. Available at http://www.eurunion.org/eu/EU-US-Relations/Agendas-Dialogues-Summits.html (accessed 15 April 2011).

Department of Foreign Affairs and International Trade (2009), *First Meeting Held on Comprehensive Economic and Trade Agreement*. Under: *News Releases*. 10 June. Available at http://www.international.gc.ca/media_commerce/comm/news-communiques/2009/387248.aspx?lang=eng (accessed 10 April 2011).

Department of Foreign Affairs and International Trade (2010a), *Canada and the European Union Take Stock of Historic Trade Agreement Negotiations*. Under: *News Releases*. 15 December. Available at http://www.international.gc.ca/media_commerce/comm/news-communiques/2010/396.aspx?lang=eng (accessed 10 April 2011).

Department of Foreign Affairs and International Trade (2010b), *Canada and the European Union on Track to Trade Deal*. Under: *News Releases*. 18 October. Available at http://www.international.gc.ca/media_commerce/comm/news-communiques/2010/338.aspx (accessed 10 April 2011).

Department of Foreign Affairs and International Trade (2010c), *Canada Begins Third Round of Economic and Trade Negotiations with European Union*. Under: *News Releases*. 20 April. Available at http://www.international.gc.ca/media_commerce/comm/news-communiques/2010/138.aspx?lang=eng (accessed 10 April 2011).

Department of Foreign Affairs and International Trade (2010d), *Second Round of Canada-EU Economic and Trade Negotiations Starts Today*. Under: *News Releases*. 18 January. Available at http://www.international.gc.ca/media_commerce/comm/news-communiques/2010/026.aspx?lang=eng (accessed 10 April 2011).

European Commission (n/d), *Countries-Canada*. Under: *Bilateral Relations*. Available at http://ec.europa.eu/trade/creating-opportunities/bilateral-relations/countries/canada/ (accessed 28 March 2011).

European Commission (2006), *Global Europe Competing in the World a Contribution to the EU's Growth and Jobs Strategy*. Brussels.

European Commission (2009), *Joint Report on the EU-Canada Scoping Exercise*, 5 March. Available at European Trade Commission. *Countries-Canada.* Under: *Bilateral Relations.* Available at http://ec.europa.eu/trade/creating-opportunities/bilateral-relations/countries/canada/ (accessed 28 March 2011).

European Commission (2010), Europe 2020 – A European Strategy for Smart, Sustainable and Inclusive Growth. Brussels, 3 March.

European Commission (2010a), *Trade, Growth and World Affairs – Trade Policy as a Core Component of the EU's 2020 Strategy*, COM (2010) 612, Brussels.

European Commission (2010b), *Report on Progress Achieved in the Global Europe Strategy, 2006-2010* SEC(2010) 1268/2, Brussels.

European Commission (2011), *South Korea – The EU-South Korea Free Trade Agreement.* Under: *Countries and Regions.* Available at http://ec.europa. eu/trade/creating-opportunities/bilateral-relations/countries/korea/ (accessed 10 April 2011).

European Commission and Government of Canada (2008), *Assessing the Costs and Benefits of a Closer EU-Canada Economic Partnership.* Available at European Trade Commission. *Analysis-Chief Economist.* Under: *Trade.* Available at http://ec.europa.eu/trade/analysis/chief-economist/ (accessed 28 March 2011).

European Communities (1976), *Framework Agreement for Commercial and Economic Cooperation Between the European Communities and Canada.* Article IV. *Official Journal of the European Communities*, No. L260. 24 September.

European Parliament (2010), *Committee on International Trade, Speaking Points: Future Trade Policy.* EU Trade Commissioner Karel De Gucht, Brussels, 22 June.

European Union (2006), *New Trade Strategy Puts EU Trade Policy at Service of European Competitiveness and Economic Reform.* Under: *Press Releases.* 4 October. Available at http://europa.eu/rapid/pressReleasesAction. do?reference=IP/06/1303 (accessed 10 April 2011).

European Union Trade Commission (2011), *Trade and Investment Barriers Report 2011*, COM (2011) 114, Brussels.

Government of Canada (2009), *Canada-EU Summit Declaration May 6, 2009.* Under: *Canada-EU Relations, Summits and Agreements.* Available at http://www.canadainternational.gc.ca/eu-ue/bilateral_relations_bilaterales/ 2009_05_06_statement-declaration.aspx?lang=eng (accessed 20 March 2011).

Government of Canada (2010), *EU-Canada Summit Joint Press Statement.* Under: *Canada-EU Relations.* 5 May. Available at http://www.canadainternational. gc.ca/euue/bilateral_relations_bilaterales/2010_05_05_statement-declaration. aspx?lang=eng (accessed 10 April 2011).

Graziani, Giovanni (2011), 'What is New with the New Trade Policy of the EU?', in Kurt Huebner, *Europe, Canada and the Comprehensive Economic and Trade Agreement.* New York: Routledge, 59–76.

Hart, M. and W.A. Dymond (2000), *Dreams and Delusions: The Continuing Allure of a Canada-EU Free Trade Agreement.* Paper prepared for the Transatlantic Studies Conference Dundee University, 8–11 July.

Kukucha, C.J. (2011), 'Provincial Pitfalls – Canadian Provinces and the Canada-EU Trade Negotiations', in Kurt Huebner, *Europe, Canada and the Comprehensive Economic and Trade Agreement.* New York: Routledge, 130–50.

M2 Presswire (2011), 'EU Sets Out to Dismantle Trade Barriers,' 10 March. Available at http://www.presswire.net (accessed 12 March 2011).

Trade Justice Network (2010), *Trade Justice Network to Brussels for Canada-EU Free Trade Negotiations.* 9 July. Available at http://tradejustice.ca/en/section/9 (accessed 3 April 2011).

Wells, P. (2007), 'Charest, Harper and Free Trade with the EU.' *Maclean's* 120(29), 30 July.

PART IV
Deepening, Widening or Multispeed Integration?

Chapter 7

Direct Democracy:
Remedying the Democratic Deficit?

Ece Ozlem Atikcan

The European integration project started as an elitist one, without explicit approval by the public. This was a necessary exclusion of public opinion, as the post-World War II European public was highly emotional and potentially hostile to cooperation with Germany. As Charles Goerens put it:[1]

> What would have happened if we had decided whether or not the Federal Republic of Germany could join the ECSC by referendum? In the 1950s, the Luxembourgish public would have rejected it. That might have been the worst political decision taken by our country.

This elitist project has delivered what it promised – a peaceful Europe. However, as a side effect, it created a democratic deficit (Marquand 1979). The European Union (EU) has long been a non-issue in European democracies, based on a 'permissive consensus' (Inglehart 1971; Lindberg and Scheingold 1970; Norris, 1997). The member-state governments negotiated complex, technical EU policies on behalf of their citizens, while the public only tacitly approved these developments. Even though the EU acquired more governing capacities, European citizens continued to be detached from the integration project. The deepening process has accelerated significantly since the late 1980s. Attempting to boost the Union's legitimacy, some member states sought to ratify these steps by using direct democracy. Yet several of these referendums rejected the treaties and shocked Europe. Rising Euroscepticism since the 1990s has shown that the tacit approval of the public has come to an end, and that the permissive consensus has collapsed.

In this chapter, my goal is not to explain voting behaviour in EU referendums but instead to focus on referendum debates and discuss how direct democracy functions as a method of deepening European integration. Both academics and politicians have frequently presented the increased use of direct democracy as a remedy to the Union's democratic deficit. I argue that the current apolitical nature of the Union also limits the democratic potential of the referendum mechanism.

---

1 Yes campaigner, Member of the Luxembourg Parliament. Interview, 10 November 2008.

For direct democracy to provide rich debates on EU policies and its future direction, European integration needs to be debated regularly from a range of perspectives. In its current state, referendums cause sudden politicization on EU matters without providing the necessary background information. In addition, the No side has an advantage in this politicization process. It is relatively easy for No campaigns to shape referendum debates and raise controversial issues – occasionally unrelated to the proposed change (Jerit 2004; LeDuc 2005). In the EU context, No campaigners are commonly blamed for shifting the debate to 'irrelevant' issues. However, fostering discussion is what referendums are supposed to do. By providing snapshots from EU referendum debates, I will demonstrate that the real problem is the general lack of contestation on European Union issues. From an unaware and unfamiliar stance, the voting public is suddenly immerged in intense debates that are often one-sided. As long as awareness on EU matters remains low, this mechanism poses certain difficulties in regard to the deepening process.

This chapter draws its empirical evidence from a broader project that investigates the voting behaviour in six referendums: on the Treaty Establishing a Constitution for Europe (TCE) in Spain, France, the Netherlands and Luxembourg in 2005; and the double referendum on the Lisbon Treaty in Ireland in 2008 and 2009. Relying on interviews with campaigners and public opinion data from these cases, I argue that if the EU were integrated into national debates on a regular basis and not just around the time of referendums, referendum debates could involve more deliberation on treaty contents and policy options. Below I first explore the existing literature on the Union's democratic deficit. Second, by using interview and survey data I discuss how sudden politicization via referendums challenges the deepening process.

Why Might the EU Need Direct Democracy?

There is widespread consensus between scholars that the EU needs to be more democratic. Yet this is accompanied by a debate concerning the definition of democracy and what the potential remedies should be (e.g. Follesdal and Hix 2006; Moravcsik 2002). Some scholars adopt a legal perspective and recommend institutional reforms that would give the European Parliament – the only directly elected institution – more power (e.g. Wallace and Smith 1995). Others approach the question from a socio-psychological stance and argue that a European *demos* is the necessary foundation for European democracy (e.g. Weiler 1996). Regardless of the approach, the key argument within this literature concerns the lack of politicization and policy contestation (Follesdal and Hix 2006; Hix 2002, 2003; Ladrech 2007; Mair 2000; Mény 2002; Schmidt 2006).

Politicization has been a central concept in the study of European integration as the project started out as an explicitly technocratic one. For Schmitter (1969: 166), politicization is essentially an increase in controversiality of joint decision-making, which would then likely lead to a widening of the audience interested and active in integration.[2] De Wilde (2011: 566) defines it more broadly as an increase in polarization of opinions, interests or values, and the extent to which they are publicly advanced towards the process of policy formulation within the EU. Recent research has questioned whether the EU is sufficiently politicized to be considered democratic.[3] On the one hand, the European public is no longer considered to be largely indifferent as the salience of European integration has increased gradually since the 1990s (de Wilde and Zürn 2012). Hooghe and Marks (2008) suggest that rising politicization caused the EU to move from a permissive consensus to a constraining dissensus in the recent past. On the other hand though, mainstream political parties have been reluctant to politicize the subject openly due to various coalition and electoral disincentives such as the party's position on the issue in relation to other parties and the electorate; a party's ideological reputation; and the existence of internal divisions on the issue (Green-Pedersen 2012; Hooghe and Marks 2008). Ladrech (2007: 953) presents this phenomenon as 'the democratic deficit *inside* political parties'. Indeed, the great majority of European political parties remain in favor of European integration. Euroscepticism is mainly limited to parties on the periphery of the party system (Hix 1999; Taggart 1998). While far left and far right parties share Euroscepticism, parties in the middle, including most social democratic, Christian democratic, liberal, and conservative parties, are generally much more supportive of European integration (Hooghe, Marks and Wilson 2002; Marks, Hooghe, Nelson and Edwards 2006).[4] Importantly, by choosing not to politicize the EU explicitly, national political elites are missing an opportunity to educate their public (Franklin 2006; Ladrech 2007).

The EU's institutional structure also contributes to the lack of politicization. Follesdal and Hix (2006) argue that the Union lacks vehicles for encouraging a Europe-wide debate about EU policies that would feed off and mobilize political opposition. The absence of a genuine European party system and competition for a European executive office blocks any restructuring of domestic parties (Mair 2000). Without such political competition, there is no debate on different policy options, which results in a disconnection between the Union's policy agenda and its citizens. Emphasizing this lack of democratic contestation in Europe, Mény (2002) argues that the constitutionalist pillar of democracy has become stronger over time at the expense of the popular pillar. Therefore, a frequent policy recommendation that comes out of these studies is to use national referendums

---

2   Schmitter focuses on politicization in relation to the spill-over hypothesis of neofunctionalist theory. According to him, following this controversiality, 'somewhere along the line a manifest redefinition of mutual objectives will probably occur' (Schmitter 1969: 166).

3   For discussions on desirability or reversibility of such politicization (see de Wilde and Zürn 2012; Hix and Bartolini 2006; Moravcsik 2006).

4   Hooghe and Marks (2008) stress that populist (traditionalism/authority/nationalism – tan) parties, nationalists in conservative parties, and radical left parties are more sceptical.

on EU issues in order to involve the public directly in decision-making.[5] As such, direct democracy is seen as a possible remedy to the Union's democratic deficit (Hug 1997).

European political leaders have explicitly linked the use of referendums to a better quality of democracy in the policy world as well. In 2004, 10 EU member states decided to ratify the TCE using the referendum method: Czech Republic, Denmark, France, Ireland, Luxembourg, the Netherlands, Poland, Portugal, Spain and the United Kingdom. Although in the end only four – Spain, France, the Netherlands and Luxembourg – held their proposed referendums. Closa (2007) analyses the reasons behind calling for the TCE referendums. Despite the existence of other strategic considerations, governments legitimized their decisions by referring to increasing the public input in European integration, or boosting the popular legitimacy of the Union. As Valéry Giscard d'Estaing put it, 'treaties are made by states and ratified by parliaments; constitutions are made by popular assemblies and ratified by citizens'.[6] In another example, the British Foreign Office noted that the TCE referendum 'would allow for the issues to be fully debated by the public'.[7]

But did these referendums *allow for the issues to be fully debated*? I am interested in the striking contrast between the heated referendum campaigns and the usual lack of debate on the EU.[8] These periods of heightened awareness on EU issues differ markedly from the everyday apathy towards the Union.[9] Then how do these sudden referendum debates unfold? I will show that EU referendum debates may in fact not live up to expectations due to the lack of day-to-day debate on EU matters. My interview data demonstrates that politicians have a hard time shaping these debates. Yes campaigners criticize No campaigners for bringing up issues unrelated to the referendum proposals, or admit that they themselves have trouble in explaining these proposals. On the other side, No campaigners resent being labelled 'anti-EU' when they disapprove of certain EU policies. Debates do not always discuss treaty contents or EU policies because the actors are not accustomed to having such conversations.

---

5   Both Mény (2002) and Follesdal and Hix (2006) explicitly recommend this. Follesdal and Hix, however, acknowledge that referendums would not promote day-to-day competition or policy contestation.

6   Cited in (Closa 2007). CONV 658/03 'Referendum on the European Constitution' CONTRIB 291, Brussels, 31 March 2003.

7   Cited in (Closa 2007).

8   The existing EU referendum literature has focused predominantly on explaining the results (e.g. Franklin, van der Eijk and Marsh 1995; Reif and Schmitt 1980; Siune, Svensson and Tonsgaard 1994; Svensson 2002). Recent research on EU referendums has highlighted that referendum campaigns and information provided to voters during these campaigns matters (de Vreese and Semetko 2004; Hobolt 2009).

9   Also, media coverage of European affairs is virtually absent from the news agenda. It peaks around important EU events but vanishes right after (de Vreese 2007; de Wilde 2011; Fossum and Trenz 2006; Miklin 2009; Tilly and Tarrow 2007; Van de Steeg 2006).

To understand the nature of these debates better, one needs to take a closer look at referendum dynamics. The literature suggests that in a referendum campaign the No side has certain political advantages as No campaigners do not necessarily need to make a coherent case against a proposal (Jerit 2004; LeDuc 2005: 179). They need only to raise doubts in the minds of voters, play upon known fears, or link the proposal to other less popular issues or personalities (de Vreese and Semetko 2004: 56). Hence the No side is the one that guides the politicization process in referendum debates. Given that voters are unfamiliar with the Union's inner workings, it is relatively easier for No campaigners to raise doubts in the minds of voters and to introduce controversial issues, including those that do not necessarily originate from the treaty under debate. Regarding the TCE referendums, Moravcsik (2005) notes that the treaty became a 'passive receptacle – as in all previous European referendums – of voters' discontent over everything from Moroccan immigration to social-welfare cuts – almost none of which are caused by EU policies'. Referring to the same phenomenon, Fossum and Trenz (2006) argue that the TCE was largely misunderstood due to the 'de-contextualisation' of constitutional debates. Analysing the French TCE referendum debate, Glencross (2009) similarly demonstrates that the No side set the terms of the French debate around social policy, and that other important subjects such as political finality, institutional reform, the Charter of Fundamental Rights, regional aid, anti-discrimination legislation, or environmental protection were all marginalized.

One can draw a distinction between referendums on broad treaty reforms and those on specific steps in the integration project such as Euro membership, as the latter are more focused and less complicated than the former. However, de Vreese and Semetko (2004), in their in-depth case study of the Danish 2000 referendum on the Euro, find that the Yes side emphasized the economic aspects of the issue, whereas the No side broadened the debate to cover issues such as enlargement, social welfare or national sovereignty. They identify this broadening as the key winning strategy for the No campaign. Thus, even single-issue EU referendums can carry similar patterns if the campaigners succeed in bringing different items to the agenda.

This peculiar dynamic can pose an additional challenge to the deepening process. While disconnecting the Union from its citizens was desirable at the beginning of the integration project, today this unawareness is problematic given its increasing competences. Below, by using interview and public opinion data, I demonstrate how this disconnection can lead to unexpected patterns of politicization in treaty ratification via referendums.

Shaping the EU Referendum Debates

Spain, France, the Netherlands, and Luxembourg held referendums on the TCE, and Ireland had two votes on the Lisbon Treaty. These debates were not identical however they had certain characteristics in common. The two treaties were very similar – long, highly complex, and technical. A great majority of the citizens were therefore unfamiliar with their contents. In all cases, the government and the opposition came together to support the treaties. While the political mainstream called for a Yes vote, the far left and far right recommended a No vote (Crum 2007; FitzGibbon 2009; Holmes 2008). In my interviews in all five countries, the Yes side complained about the No campaign arguments that did not originate from the text, and also about the difficulty of explaining the treaties, while the No campaigners resented not being able to have a debate, as the Yes side had painted them as extremists.

An important difference was that the Spanish debate was less intense than the other ones.[10] When asked about the low level of interest in the TCE, Spanish campaigners connected this to lack of contestation. Popular Party (PP) Senator Alejandro Muñoz Alonso opposed the idea of having a referendum on such a long and complicated text: 'I thought that it would be better to have a referendum on the first part of the treaty which was about the principles and values, which would be much easier to explain to citizens. And not on the concrete policies of the Union that were very difficult to understand for people'.[11] He added, that 'there was no controversy or confrontation between parties, so there was lack of interest'. In PP MP Ignacio Cosidó Gutiérrez's words, 'the public's knowledge of the TCE was quite low. It was a complex text, but also we did not have a real debate. Because everybody agreed, we did not debate. The result was low participation'.[12] With 42%, Spain indeed had the lowest turnout level of the six referendum cases. However, its debate shared key similarities with the other cases. Below I provide selected quotes from campaigners in all five countries as examples of these common aspects.

Especially where all-encompassing EU treaties such as the TCE or the Lisbon Treaty are concerned, No campaigners can raise a wide range of issues to persuade the public to vote No. For instance, they argued that treaty ratification would increase immigration, decrease welfare benefits, undermine national sovereignty, and interfere in domestic laws on military neutrality or even abortion and drug policies. Importantly, the No side does not necessarily need to build a coherent case. In the Netherlands, International Secretary of the Labor Party (PvdA) Marije Laffeber noted this as a significant problem: 'There is something for everybody to

---

10   See (Hobolt 2005, 2009) for the measurement of campaign intensity based on political opposition to the ballot in parliament, difference between the Yes and No vote intentions in the polls, and news coverage.

11   Yes campaigner, Spain. Interview, 2 October 2008.

12   Yes campaigner, Spain. Interview, 1 October 2008.

dislike. In the Yes camp you are in a defensive position, and you have to explain everything'.[13] In Ireland, Lucinda Creighton, Fine Gael MP, commented that 'People only need one good reason to vote against. It is a major difficulty'.[14] Karen White, member of Irish Alliance for Europe, similarly stated that 'If you are on the No side, you can appeal to different groups with different messages. We had to counter all these different arguments'.[15] In Luxembourg, François Biltgen, the Chairman of the Christian Social People's Party (CSV) and the Minister of Labor and Employment, echoed the same point, emphasizing that it was easier to be on the No side.[16] Charles Goerens, Democratic Party (DP) MP, agreed, noting that 'destruction is easier than the building process'.[17] Dutch Socialist Party (SP) MP Harry van Bommel acknowledged this as advantageous to the No side and that 'There was a basket of arguments. People sometimes have the wrong reasons to come to the right conclusions. I never mentioned Turkey's membership, but if that was somebody's trigger to vote No, that was fine by me'.[18] An Irish campaigner, Executive Director of the Libertas Naoise Nunn compared the No campaign to guerilla warfare in this regard:[19]

> You picked one little issue on which there was some doubt and contention, and then you sold and created enough doubt in the minds of the audience. ... Some of the language in the treaties is quite vague and open to interpretation. If you are on the No side you can interpret anyway you want, and it is up to the Yes side to disprove it, and it is very, very difficult to disprove it. Especially if you do not know what it means in the first place. That makes being on the attack very easy.

The result of this dynamic is often a campaign where the subject becomes much broader than the Yes campaigners expect. Campaign themes may not necessarily originate from the referendum proposals. Frustrated with this broadening in the Irish campaigns, Dick Roche, Minister of Europe, gave examples: 'They always come up. Ireland will lose neutrality. ... Ireland will lose its character. ... We will be subsumed in Europe. ... We will lose our culture'.[20] Brigid Laffan, Chairperson of Ireland for Europe, characterized the No campaign themes such as neutrality and abortion as Ireland's 'neuralgic issues'.[21] Similarly, Enrique Baron Crespo,

---

13   Yes campaigner the Netherlands. Interview, 22 October 2008.

14   Yes campaigner, Ireland. Interview, 19 April 2011.

15   Yes campaigner, Ireland. Interview, 28 April 2011.

16   Yes campaigner, Luxembourg. Interview, 12 November 2008.

17   Yes campaigner, Luxembourg. Interview, 10 November 2008.

18   No campaigner, the Netherlands. Interviews, first 8 April 2008, second 31 October 2008.

19   No campaigner in the first round, Yes campaigner in the second round, Ireland. Interview, 12 April 2011.

20   Yes campaigner, Ireland. Interview, 27 April 2011.

21   Yes campaigner, Ireland. Interview, 29 April 2011.

Member of European Parliament (MEP) with the Spanish Socialist Workers' Party (PSOE), emphasized that some of the No campaign arguments were not accurate.[22] In Luxembourg, CSV MP Laurent Mosar referred to the same phenomenon: 'If somebody says that with the TCE we would lose our independence, people immediately believe [it]'.[23] In France, Pierre Kanuty from the French Socialist Party (PS) agreed as well, noting that 'the No camp tried to use everything to convince people'.[24] Olivier Ubéda of the Union for a Popular Movement (UMP) explained that unrelated issues became a major obstacle for the Yes side:

> [There were arguments such as] Turkey would come into the EU with the TCE. Or that you would have 80 millions of Muslims coming into Europe. ... We had an argument about the Polish plumber, because in the treaty we said that everybody could work everywhere. As if a wave of Polish plumbers would have arrived in France. This is just fears. This is human, you fear things you do not understand, you do not know about ... All this from the No camp was just nonsense.[25]

Chirac experienced a similar moment on a televized debate with French youth. When confronted with wide-ranging socioeconomic worries, he 'bemoaned on no fewer than four occasions this pessimism and twice exhorted his audience to set aside their fears – *n'ayons pas peur*' (Glencross 2009).

Naturally, the No campaigners had more liberty in introducing themes to these debates, and their arguments ranged from treaty-based concerns to those that had no connection to the text. In Spain, United Left campaigner José Manuel Fernández stated that a text-based argument they have used involved mathematics: 'In the TCE, words "free market" and "competition" existed more than 300 times.[26] The word "social" appeared only about 15 times'. As an example of unrelated themes being brought into the debate, Wim van de Donk, the chairman of the Dutch Scientific Council for Government Policy (WRR), mentioned that the Dutch No camp was successful in bringing up bizarre European policies such as those determining the length of sausages.[27] Yes campaigners highlighted the difficulty of responding to these diverse arguments. This is not surprising as the voting public is not exposed to arguments concerning the EU on a daily basis. In order to counter the various No arguments, the Yes campaigners needed to quickly educate the public on the technicalities of EU decision-making. Anthony Brown, Director of Research for Ireland for Europe, explained that in order to reply to arguments on

---

22   Yes campaigner, Spain. Interview, 16 October 2008.
23   Yes campaigner, Luxembourg. Interview, 14 November 2008.
24   Yes campaigner, France. Interview, 8 September 2008.
25   Yes campaigner, France. Interview, 9 September 2008.
26   No campaigner, Spain. Interview, 7 October 2008. The interviewee noted that he did not remember the exact number.
27   Interview, 23 October 2008.

neutrality or abortion, the answer had to be related to the EU's 'competences', which he referred to as a 'dread-word' in a political debate.[28] EU competence simply refers to its decision-making power but a discussion on EU competences is rather technical as the Union has multiple decision-making systems applying to different issue areas. In Luxembourg Socialist Workers' Party LSAP) MP Ben Fayot's words, 'citizens have not yet understood the institutional framework and are misinformed about the actual competences of the Union'.[29] It is revealing that a crucial term as EU competence is not part of regular political debate in Europe. Many politicians, just like voters, are unaware of the list of areas in which the EU legislates. Pat Cox, Campaign Director of Ireland for Europe, noted that many Yes campaigners found it difficult to campaign on the content of the treaty, 'because of the complexity of Article 48A Paragraph 3 … it is not the easiest terrain'.[30] In the Netherlands, People's Party for Freedom and Democracy (VVD) member Patrick van Schie agreed:

> We never had a public debate on Europe. … There were few specialists, sometimes it would be debated in the national parliament, not often. In the Netherlands, it is considered as a topic of International Relations specialists and the MEPs. … The problem of the Yes campaign was this. They did not have to think of arguments for further European integration because there was never a public debate.[31]

A striking example of how lack of awareness on EU issues can cause problems during intense campaign discussions comes from the Dutch TCE referendum. One week before the vote, the Dutch government sent every household a short leaflet, which explained the content of the TCE. This text was approved by the Referendum Commission but it became controversial due to a factual error. This leaflet mentioned that by saying Yes the Netherlands would accept the superiority of EU laws over national laws. This legal doctrine, known as the supremacy of EU law, was actually not introduced by the TCE and has been long established. Atzo Nicolaï, Dutch Minister of EU Affairs, specified this as one of the mistakes, an unfortunate statement, as people did not know that the EU laws were already superior to national laws.[32] According to Christian Democratic Appeal (CDA) MP Jan Jacob van Dijk also, this reinforced the feeling among Dutch citizens that

---

28   Yes campaigner, Ireland. Interview, 20 April 2011.
29   Yes campaigner, Luxembourg. Interview, 14 November 2008.
30   Yes campaigner, Ireland. Interview, 28 April 2011.
31   Director of the think tank that is related to the VVD – the Dutch Liberal Party. Interview, 6 November 2008. Van Schie added that the only politician, who seriously started a debate on Europe, was VVD-leader Frits Bolkestein (1990–1998). He explained that when Bolkestein left the national political arena, no one took over from him.
32   Yes campaigner, the Netherlands. Interview, 29 October 2008.

they would lose control over their own legislation.[33] Once again, it is telling that EU citizens were not aware of the supremacy of EU law, which was introduced in 1964. If they hear about this doctrine for the first time in the midst of a heated referendum campaign, it can be difficult to reverse the misunderstanding.

In addition, prominent Yes campaigners occasionally made controversial statements. In Ireland several key Yes campaigners acknowledged that they had not read the Treaty (Holmes 2008). Taoiseach Brian Cowen said he had not read the treaty 'from cover to cover', whereas Irish Commissioner Charlie McCreevy mentioned that 'no sane or sensible' person could be expected to read the document. In the Netherlands, certain Yes campaigners warned the public explicitly not to vote against the text (Anker 2006). Minister of Foreign Affairs Ben Bot recommended that voters abstain in case of doubt, while former Prime Minister Ruud Lubbers repeated this position one day before the vote. These kinds of remarks could easily give the impression that the Yes campaigners did not know what was in the treaty, or even worse, that they were not interested in the public's opinion when the point of holding a referendum is theoretically the exact opposite.

Conversely, the No campaigners complained about not being able to discuss EU policies, and about being immediately perceived as extremists or as against European Union membership. In France, Christophe Beaudouin, member of the Gaullist No campaign 'Group for a Confederation of the States of Europe', explained his experience:

> When you criticize Europe, you are in the camp of evil. They put morality everywhere, there is the camp of the good and the evil. When you take a position, even with arguments, they do not say 'I don't agree with you, your arguments are wrong and I will demonstrate that you are wrong with this and this'. That would have been normal and a balanced debate. They instead said 'you cannot say that, it is not your right, remember all the people who died in WW2'.[34]

Daniel Cirera of the French Communist Party (PCF) also stated that Yes campaigners portrayed No campaigners as against Europe.[35] ATTAC member Maxime Combes echoed the same point, specifying the Yes side's tone as 'you have to vote Yes', or 'you do not understand the philosophy of European construction'.[36] As Claude Debons of the General Workers' Confederation (CGT) put it: 'The Yes campaigners were very defensive. Sometimes they were making mistakes. In the debates especially, they did not know the text. When the No vote increased in the polls, they started accusing us of xenophobia.'[37] UMP MP Nicolas Dupont-Aignan, a prominent No campaigner, similarly noted: 'As soon as we

---

33   Yes campaigner, the Netherlands. Interview, 29 October 2008.
34   No campaigner, France. Interview, 15 September 2008.
35   No campaigner, France. Interview, 10 September 2008.
36   No campaigner, France. Interview, 8 September 2008.
37   No campaigner, France. Interview, 19 September 2008.

avoided the trap of being extremists, we won'.[38] In Spain, Initiative for Catalonia Greens (ICV) campaigner Marc Giménez Villahoz also explained that the Yes side frequently portrayed the No side as against Europe, and he identified this as an 'easy counterargument' to their arguments.[39] In Luxembourg too, Trade Unionist Nico Clement (OGBL) criticized certain Yes campaigners for following the logic that 'if you are not for the TCE then you are against Europe, then you are in fact for World War in Europe'.[40] In the Netherlands, member of the Constitution No group, Erik Wesselius, described the same phenomenon: 'There was a taboo. The No campaign and the No vote were being put in the corner of xenophobia. ... They tried to move us in that corner'.[41] This was an issue in Ireland too. Mary Lou McDonald, Sinn Féin MP, mentioned that the Yes side portrayed the No side as extremists.[42] In fact, former Taoiseach Bertie Ahern dismissed the No campaigners as 'loolah's' ['lunatics'] (Holmes 2008). Killian Forde, Sinn Féin's Director of Strategy in the first Lisbon campaign, similarly noted that the Yes side used an emotional argument: 'we had to vote Yes, because we were good Europeans'.[43] This, once again, is a reflection of the Union's democratic deficit. Given the lack of contention on the subject, being against an EU treaty can easily be conflated with being against the EU or even being against European peace in general.

As a result of these factors, referendum debates may not always fully achieve what they are intended to achieve – democratic deliberation and contestation on treaty reforms. 'Until the beginning of 1990s nobody asked which kind of EU policies people wanted', Patrick van Schie, member of the VVD, emphasized.[44] Hence sudden EU referendum debates may not generate in-depth discussion on EU policies. Neither the public nor the politicians are used to this dialogue. José Ignacio Torreblanca's summary of the Spanish campaign captures the essence of the problem:

> Since Europe was a non-issue, the referendum was a disappointment. ... Instead of having a policy debate on what sort of Europe we want, we had sportsmen reading Article 7 of the Charter of Fundamental Rights on television. It was only black and white messages. 'Europe is good', without debating the policy implications, there was no debate on political vs. economic Europe, or social vs. political Europe, or enlarged vs. core group. ... The referendum showed that we

---

38   No campaigner, France. Interview, 24 September 2008.

39   No campaigner, Spain. Interview, 15 October 2008.

40   Interview, 17 November 2008. OGBL is the Confederation of Independent Trade Unions of Luxembourg, affiliated with the LSAP.

41   No campaigner, the Netherlands. Interview, 4 November 2008.

42   No campaigner, Ireland. Interview, 26 April 2011.

43   No campaigner, Ireland. Interview, 12 April 2011.

44   Director of the think tank that is related to the VVD – the Dutch Liberal Party. Interview, 6 November 2008.

were not yet able to discuss European issues in a material way, with complex options.[45]

From the Public's Perspective

How did the voting public perceive these debates? There are detailed post-referendum studies of the TCE and Lisbon Treaty referendums.[46] These surveys seek to explain the voting behavior, therefore there are no direct questions focusing on the public's perception of the referendum debates. Nevertheless, questions asking the voters to specify the reasons behind the way they voted reveal the public's perspective to some extent. First of all, when looking at the motivations of Yes voters, we see that it was rare when the reasons for how they voted were directly linked to the treaty contents. In all five countries, answers such as 'it is essential for continuing the European construction', 'it increases the influence of Europe vis-à-vis the US and China', 'in order to further deepen', or the 'place of our country in Europe' ranked highly. These answers are all supportive of the integration project in general, but they are not necessarily related to the policies or reforms contained in the TCE and Lisbon Treaty. In an example, 15% of the Spanish Yes voters said that they approved the TCE because it created EU citizenship, which was in fact created by the Maastricht Treaty a decade ago. However, this was not a misperception on the part of the citizens. Spanish Yes campaign documents emphasized this as a positive aspect of the TCE. Similarly, Yes campaigners in all countries highlighted benefits received from European integration in the past, which are visible in voters' responses in these post-referendum surveys in justifying their vote decision. While this is a very important argument, it does not necessarily invoke a policy debate for the future.

These surveys also demonstrate that not knowing enough about the complex referendum proposals leads an important part of the public to reject them. In Spain,

---

45   Yes campaigner, Spain, Senior Analyst for EU Affairs, Elcano Royal Institute for International Affairs. Interview, 6 October 2008.

46   For Spain, the CIS survey is available at: http://www.cis.es/cis/opencm/ES/1_encuestas/estudios/ver.jsp?estudio=4617. For France, the SOFRES data can be obtained from http://www.tns-sofres.com/; the CSA data is available at: http://www.csa.eu/dataset/data2005/opi20050529d.pdf; and the IPSOS data is available at: http://www.ipsos.fr/canalipsos/poll/8074.asp. For Luxembourg, the TNS-ILRES survey is available at: http://www.tns-ilres.com/cms/Home/News/Publications/Archive/Referendum-vum-10-Juli-2005. For Ireland see (Sinnott and Elkink 2010; Sinnott, Elkink, O'Rourke and McBride 2009), for Luxembourg see (Dumont, Fehlen, Kies and Poirier, 2007), for the Netherlands see (Aarts and van der Kolk 2005). The data in the Netherlands was originally collected by GfK Benelux on behalf of Kees Aarts and Henk van der Kolk, both of the University of Twente. The study was made possible by a grant from the Ministry of Home Affairs and Kingdom Relations. The original collectors of the data do not bear any responsibility for the analyses or the interpretations published here.

24% of the No voters specified lack of information as their motivation to vote No. In the Netherlands, 9% of the No voters mentioned the same. In France, 34% of the No voters said they rejected the treaty because the text was too difficult. In Luxembourg, 59% of the No voters specified the same reason for voting No. In Ireland, in the Lisbon referendums, respectively 42% and 20% of the No voters rejected the treaty because of lack of information.

Other reasons cited by the No voters are also quite interesting. Thomassen (2005) reports a small conversation from an interview conducted on the street during the Dutch TCE campaign. The respondent says that he would certainly vote No, and the two reasons he provides are the Euro and Turkish enlargement. When the interviewer reminds him that the TCE is not about these issues, he responds that his opinion on these themes was never asked before. In France as well, post-referendum surveys found that Turkish accession to the EU was ranked highly among the reasons for rejecting the TCE, even if this issue had nothing to do with the treaty. In Luxembourg, a detailed focus group study highlighted four main concerns that were decisive in the final vote: social cohesion, employment, education, and enlargement (Dumont et al. 2007). However, this study also found that these issues were not built around the categories and policies specified in the TCE, which confirms that the treaty contents did not capture the public's attention. In Ireland too, detailed studies showed that perceptions that the introduction of conscription, the erosion of Irish neutrality, the end of Ireland's control over its policy on abortion, and the end of Irish control over Irish corporate tax rate were in the treaty contributed to the No vote (Sinnott et al. 2009). Just as in the examples above, these were all inappropriately perceived to be in the treaty.

I do not present these figures to argue that the treaties were approved or rejected for entirely unrelated reasons. There were also treaty-related factors that contributed to referendum results. However, these survey responses reveal the extent to which lack of information and lack of familiarity with the Union can limit democratic deliberation and in turn affect the deepening process.

Direct Democracy in an Ever Closer Union

Direct democracy is a frequent policy recommendation to decrease the Union's democratic deficit. But does the referendum method provide the Union with the democratic contestation it needs? I argued that for this to happen, national politicians and the voting public need to be more familiar with EU affairs on a day-to-day basis. As long as the EU remains distant to them, the referendum mechanism may lead to debates that do not necessarily reflect the contents of the treaty reforms.

Does this imply that increased use of referendums would block the Union from integrating further? Moravcsik (2005) states that 'politics by plebiscite generates political chaos'. Hug (1997) warns that while the use of the referendum method would increase the social legitimacy of the project, it would also cause a heavily fragmented integration as the number of veto players increase. Paralleling these concerns, CDA MP Jan Jacob van Dijk notes: 'My impression is that referendum is a conservative instrument. It would be an instrument which would block new developments'.[47] However, it does not automatically follow that direct democracy would hinder deepening. A lot depends on the level of awareness. Campaigners perceive EU referendums to be conservative because this mechanism causes sudden politicization and they are not used to having such debates. They do not have ready arguments that they always use regarding EU policies, as they do for domestic policies such as social security. If they did, EU referendum debates would be more predictable and focused on EU policy and institutional reforms. De Wilde and Zürn (2012) propose to observe the EU's politicization using three indicators: rising awareness, mobilization, and polarization.[48] A healthy increase in these three components would enhance the Union's direct democracy experience for the reasons I outlined in this chapter. With rising awareness, Yes campaigners would have less responsibility to educate the public during short referendum campaigns. With more mobilization and polarization on the other hand, No campaigners would obtain a more legitimate standing in these debates.

Another strand of literature questioned whether ordinary citizens have the necessary interest and expertise to make informed decisions in referendums (Sartori, 1987). Laurent Mosar, CSV MP, expresses the same concern: 'It is really complex and difficult. Therefore referendum is not the right way to continue with European policy-making. … It is too complicated to explain'.[49] In fact, it has been repeatedly shown that referendum voters are capable of making informed decisions (e.g. Cronin 1989; Lupia 1994; Magleby 1984). We have no reason to believe that EU citizens are inherently incapable of deciding on EU matters. Recent research demonstrated that in EU referendums, overall, citizens vote in line with their underlying broad attitudes towards European integration, rather than simply voting on national issues (Hobolt 2009). In the future, with more sophisticated debates involving competing justifications for EU policies, citizens could be expected to develop more specific policy preferences on European integration.

As a first step forward, the Union needs better communication (e.g. Fossum and Trenz 2006; Meyer 1999). European citizens need to be accustomed to discussing the EU's policies just like they discuss their national governments' policies. Charles Goerens, DP MP, raised a significant point:

---

47   Yes campaigner, the Netherlands. Interview, 29 October 2008.

48   They define rising awareness as a greater interest and engagement of citizens in EU affairs, mobilization as an increase over time in the amount of resources spent in conflict on EU issues and the number of political actors engaged, and polarization as co-occurrence of conflicting demands for collective goods, the extremity of such demands and the depletion of nuanced or underdeveloped positions.

49   Yes campaigner, Luxembourg. Interview, 14 November 2008.

The EU integration process, despite having started in the 1950s, generated institutions that are still very young. Nobody says 'we have to renounce our national parliament' because of the bad decisions taken there. But if you have taken a decision in the EP or Commission or the Council, which does not please everybody, then you get opposition. At the end of the day this opposition can even lead to the rejection of the EU institutions.[50]

Indeed, detailed studies reveal the European public's limited knowledge of the EU institutions, which often results in an 'uninformed' politicization (Hurrelmann, Gora and Wagner 2012). If the Union removed this communication deficit, the public would be exposed to more information on EU policies concerning environment, crime-prevention, energy, science and technology, and many others that affect their lives on a daily basis. This would likely lead to increasing contestation on these policies, which is in fact what the Union needs to create a genuine link with its citizens. Only then direct democracy can be expected to fully deliver its promise.

References

Aarts, K. and H. van der Kolk (eds). (2005), *Nederlanders en Europa: Het Referendum over de Europese Grondwet*. Amsterdam: Utigeverij Bert Bakker.

Anker, H. (2006), 'The Netherlands, Referendum on the European Constitution, June 1: A Referendum on the Gap between the Citizens and the Political Establishment', in S. Hartinger (ed.), *Election Time 2005: The European Yearbook of Political Campaigning 2005*: European Association of Political Consultants and Hartinger Consulting Communications.

Closa, C. (2007), 'Why Convene Referendums? Explaining Choices in EU Constitutional Politics'. *Journal of European Public Policy* 14(8), 1311–32.

Cronin, T. (1989), *Direct Democracy: The Politics of Initiative, Referendum, and Recall*. Cambridge: Harvard University Press.

Crum, B. (2007), 'Party Stances in the Referendums on the EU Constitution: Causes and Consequences of Competition and Collusion'. *European Union Politics* 8(1), 61–82.

de Vreese, C. (2007), 'No News Is Bad News! The Role of the Media and News Framing in Embedding Europe'. *WRR Scientific Council for Government Policy Web Publications* 20.

de Vreese, C. and H. Semetko (2004), *Political Campaigning in Referendums: Framing the Referendum Issue*. Abingdon: Routledge.

de Wilde, P. (2011), 'No Polity for Old Politics? A Framework for Analyzing the Politicization of European Integration'. *Journal of European Integration* 33(5), 559–75.

---

50   Yes campaigner, Luxembourg. Interview, 10 November 2008.

de Wilde, P. and M. Zürn (2012), 'Can the Politicization of European Integration Be Reversed?' *Journal of Common Market Studies* 50(1), 137–53.

Dumont, P., Fehlen, F., Kies, R. and P. Poirier (2007), *Le Référendum sur le Traité Etablissant une Constitution pour l'Europe: Rapport Elaboré pour la Chambre des Députés.* Luxembourg: University of Luxembourg.

FitzGibbon, J. (2009), 'The Second Referendum on the Treaty of Lisbon in the Republic of Ireland, 2nd October 2009'. *European Parties Elections and Referendums Network, Referendum Briefing Paper*, 17.

Follesdal, A. and S. Hix (2006), 'Why There is a Democratic Deficit in the EU: A Response to Majone and Moravcsik'. *Journal of Common Market Studies* 44(3), 533–62.

Fossum, J. and H.-J. Trenz (2006), 'When the People Come In: Constitution-Making and the Belated Politicisation of the European Union'. *European Governance Papers C-06-03*.

Franklin, M. (2006), 'European Elections and the European Voter', in J. Richardson (ed.), *European Union: Power and Policy-making*, 3rd edn. London: Routledge.

Franklin, M., van der Eijk, C. and M. Marsh (1995), 'Referendum Outcomes and Trust in Government: Public Support for Europe in the Wake of Maastricht'. *West European Politics* 18(3), 101–17.

Glencross, A. (2009), 'The Difficulty of Justifying European Integration as a Consequence of Depoliticization: Evidence from the 2005 French Referendum'. *Government and Opposition* 44(3), 243–61.

Green-Pedersen, C. (2012), 'A Giant Fast Asleep? Party Incentives and the Politicisation of European Integration'. *Political Studies* 60(1), 115–30.

Hix, S. (1999), 'Dimensions and Alignments in European Union Politics: Cognitive Constraints and Partisan Responses'. *European Journal of Political Research* 35(1), 69–106.

Hix, S. (2002), 'Why the EU Should Have a Single President, and How She Should Be Elected'. *Paper for the Working Group on Democracy in the EU for the UK Cabinet Office.*

Hix, S. (2003), 'The End of Democracy in Europe? How the European Union (As Currently Designed) Restricts Political Competition'. Unpublished manuscript.

Hix, S. and S. Bartolini (2006), 'Politics: The Right or the Wrong Sort of Medicine for the EU?' *Notre Europe* 19.

Hobolt, S. (2005), 'When Europe Matters: The Impact of Political Information on Voting Behaviour in EU Referendums'. *Journal of Elections, Public Opinion and Parties* 15(1), 85–109.

Hobolt, S. (2009), *Europe in Question: Referendums on European Integration.* New York: Oxford University Press.

Holmes, M. (2008), 'The Referendum on the Treaty of Lisbon in the Republic of Ireland, 12 June 2008'. *European Parties Elections and Referendums Network, Referendum Briefing Paper*, 16, 1–9.

Hooghe, L. and G. Marks (2008), 'A Postfunctionalist Theory of European Integration: From Permissive Consensus to Constraining Dissensus'. *British Journal of Political Science* 39(1), 1–23.

Hooghe, L., Marks, G. and C. Wilson (2002), 'Does Left/Right Structure Party Positions on European Integration?' *Comparative Political Studies* 35(8), 965–89.

Hug, S. (1997), 'Integration through Referendums?' *Aussenwirtschaft* 52(1–2), 287–310.

Hurrelmann, A., Gora, A. and A. Wagner (2012), 'The Politicization of European Integration: More than an Elite Affair?' *Paper presented at the 9th ECSA-C Biennial Conference*, Ottawa, Ontario, Canada.

Inglehart, R. (1971), 'Public Opinion and European Integration', in L. Lindberg and S. Scheingold (eds), *European Integration*. Cambridge: Harvard University Press.

Jerit, J. (2004), 'Survival of the Fittest: Rhetoric during the Course of an Election Campaign'. *Political Psychology* 25(4), 563–75.

Ladrech, R. (2007), 'National Political Parties and European Governance: The Consequences of "Missing in Action"'. *West European Politics* 30(5), 945–60.

LeDuc, L. (2005), 'Saving the Pound or Voting for Europe? Expectations for Referendums on the Constitution and the Euro'. *Journal of Elections, Public Opinion & Parties* 15(2), 169–96.

Lindberg, L. and Scheingold, S. (1970), *Europe's Would-Be Polity: Patterns of Change in European Community*. Cambridge: Harvard University Press.

Lupia, A. (1994), 'Shortcuts versus Encyclopedias: Information and Voting Behavior in California Insurance Reform Elections'. *American Political Science Review* 88(1), 63–76.

Magleby, D. (1984), *Direct Legislation: Voting on Ballot Propositions in the United States*. Baltimore: Johns Hopkins University Press.

Mair, P. (2000), 'The Limited Impact of Europe on National Party System'. *West European Politics* 23(4), 27–51.

Marks, G., Hooghe, L., Nelson, M. and E. Edwards (2006), 'Party Competition and European Integration in the East and West: Different Structure, Same Causality'. *Comparative Political Studies* 39(2), 155–75.

Marquand, D. (1979), *Parliament for Europe*. London: Jonathan Cape.

Mény, Y. (2002), 'De la démocratie en Europe: Old Concepts and New Challenges'. *Journal of Common Market Studies* 41(1), 1–13.

Meyer, C. (1999), 'Political Legitimacy and the Invisibility of Politics: Exploring the European Union's Communication Deficit'. *Journal of Common Market Studies* 37(4), 617–39.

Miklin, E. (2009), 'Government Positions on the EU Services Directive in the Council: National Interests or Individual Ideological Preferences?' *West European Politics* 32(5), 943–62.

Moravcsik, A. (2002), 'In Defense of the "Democratic Deficit": Reassessing Legitimacy in the European Union'. *Journal of Common Market Studies* 40(4), 603–24.

Moravcsik, A. (2005), 'The Politics of Plebiscites'. *Newsweek International.*

Moravcsik, A. (2006), 'What Can We Learn from the Collapse of the European Constitutional Project?' *Politische Vierteljahresschrift* 47(2), 219–41.

Norris, P. (1997), 'Representation and the Democratic Deficit'. *European Journal of Political Research* 32(2), 273–82.

Reif, K. and H. Schmitt (1980), 'Nine Second-Order National Elections: A Conceptual Framework for the Analysis of European Election Results'. *European Journal of Political Research* 8(1), 3–44.

Sartori, G. (1987), *The Theory of Democracy Revisited.* Chatham: Chatham House Publishers.

Schmidt, V. (2006), *Democracy in Europe: The EU and National Polities.* Oxford: Oxford University Press.

Schmitter, P. (1969), 'Three NeoFunctional Hypotheses about International Integration'. *International Organization* 23(1), 161–6.

Sinnott, R. and J. Elkink (2010), 'Attitudes and Behaviour in the Second Referendum on the Treaty of Lisbon'. *Report for the Department of Foreign Affairs.*

Sinnott, R., Elkink, J., O'Rourke, K. and J. McBride (2009), 'Attitudes and Behaviour in the Referendum on the Treaty of Lisbon'. *Report for the Department of Foreign Affairs.*

Siune, K., Svensson, P. and O. Tonsgaard (1994), 'The European Union: The Danes Said "No" in 1992, But "Yes" in 1993: How and Why?' *Electoral Studies* 13(2), 107–16.

Svensson, P. (2002), 'Five Danish Referendums on the European Community and European Union: A Critical Assessment of the Franklin Thesis'. *European Journal of Political Research* 41(6), 733–50.

Taggart, P. (1998), 'A Touchstone of Dissent: Euroscepticism in Contemporary Western European Party Systems'. *European Journal of Political Research* 33(3), 363–88.

Thomassen, J. (2005), 'Nederlanders en Europa. Een Bekoelde Liefde?', in K. Aarts and H. van der Kolk (eds), *Nederlanders en Europa: Het Referendum over de Europese Grondwet.* Amsterdam: Utigeverij Bert Bakker.

Tilly, C. and S. Tarrow (2007), *Contentious Politics.* London: Paradigm Publishers.

Van de Steeg, M. (2006), 'Does a Public Sphere Exist in the European Union? An Analysis of the Content of the Debate on the Haider Case'. *European Journal of Political Research* 45(4), 609–34.

Wallace, W. and J. Smith (1995), 'Democracy or Technocracy? European Integration and the Problem of Popular Consent'. *West European Politics* 18(3), 137–57.

Weiler, J.H.H. (1996), 'European Neo-Constitutionalism. In Search of Foundations for the European Constitutional Order'. *Political Studies* 44(3), 517–33.

Chapter 8

Europe After the Greek Default: Widening, Deepening, or Splitting?

Imtiaz Hussain

What led to Greece's financial collapse? Why could the Eurogroup not preempt it? How does the future look for European regional integration? Analysis points to a Europe divided by economic culture, and overly top-heavy decision-making. This is evident in (a) public sectors expanding alongside market reforms; (b) credit agencies literally toying with EU members; (c) 'fringe' movements exploiting the growth-versus-austerity debate to flaunt nationalism over Europeanism; (d) EU dependence on 'external' input weakening regional bonds; and (e) democratic preferences challenging integration. A mixture of Hoffmann's statism, Moravcsik's inter-governmentalism, and Haas's turbulence better explain European dynamics today than any regional integration model.

Puzzle: Greece's European Tragedy – Crocodile Tears?

From being the fountainhead of European democracy, Greece today pits democracy against European integration. This reincarnated folkloric tragedy (Zingales 2012), raises serious questions: how could Greece's debt deepen without European Central Bank (ECB) oversight? Why is it casting a long global shadow? What makes 'normalcy' so elusive?

By attracting buyers for its bonds on March 9, 2012 Greece's government officers were able to call it a 'good day' (BBC 2012h), yet elections in May and June exposed the political economic frailty of both Greece and its European membership (Milner 2012; Sivy 2012). With unprecedented joblessness, austerity, and a recession plaguing the continent (Pylas 2012; Guarascio and Dumore 2012; Isidore 2012), it was unclear if the second election, in June, would give Greece 'breathing space' and Europe 'a respite' from the stalemated May election, when the idea of Greece exiting the Eurogroup and returning to the *drachma* was real (*Financial Times* 2012; Rachman 2012: 11). Greece's woes could easily have been a 'warm-up act for Europe' (*USA Today* 2012), since Spain was 'in cross hairs' (Forelle and Schaefer 2012: 1), and Italy owned 'the third largest debt stock in the world' (Rachman 2012) Greece's 'poll honeymoon' was 'short-lived' (Wigglesworth et al. 2012), lasting just one day (18 June), while the anticipated fiscal/market 'clash with Germany' yielded to a soccer clash (Paris et al. 2012).

Needing at least 66.6% of its creditors to 'voluntarily' purchase new bonds to invoke the 'collective' action clauses of bond agreements to prevent a default (Rooney 2012), Greece sold 95% on 9 March, worth €177 billion, through a series of discounts: debt repayment values were slashed (so-called 'haircuts') by 53.4%, interest rates lowered, maturation dates extended, and the ballooned 'contingent liabilities' that the Institute of International Finance (IIF) estimated would touch €1 trillion (CNN Money 2012c), were braced.

Even then, avoiding another *Echternach* Waltz was impossible. On the one hand, the 'largest sovereign debt overhaul in history' provided Greece with €130 billion from the European Union (EU) and the International Monetary Fund (IMF) in February 2012 (Reguly 2012a); on the other, private creditors opted for a 70.5% haircut to a complete loss (CNN Money 2012c). Finance Minister Evangelos Venizelos promised an 'ambitious program of reform and adjustment', even as creditors predicted another default and debt restructuring later in the year.

Leading PASOK (Panhellenic Socialist Movement), Venizelos failed twice – he could not form a coalition government after the May 2012 election (*The Economist* 2012a), then could not retain the seats won in May in the June election. His PASOK bagged 13.2% of the May vote, the anti-austerity and anti-Europe SYRIZA (Left Coalition) 16.8%, and the NDP (New Democratic Party) 18.9% – the three parties receiving 41, 52, and 108 seats, respectively, against the 160, 13, and 91 each correspondingly held in 2009; yet in June 2012, they received 12.3%, 26.9%, and 29.7% of the votes, respectively, winning 33, 71, and 79 seats. By gaining an additional 50 seats as the leading party, Antonis Samparas could still only tally 129 out of the 300 seats, needing Venizelos to bail him out against a soaring anti-bailout SYRIZA (Granitsas et al. 2012 A9; Hope 2012: 2). EU negotiators had argued against an election in providing the February 2012 bailout. Though a large majority of Greeks want to remain in the eurozone, they like the fiery and popular SYRZIA leader, Alexis Tsipras, who asked the PASOK and NDP leaders to write a repentance letter for accepting EU bailouts.

The following five sections of this chapter explore: (a) Greece's painful bailout consequences; (b) the political fallout of not adapting socio-culturally to a market economy; (c) increasing EU intervention and German stridency; (d) resorting to non-European bailout funds to hedge against future crises; and (e) credit agencies threatening state sovereignty and regional integration. The subsequent conclusions and implications intertwine with the theoretical arguments.

Greek Default

The February 13, 2012 EU/IMF bailout was not Greece's first, nor may it be the last. Since 'the markets had not responded positively to the austerity measures designed to reduce the country's debt' (BBC News 2010), on 22 April 2010 Prime Minister George Papandreau sought Eurogroup support through Finance Minister George Papaconstantinouon. The bailout required reducing the fiscal deficit to

5% of GDP during 2010 and to 3% by 2014, hiking value-added taxes (VAT) from 21% to 23%, imposing excise taxes on fuel, cigarettes, and drinks by 10%, adopting windfall and property taxes, as well as clipping Christmas and Easter bonuses, pensions, and premature retirements (Georgiev 2010).

Greece could not repay €54 billion of the €300 billion 2010 debt. Hoping that the €110 billion rescue package would 'revive growth, and modernize the economy' (International Monetary Fund 2010), the Troika (the European Commission, ECB, and IMF), raised unnecessary expectations: IMF Managing Director Dominique Strauss-Kahn believed that Greece would 'contribute to the broad international effort underway to help bring stability to the euro area and secure recovery in the global economy' (ibid.); Ewald Nowotny, an ECB Governing Committee member, similarly postulated there was 'no economic basis for negative news' (BBC News 2010); while U.S. Treasury Secretary, Timothy Geithner, added that any 'threat of cascading default, bank runs, and catastrophic risk must be taken off the table' (Simms 2011).

How would Greece repay, why had the austerity measures stalled, and what the European spread-effects were ignored questions, making Europe look like the Latin America of the 1980s or the Far-east/Southeast Asia of the late 1990s, with Cyprus, Ireland, Italy, Portugal, and Spain also lining up for a bailout (Wishart 2011). Comparison to Argentina's crippling 2001 case depicted Greece's predicament as 'five times greater': Argentina's dollar was managed by a currency board, while Greece follows euro rules (Simms op. cit.); symbolically, the spillover effects of Greece's crisis, which distinguishes the *more* from the *less* fiscally responsible euro members, were larger than Argentina's (CNN Money 2012b).

Also exposed was a eurozone ambiguity: debt/deficit prohibitions belied their regular occurrences. The February 2012 bailout proved sticky because of Greece's unreliable tax/finance management reputation (Lynn 2011: Ch. 10). Even after upgrading Greece to CCC from a selective default category after the February 2012 bailout, John Chambers, chief of the Standard & Poor (S&P) sovereign ratings department, predicted a 'selective default' ranking by fall 2012 (BBC 2012i), precisely because of Greece's 'very high' burden and 'very low' credit rating (Tymkiw and Rooney 2012). How could Greece adopt the euro and persist with questionable credentials without EU scrutiny?

Greece's Political Fallout

Pitched battles between the public and police in Athens' Syntagma Square captured as much of the headlines as the Greek Parliament approving the €110 billion bailout on 13 February 2012 did (CNN 2012a), depicting a vicious cycle (Rooney 2012): protests against physically downsizing a vast and lavish public sector reduced tourism, one of Greece's largest foreign exchange suppliers, by fifteen per cent (Granitsas and Stevens 2012), beginning a vicious cycle.

Even though Christos Papoutsis, a former Civil Defense Minister, thus managing immigration, called the stubborn European approach 'sheer blackmail' (Papadimas and Strupczewski 2012) – absorbing present pain against future benefits in 2012 when it did not work in 2010, fuels pessimism and worsens immigration problems; it also promotes fringe parties, like the Golden Dawn, whose May tally of 21 seats and 18 in June – figures from out of the blue – demonstrates staunch opposition capable of overnight growth. The original sin of expecting Greece's economic transformation overnight upon EU admission in 1981 was obscured by the false promise that after the Cold War liberalism and pluralism would inevitably and automatically come.

Blaming the 2010 austerity plans for the five-year recession, the 20+% unemployment rate, and Greece's €330 billion debt (equal to an unsustainable 160% level of its gross domestic product), the February 2012 protestors were incensed by the bailout terms: 150,000 lay-offs in the public sector by 2015, a 22% minimum wage reduction, large-scale privatization, and defense cut-backs (Reguly 2012b). Democracy, an integrative *sine qua non* (Nye 1971), challenged regional integration rules.

Greece's 'mainstreaming of extremism' and 'rejection of the rule of law' flowed from its EU membership. Defending the bailout, center-left PASOK and Antonin Samaras's center-right NDP scraped through in June (Gerodimos 2012; Hope and Spiegel 2012), but a thriving Golden Dawn (Mortensen et al. 2012b), and Tsipras's description of the bailout as 'barbarous' (Reguly 2012c; Mortensen et al. 2012a), created ghosts where there were none. Questions arose regarding which precedes the other in a collision – democratic expressions within domestic confines or integrative norms/rules from abroad? At stake, Peter Ludlow (2012) grimly notes, were 'fundamental differences in political philosophy, culture and outlook'. With intra-EU clashes becoming a norm and Germany pushing austerity, anchoring Greek recovery and dubiously claiming fiscal responsibility, the puzzle only worsened.

Germany's Stewardship and European Spillovers

Germany's weight exertion was couched in Chancellor Angela Merkel's 'full European political union' call. This, the 'great European project', she explained, of a 'fiscal compact', was developed in an EU Brussels summit during December 2011 (Wilkinson and Chapple 2012), and fleshed out in a 2012 inter-governmental treaty seeking a 'stability union' (Mullen and Meilhan 2011). Enmeshed in the European Council's Title III of the 30 January 2012 Treaty on Stability, Coordination and Governance in the Economic and Monetary Union (TSCG), it exposes 'German power', and Merkel's ability 'to change the European treaties', for 'a new treaty as the second-best solution' (Krielinger 2012). With France's Sarkozy acquiescing, the resultant media-labelled 'Merkozy' plan found Eurogroup support, plus that of six other EU members (for a total of 23 initially, but 25 eventually after Hungary and Sweden reconsidered; Britain and the Czech Republic opted out) (Neild and Chapple 2012; BBC 2012a); for ECB bailouts, Franco-German leaders wanted EU veto-power, sanctions against persistent deficits, and European Court of Justice (ECJ) dispute jurisdiction determination.

With Sarkozy's May 2012 election defeat (*The Economist* 2012b: 23–6), Socialist François Hollande is not only conditioning fiscal-pact support (BBC News 2012g), but also rallying Italy and Spain against Germany (Steinhauser and Horobin 2012: A8). His Finance and Foreign Trade Minister, Pierre Moscovici, confirmed that 'France would not ratify a European pact [without] measures to boost growth', while the new Foreign Minister, Laurent Fabius, spoke of the need of 'a different Europe' (CNN 2012b). Mario Draghi, the ECB President, preferred growth over austerity for structural reforms (Day and Jones 2012; Rubin 2012), just like the May 18–19, 2012 Washington G8 Summit and the June 18–19 Los Cabos G20 meet also did. Inheriting a 90% debt-GDP ratio and 5.2% 2011 deficit, Hollande has his work cut out for him if he wants to be what he desires, a 'normal president' (Vaïsse 2012), but the ideological resurgence in the French and Greek elections, and the mounting external pressures against the EU's 'toughest fiscal disciplinarian' – Merkel – softened regionalism significantly (Faiola and Schneider 2012; Milner and McKenna 2012).

Queen of austerity, Merkel may accept the 'growth compact' if she wins her own 2013 election (Carmichael 2012), but prefers the ECB adopt Bundesbank's fundamental inflation-control goal (relinquishing a lender of last resort role). Avoiding the Weimer ghost (of purchasing loaf for a wheelbarrow of cash), surreptitiously enhances German unilateralism. Merkel refuses (a) to accept Eurobonds, which private creditors advocate (Jones, B. 2012); (b) EFSF/ESM (European Financial and Stability Fund/European Stability Mechanism) money to recapitalize private banks; and (c) EFSF/ESM dipping into ECB credit (Dalton 2012).

Even though a disciplined Germany violates ECB's fiscal rules, the Greek crisis permitted Merkel to (a) reverse her sharp popularity crash; (b) vaunt Germany's resiliently strong economy and vault German banks, and (c) prevent any Europe-wide 'contagion' (Véron 2012).

With the private bank 'haircut' rising from 21% to 60% within the year (Evans-Pritchard 2011), German Finance Minister Wolfgang Schäuble recapitalized private banks, as IMF sources estimated losses of up to €200 billion. Merkel and Sarkozy turned to external cash to fill EFSF vaults, particularly from surplus-flushed China (*The Telegraph* 2011). This stop-gap institutional innovation hastened the ESM initiation from March 2013 to July 2012 (Wilkinson and Chapple 2012). With a projected €500 billion fund from ostensibly paid-in Eurogroup capital and by increasing the EFSF lending capacity to €440 billion from €250 (U.S. $326 billion), the EU's bailout 'firepower' fuel was boosted to €1 trillion. EU pressure streamlined Germany's. Jean-Claude Juncker, the 17-member Eurogroup chief, demanded Greece fulfill its bailout terms regardless of election outcomes, and pay €325 million for 'structural expenditures'. Olli Rehn, the European

Commissioner for Economic and Monetary Affairs, asked the Greek government to 'take responsibility' and show eurozone 'solidarity' (Lister 2012), while his trade counterpart, Karel de Gucht, denied a Grexit (Greek exit) meant 'the end of the euro' (*Globe and Mail* 2012b). By leaving a Grexit to the Greeks (*Economist* 2012d; Moffett and Peacock 2012), Germany's Schäuble, who sees Greece as having a 'bottomless pit', also suggested that Greece 'will die a slow death' if it stays, but face only a 'crisis' if it leaves (Lapavitsas 2012: 11).

Germany supported the February 2012 bailout, but demanded a pension-cut against Greece's resistance (BBC News 2012b). Both Schäuble and Juncker (Luxembourg's prime minister) constantly remind Greece of the many unsettled 'uncertainties' (Paphitis and Steinhauser 2012), yet any Greek default would immensely damage fragile post-recession European economies, especially those already indebted, and near-bankrupt banks (Jenkins et al. 2012; Rooney and Isidore 2012; Slater and Laurent 2012). While the euro value continues falling (Ross et al. 2012: 1), funds like Amundi (Europe's second-largest), Threadneedle, and Merk Investment have abandoned the euro in case of a Grexit (Oakley and Ross 2012: 1), French retailer Carrefour has left Greece, global stock market recovery from the June election was 'tepid', investors 'will not stop punishing Europe until its leaders devise a comprehensive program with a lot of money to backstop the Continent's banks and governments' (Popper 2012); and Chinese and the U.S. economic slippage reduces European export-based recovery (Hilsenrath and Mitchell 2012: 1).

Eurogroup borrowing rules were established through the 1992 Maastricht Treaty's convergence criteria over the inflation rate, fiscal performance, exchange-rate, and interest rate (Watson 1997: 69–71). Whereas the inflation rate stipulation prohibits exceeding the average of the top-three EU consumer price index levels by more than 1.5%, the fiscal discipline caps the national budget deficit to 3% of the gross domestic product; similarly, the exchange-rate stipulation is to maintain the normal EU fluctuation margins and avoid devaluations, while the interest rate criterion is for long-term rates to not exceed the average in the top-three countries by more than 2%. Germany leads this violation (Lorca-Susino 2010: 185), with the fiscal discipline as the favourite 'escape valve': Germany and Italy were the first to break the 3% borrowing limit – the former breaking it four times, the latter six (Spain has had no violations, France three, and Greece every year since joining in 2001) (BBC News 2011b). Against the eurozone's prescribed 60% debt-GDP ratio, Germany had one of the lowest debts and the slowest debt growth-rate (from 62% of annual economic output in 2000 to 77% in 2010 of government debt, and from 165% to 164% during that time for private debt, for a total of 226% and 241%, respectively). The higher debts and faster debt-growth rates in Mediterranean countries reflected greater imports from Germany, especially after the 2007 mortgage crisis, when France's debt spiraled to 321%, Italy's 310%, and Spain's 355% – much of that in the private sector (purchasing houses). Greece's EU social security debt ratio of GDP was over 125% – the highest – followed by Italy's 110%. Except for Finland and Spain, all members have a higher-than-50%

ratio (Gimenez-Roche 2011: 13). Germany's lowest interest rate and a complete disinterest in borrowing attract creditors, but Mediterranean countries carry low creditor confidence and remain globally uncompetitive (BBC News 2011a).

Remodeling Germany's image remains Merkel's European (and 2013 electoral) challenge, but faces French circumspection after Sarkozy. Even the third largest eurozone economy, Italy, might have to reconsider after toeing the German line under Mario Monti (D'Emilio 2012), its technocrat Europeanist (who promised to bail Italy out).

Franco-German monetary relations have historically depended on *quid pro quo* bargaining, with Germany conceding monetary discipline to France to get French support for a political union (Szász 1999: 217–18, 224–5). But with optimistic German economic performance (Mclean 2012), and a growing German distaste for the euro and the European Union, Hollande's *growth* priority may profoundly impact the intertwining Greek crisis, Germany-anchored bail-outs, and the absence of any EU game-plan.

Since Greece has not privatized a single public sector, its Greek financial/ monetary tragedy has been blamed on deception, for example, supplying the wrong information; abandonment as a bond-collateral by the private sector and the ECB; and having its sovereign debt abandoned (Lorca-Susino 2010: 185–6).

Any Greek restructuring was expected to reduce Greece's debt load to 120% by 2020 from 160 today, through a voluntary write-down of 50% of the value of Greece's bonds (Smith 2012). Corporatist practices rather than pluralist, fading Eurogroup capacity to repay (when they do have any golden source of automatic income), and time (without undergoing the commensurate and irreversible movements towards a freer economy), took their toll. Among the consequences, Greece was unable to pay (Lynn 2011: Ch. 10), Spain succumbed to the 2007–10 recession, and both Italy and Ireland, as well as Portugal remain on the brink. Just as economic cultures could not be conquered by neo-functionalism, the free-market western/northern variety did not become the 'be-all and end-all' of all European economic formulas (Ibid.: Ch. 11), and ECB decision-making 'dysfunctionality' (Tymkiw and Rooney 2012) or option overload (Fidler 2012: A9; *Economist* 2012c: 12), was not redressed, the sub-4% Eurogroup preference with longer maturities for new securities did not gel with the supra-3.5% private investor preference. EU-private sector negotiations became 'coercive': 'We were led to believe that what we put on the table was middle ground', Hans Hume, representing the private sector, confided, but 'they came back and said that's not true', hitting the 'threshold of what [could] be considered voluntary' (Tymkiw and Rooney 2012). The ECB refrained from buying more Greek bonds in March 2012. With a 50% voluntary Greek-bond haircut amounting to a €100 billion loss, the expected stability from reducing Greece's debt proportion to 120% (from 160) was constrained by private sector apprehension of the haircut spiraling beyond 70% (which is what did happen), at low interest rates. S&P's simultaneous Greece and EFSF downgrading suggest insufficient creditworthiness for the former but evaporating institutional 'sweetness' for the latter (Rooney 'Greek debt …' 2012).

European spread-effects varied. As previously observed, other Mediterranean countries simultaneously face huge fiscal constraints (Reguly 2012a; Giles 2012), while Belgium, Greece, Italy, and Portugal remain locked in a recession (Emmott and Flynn 2012). No cure has evolved for repeat offenders (Elliott 2011; RT 2011), or trapped foreign banks (Inman and Smith 2011). Maria Lorca-Susino's study of what she calls the eurozone's 'first economic crisis' reveals how France leads all countries in the exposure to a Greek default – to the tune of €55 billion, followed by Switzerland with €47 billion and Germany with €32 billion out of a total €222 billion at stake (2010: 187). Just for the 2010 bailout, France provided €16.8 billion of the total €79.59 billion bilateral loans, behind Germany's €22.30 billion, but ahead of Italy's €14.7 billion and Spain's €9.8 billion (Fernandes and Rubio 2012).

More troubling, the December 2011 EU unemployment rate hit the highest level since the euro was adopted in 1999 (Pylas 2012): Greece's 20+% and Spain's 23% topped the list and Austria's 4.1% and the Netherlands's 4.9% brought up the bottom, with Germany's 6.7% (the lowest recorded in unified Germany) in between (Emmott 2012a). The 16.5 million unemployment figure for December marked a steady increase throughout 2011 – sharpening the North Sea-Mediterranean divide (Emmott 2012b). Attached to this is what David Howden calls the 'shadow economy' (Howden 2011: 61–3); that is, illegal business activities not being reported or monitored, like drugs, prostitution, pornography, and so forth. Needless to say, the shadow economy accounts for 20+% of Mediterranean GDPs (the OECD average is 14.6%) – almost a quarter of all employment during 2007, with Greece leading the list with 38.6% (Ibid: 66).

Simultaneously, the European Commission predicted a 0.3% eurozone contraction in 2012 – a reverse punch from the November 2011 forecast of a 0.5% growth. Greece was predicted to contract by 4.4%, while Belgium, Cyprus, Italy, the Netherlands, Portugal, Slovenia, and Spain were also expected to follow (BBC News 2012d). While Italy and Spain have emitted positive signals (Unmack 2012), and the January 2012 EU fiscal compact is regaining market confidence (*CNN Money* 2012a), optimism remains thin.

According to the fiscal compact, signatories will be required to show a balanced budget and announce ahead of time any debt, while ESM decisions would require 85% qualified majority voting (Neild and Chapple 2012). There is concern over the implied sovereignty loss, as evidenced in the Greek discontent (Varoufakis 2012): Venizelos rejected an EU budget commissioner overseeing Greece's reforms, that too with veto-wielding powers over tax and spending decisions (Spiegel and Hope 2012). As both Greece and Germany face constraints (Jones, B. 2012; Kreilinger 2012; Reguly 2012a), the fiscal compact exposes three major problems. First, the prior fiscal union was apparently not conducted nor completed effectively: this was in the common market stage before the shift to a common currency, begun before Greece, Portugal, and Spain became members, but apparently not adequately applied to these new members or since their membership to others (Glenn 2004: 3–28). EU agencies would have to have more sovereignty-biting, intrusive, and regulatory powers to eliminate such gaps.

Second, bureaucracy will not only grow, especially at the EU level, but unnecessarily parallel national counterparts. This process began with the Common Agricultural Policy in the 1960s, but has since mushroomed and diversified, entrenched regulations, and reduced policy efficiency through subsidies (Ellison 2006: 150–65; Kopstein and Reilly 2006: 140–49).

Finally, the fiscal compact continues the two-track tradition introduced with the common currency: without all countries on-board, control is sacrificed, in this case leaving private firms to exploit the opportunity. Above all, future convergence seems traded away.

Global Paymasters and European Bailouts

Whether it is a multilateral agency like the IMF, a privileged group such as the G8 or G20, or financial-surplus countries, Europe's crisis depends on the external milieu for a solution. This accelerates (a) the financial fulcrum-shift from the Atlantic towards Asia, and (b) the waning of regional integrative identity, much as observed a generation earlier (Haas 1975).

China agreed to contribute to an EU fund after its forecasted 2012 growth rate of 9 slipped (to 8.2 under normal circumstances, according to the IMF, or to 7.2 if the European recession deepens), aggravating China's exports and Europe's recovery (Anderlini 2012). EU porosity was evident, for example, in the China-EU annual summits. The Fourteenth such summit, held in Beijing on 14 February 2012, dramatized this: the European Council President Herman Van Rompuy and European Commission President José Manuel Barroso pleaded for help, which Premier Wen Jiabao expeditiously accepted (Voigt 2012).

Yet Chinese enthusiasm was absent in business circles and at the technocratic level. Among businesses, a growing recommendation is to 'lessen [China's] exposure to euro assets in the short term … [and] reduce its dependence on exports to Europe' over the long-term (Jing and Tian 2012: 13). When Merkel invited Investment Company to 'invest in euro debt bonds' in her March 2012 visit, its disinterested chairman, Lou Jiwei, and central bank advisor, Xia Bing, conveyed a shared view: 'We may be poor', they proudly conceded, but 'we aren't stupid'. While the technocratic debt-purchase distaste combined with the political desire to dip into it informs us more of Europe's growing external dependence than of China's internal policy tussles; indeed building the €500 billion (U.S. $665 billion) ESM fund cannot but carry more external strings than Europe may be willing to accept, European regionalism shows more a spaghetti-bowl variety than pure regionalism (Baldwin 2006). EU membership expansion might stall, but then membership interest may also evaporate, as being suggested in Turkey (Bagic 2012).

Credit-agency Challenge

Even more mysterious is the growing role of credit rating agencies (CRAs). Though Western Europe's integrative efforts have historically been cast within a fuzzy sovereignty-supranational tussle, evident most conspicuously in the fate or fortune of neo-functional theory (Haas 1958; Hoffmann 1966; Moravcsik 1991; and Nye 1971), CRAs threaten state sovereignty and the rubrics of regional economic integration more directly and dramatically. Evidence suggests so over trade liberalization in another context (Biglaiser and DeRouen 2007: 121–38), but the Greek crisis suggests a neglected CRA practice may suddenly summon more scrutiny. Fitch, Moody's, and S&P set the tone: their routine state-rankings shook the market, altered trajectories, and thwarted routine expectations. On the eve of the December 2011 EU fiscal compact, Fitch immediately placed Belgium, Cyprus, Ireland, Italy, Spain, and Slovenia on a negative list, even warning the Eurogroup that a 'comprehensive solution' to the debt crisis 'was beyond reach' (*Globe and Mail* 2012a).

Standard & Poor's rankings even took France's AAA ranking away, while downgrading Cyprus, Italy, Portugal, and Spain two notches, and Malta, Slovakia, and Slovenia one notch. Making the unprecedented move of removing the United States from AAA to AA+ in August 2011, S&P's (like Fitch and Moody's) have downgraded the European Union and virtually condemned Greece to a default later in the year (*The Guardian* 2010).

David Riley of Fitch, while acknowledging France to be 'the weakest AAA country in the eurozone', pinned greater blame on the ECB for not buying more EU debt, especially Italy's. 'It is hard to believe the euro will survive', he argued, 'if Italy does not make it through', predicting any end to the euro 'would be cataclysmic' (Jones, M. 2012). Never before had EU's fulcrums been so exposed, criticized, and threatened.

Around the time of the February 2012 bailout, Moody's downgraded Italy, Portugal, and Spain, on the one hand, and Austria, France, and the United Kingdom, on the other, while Fitch downgraded Greece to the lowest credit rating even after receiving the bail-out – suggesting the low business confidence continued to remain low (Paphitis 2012).

Conclusions

The Greek crisis confirms that (a) nationalistic flames and firepower are far from being spent across West Europe, and especially cultural differences over economic practices; (b) consolidated economic asymmetry in contradiction to economic integrative expectations, indicating how realist power considerations continue to lurk behind economic integrative efforts and expectations, that without a Germany in charge, at least the economic/financial substructure would simply fall apart; (c) the potency of the theoretically neglected 'external influence' in weakening regional integration; (d) West Europe's identity crisis from not streamlining different degrees of market economy adjustments; (e) how downgrading national public sectors is being contradicted by upgrading regional-level public sectors, such as the creation of new EU institutions and safeguards; and (f) given the fissiparous dynamics, that West Europe is too multi-speed an experiment to be categorized as purely nationalistic, regional, supranational, or global.

Implications

The Greek crisis becoming a euro crisis and carrying global 'spillovers' may be opening a post-regionalism analytical space to further explore (a) what regional trade-offs can be made with external actors without splintering the region; (b) if the diminishing EU regional model being offset by increasing global bargaining positions can continue to be explained by regional integration theories or necessitate moving beyond; and (c) the need for multiple models to explain EU dynamics – from neo-functionalism to inter-state bargaining and beyond the state.

References

Aderlini, J. (2012), 'IMF Warns China on Eurozone Fallout'. *CNN*. 6 February 2012. Available at http://edition.cnn.com/2012/02/06/business/china-imf-eu/index.html?hpt=hp_bn1 (accessed 7 February 2012).

Bagic, E. (2012), 'Turkey's Minister for EU Affairs'. Available at http://egemenbagis.com/tr/4178 (accessed 28 May 2012).

Baldwin, R. (2006), 'Multilateral Regionalism: Spaghetti Bowls as Building Blocks on the Path to Global Free Trade'. National Bureau Economic Research, Working paper #12545. Cambridge, MA. Available at http://www.nber.org/papers/w12545 (accessed 24 March 2012).

BBC News (2010), 'Greece Calls on EU-IMF Rescue Loans'. 23 April 2010. Available at http://news.bbc.co.uk/2/hi/8639440.stm (accessed 20 January 2012).

BBC News (2011a), 'Europe's Four Big Dilemmas'. 27 October 2011. Available at http://www.bbc.co.uk/news/business-14934728 (accessed 14 February 2012).

BBC News (2011b), 'What Really Caused the Eurozone Crisis?' 22 December 2011. Available at http://www.bbc.co.uk/news/business-16301630 (accessed 20 January 2012).

BBC News (2012a), 'EU Summit: UK and Czechs Refuse to Join Fiscal Compact'. 30 January 2012. Available at http://www.bbc.co.uk/news/world-europe-16803157 (accessed 30 January 2012).

BBC News (2012b), 'Greece Bailout: Eurozone Ministers Set New Conditions'. 9 February 2012. Available at http://www.co.uk/news/world-europe-16976520 (accessed 9 February 2012).

BBC News (2012c), 'Greek Bailout Crisis: EU Welcomes Austerity Vote'. 13 February 2012. Available at http://www.bbc.co.uk/news/world-europe-17012604 (accessed 13 February 2012).

BBC News (2012d), 'EU Says Eurozone Economy to Shrink in 2012'. 23 February 2012. Available at http://www.bbc.co.uk/news/business-17138207 (accessed 23 February 2012).

BBC News (2012e), 'Greek Debt Swap "Success" Welcomed by European Leaders'. 9 March 2012. Available at http://www.bbc.co.uk/news/business-17308804 (accessed 9 March 2012).

BBC News (2012f), 'Greek Debt Raised Out of Default by Standard and Poor's'. 2 May 2012. Available at http://www.bbc.co.uk/news/business-17922385 (accessed 2 May 2012).

BBC News (2012g), 'French Finance Minister Moscovici Questions Fiscal Pact'. 17 May 2012. Available at http://www.bbc.co.uk/news/business-18101338 (accessed 17 May 2012).

Biglaiser, G. and K. DeRouen, Jr. (2007), 'Sovereign Bond Ratings and Neoliberalism in Latin America'. *International Studies Quarterly* 51(1) (March), 121–38.

Carmichael, K. (2012), 'Why Germany Holds the Key to Europe's Economic Revival'. *The Globe and Mail*. 9 May. Available at http://www.theglobeandmail.com/report-on-business/economy/economy-lab/why-germany-holds-the-key-to-europes-economic-revival/article4105751/ (accessed 9 May 2012).

CNN (2012a), 'Amid Clashes, Greek Parliament Approves Austerity Measures'. 13 February 2012. Available at http://edition.cnn.com/2012/02/12/world/europe/greece-debt-crisis/index.html?hpt=hp_t1 (accessed 13 February 2012).

CNN (2012b), 'French Finance Minister Says No EU Fiscal Pact Without Growth'. 17 May 2012. Available at http://edition.cnn.com/2012/05/17/world/europe/france-politics/index.html?hpt=hp_t1 (accessed 17 May 2012).

CNN Money (2012a), 'Stocks: Investors Welcome Europe's Fiscal Pact'. 31 January 2012. Available at http://money.cnn.com/2012/01/31/markets/premarkets/index.htm?hpt=hp_13. (accessed 31 January 2012).

CNN Money (2012b), 'Greece's Fate Uncertain as Hard Deadline Looms'. 7 March. Available at http://money.cnn.com/2012/03/07/markets/greece_debt_crisis/index.htm?hpt=hp_bn1 (accessed 7 March 2012).

CNN Money (2012c), 'Greece's Debt Swap Down to the Wire'. 8 March 2012. Available at http://money.cnn.com/2012/03/08/markets/greece-debt-creditors/indes.htm?hpt=hp_t1 (accessed 8 March 2012).

D'Emilio, F. (2012), 'Italy's Prime Minister Says Rest of Europe Needs to Step it Up in Debt Crisis'. *The Globe and Mail*. 7 January 2012. Available at http://twittweb.com/italy+s+prime+minister+-15443494 (accessed 7 January 2012).

Economist (2012a), 'There Are All Too Many Alternatives'. 12–18 May 2012, 27–8.

Economist (2012b), 'An Ever-deeper Democratic Deficit'. 26 May 2012, 23.

Economist (2012c), 'Europe's Choice: The Future of the European Union'. 26 May 2012, 12.

Economist (2012d), 'The Cutting Up Rough: The Costs of a Greek Exit'. 26 May 2012, 26.

Ellison, D.L. (2006), 'Divide and Conquer: The European Union's Enlargement's Successful Conclusion'. *International Studies Review* 8(1) (March), 150–65.

Emmott, R. (2012a), 'Euro Zone Jobless Rate Hits Highest Level since Birth of Euro'. *The Globe and Mail.* 31 January. Available at http://www.reuters.com/article/2012/01/31/us-eurozone-unemployment-idUSTRE80U0K920120131 (accessed 31 January 2012).

Emmott, R. (2012b), 'Eurozone Retail Sales, Sentiment Point to Mild Recession'. *The Globe and Mail.* 6 January. Available at http://www.reuters.com/article/2012/01/06/eurozone-economy-idUSL6E8C60YD20120106 (accessed 21 January 2012).

Emmott R. and D. Flynn (2012), 'North and South Split as Eurozone Economy Shrinks'. *The Globe and Mail.* 15 February. Available at http://www.theglobeandmail.com/report-on-business/international-business/north-and-south-split-as-euro-zone-economy-shrinks/article4171645/ (accessed 16 February 2012).

Evans-Pritchard, A. (2011), 'German Push for Greek Default Risks EMU-wide "Snowball"'. *The Telegraph.* 10 October. Available at http://www.telegraph.co.uk/finance/financial/crisis/8819195/German-push-for-Greek-defa (accessed 20 January 2012).

Faiola, A. and H. Schneider (2012), 'Greek Election Offers No Relief: Vote Doesn't Calm Fears on Europe: G20 Leaders Press for Bolder Action on Euro'. *The Washington Post.* 19 June, A1.

Fernandes, S. and E. Rubio (2012), 'Competition, Cooperation, Solidarity: Solidarity within the Eurozone: How Much, What For, How Long?' *Notre Europe.* Policy paper #51.

Fidler, S. (2012), 'Euro Crisis Needs Mix of Solutions'. *Wall Street Journal.* 26–7 May, A9.

Financial Times (2012), 'Greece Gains Some Breathing Space'. 19 June 2012: 10 Editorial.

Forelle, C. and S. Schaefer Muñoz. (2012), 'Spain Back in Cross Hairs: Greek Election Results Fade Quickly as Madrid's Borrowing Costs Set Record'. *The Wall Street Journal.* 19 June, 1.

Gerodimos, R. (2012), 'Opinion: Extreme Measures Breeds Extreme Politics'. *CNN.* 13 February. Available at http://edition.cnn.com/2012/02/13/opinion/greece-politics-opinion/index.html?hpt=hp_c1 (accessed 13 February 2012).

Globe and Mail (2012a), 'Fitch Sees 1-2 Notch Downgrade for Some Euro States'. 19 January 2012. Available at http://www.theglobeandmail.com/report-on-business/international-business/fitch-sees-1-2-notch-downgrade-for-some-euro-states/article4197494/ (accessed 21 January 2012).

Globe and Mail (2012b), 'EU, ECB Working on Greece Exit Contingency'.
    18 May 2012. Available at http://www.theglobeandmail.com/report-on-business/
    international/international-news/eu-ecb-working (accessed 18 May 2012).
Granitsas, A., Paris, C. and M. Stevis (2012), 'Three Greek Parties Form Coalition'.
    The Wall Street Journal. 21 June, A9.
Granitsas, A. and L. Stevens (2012), 'Tourists also Tell Greece No:
    No Escape: Drop in Summer Bookings is Last Thing its Ailing Economy
    Needs'. *The Wall Street Journal*. 26–7 May, A9.
Guardian, The (2010), 'Credit Ratings: How Fitch, Moody's and S/P Rate Each
    Country'. Datablog. *The Guardian*. Available at http://www.guardian.co.uk/
    news/datablog/2010/apr/30/credit-ratings-country-fitch-moodys-standard
    (accessed 20 January 2012).
Haas, E.B. (1958), *Uniting of Europe: Political, Economic, and Social Forces,
    1950–1958*. Stanford, CA: Stanford University Press.
Haas, E.B. (1975), *The Obsolescence of Regional Integration Theory*. Berkeley,
    CA: University of California Press.
Hilsenrath, J. and J. Mitchell (2012), 'New Signs of Global Slowdowns: Weak
    Reports in US, Europe and China Suggest Economies are Slipping in Sync'.
    Wall Street Journal, 25 May, 1.
Hoffman, S. (1966), 'Obstinate or Obsolete? The Fate of the Nation State'.
    Daedalus 95, 862–915.
Hope, K. (2012), 'Samaras Scrambles to Agree Coalition Pact'. *Financial Times*,
    19 June, 2.
Hope, K. and P. Spiegel (2012), 'Greek Rhetoric Turns into Battle of Wills'. *CNN*.
    16 February. Available at http://www.cnn.com/2012/02/16/business/greek-
    debt-crisis-battle-wills/index.html (accessed 16 February 2012).
Howden, D. (2011), 'Europe's Unemployment Crisis: Some Hidden Relief', in D.
    Howden (ed.), *Institutions in Crisis: European Perspectives on the Recession*,
    ch. 4. Northampton, MA: Edward Elgar.
Inman, P. and H. Smith (2011), 'Banks Must Take Bigger Losses on Greek Loans,
    Says German Finance Minister'. *The Guardian*. 16 October. Available at http://
    www.guardian.co.uk/business/2011/oct/16/banks-bigger-losses-loans-greece
    (accessed 20 January 2012).
International Monetary Fund (2010), 'Greece Program: IMF Appraises €30 bln.
    Loan for Greece on Fast Track'. *IMF Survey Magazine: In the News*. 9 May.
    Available at http://www.imf.org/external/pubs/ft/survey/so/2010/new050910a.
    htm (accessed 20 January 2012).
Isidore, C. (2012), 'Eurozone Unemployment Hits Record 10.9%'. *CNN Money*.
    2 May. Available at http://money.cnn.com/2012/05/02/news/economy/europe-
    unemployment/?hpt-hp_t3 (accessed 2 May 2012).
Jenkins, P., Oakley, D. and R. Atkins. (2012), 'Banks Set to Double Crisis Loans
    from ECB'. *Financial Times*. 30 January. Available at http://www.ft.com/intl/
    cms/s/0/09ab9542-4b6d-11e1-b980-00144feabdc0.html#axzz2HyPLNJur
    (accessed 31 January 2012).

Jing, F. and W. Tian (2012), 'China "Should Prepare" a Euro Exit'. *China Daily*. 25–7 May: 13, 15.

Jones, B. (2012), 'Why Does the Euro Mean So Much to Germany'. *CNN*. 13 January, Available at http://edition.cnn.com/2011/12/09/world/europe/germany-euro-importance/indexc.html (accessed 30 January 2012).

Jones, M. (2012), 'ECB Must Do More to Prevent "Cataclysmic" Euro Collapse: Fitch'. *The Globe and Mail*. 11 January 2012. Available at http://www.theglobeandmail.com/report-on-business/international-business/ecb-must-do-more-to-prevent-cataclysmic-euro-collapse-fitch/article1358000/ (accessed 21 January 2012).

Kopstein, J. and D. Reilly. (2006), 'As Europe Gets Larger, Will it Disappear?' *International Studies Review* 8(1), 140–49.

Krielinger, V. (2012), 'The Making of a New Treaty: Six Rounds of Political Bargaining'. *Notre Europe*, Policy Brief # 32. February.

Lapavitsas, C. (2012), 'Why it is in Greece's Best Interest to Leave the Euro'. *Financial Times*. 24 May, 11.

Lister, T. (2012), 'Greece: Why Not Let It Sink'. *CNN*. 10 May. Available at http://edition.cnn.com/2012/05/10/world/europe/greece-why-care/index.html?hpt=hp_cl (accessed 10 May 2012).

Lorca-Susino, M. (2010), *The Euro in the 21st Century: Economic Crisis and Financial Uproar*. Farnham, Surrey, UK: Ashgate.

Ludlow, P. (2012), *The European Council of 8/9 December 2011*. 12 January.

Lynn, M. (2011), *Bust: Greece, the Euro, and the Sovereign Debt Crisis*. Hoboken, NJ: John Wiley & Sons.

McLean, C. (2012), 'For Many Germans, the Euro Crisis Remains a Non-event'. *The Globe and Mail*. 29 January. Available at http://www.theglobeandmail.com/report-on-business/for-many-germans-the-euro-crisis-remains-a-non-event/article542655/ (accessed 31 January 2012).

Milner, B. (2012), 'Greece's Membership in Euro Zone at Risk Again'. *The Globe and Mail*. 8 May. Available at http://www.theglobeandmail.com/report-on-business/international-news/european/greece (accessed 9 May 2012).

Milner, B. and B. McKenna (2012), 'France and Greece Spur New Era of Uncertainty'. *The Globe and Mail*. 7 May. Available at http://www.theglobeandmail.com/report-on-business/economy/economy-lab/france-and-greece-spur-new-era-of-uncertainty/article4105327/ (accessed 9 May 2012).

Moffet, S. and M. Peacock (2012), 'Europe Thinks the Unthinkable on Greece'. *The Globe and Mail*. 18 May. Available at http://m.theglobeandmail.com/report-on-business/international-business/europe-thinks-the-unthinkable-on-greece/article4186851/?service=mobile (accessed 18 May 2012).

Moravcsik, A. (1991), 'Negotiating the Single European Act: National Interests and Conventional Statecraft in the European Community'. *International Organization* 45(1) (Winter), 19–56.

Mortensen, A., Chance, M. and E. Labropoulou (2012a), 'Radical Greek Leftist Gives Up Effort to Form Government'. *CNN News*. 10 May. Available at http://edition.cnn.com/2012/05/10/world/europe/greece-politics/index.html?hpt=hp_t3 (accessed 10 May 2012).

Mortensen, A., Chance, M. and E. Labropoulou (2012b), 'Greek Socialist Leader Gets Chance to Form Government'. *CNN News*. 11 May. Available at http://edition.cnn.com/2012/05/10/world/europe/greece-politics/index.html?hpt=hp_t2 (accessed 11 May 2012).

Neild, B. and I. Chapple (2012), 'Q & A: Will New Seal Solve Europe's Problems?' *CNN*, 29 February. Available at http://edition.cnn.com/2011/12/09/business/euro-deal-qanda/index.html?hpt=hp_cl (accessed 29 February 2012).

Nye, J.S. (1971), 'Comparing Common Markets: A Revised Neofunctionalist Model', in Leon N. Lindberg and Stuart A. Scheingold (eds), *Regional Integration: Theory and Research*. Cambridge, MA: Harvard University Press.

Oakley, D. and A. Ross (2012), 'Big European Funds Dump Euro Assets amid Greece Exit Fears'. *Financial Times*. 25 May, 1.

Papadimas, L. and J. Strupczewski (2012). 'Greece, EU, "Almost There" on Bailout'. *The Globe and Mail*, 17 February. Available at http://m.theglobeandmail.com/report-on-business/international-business/greece-eu-almost-there-on-bailout/article547107/?service=mobile (accessed 17 February 2012).

Paphitis, N. (2012), 'Greece Downgraded Deeper into Junk Status'. *The Globe and Mail*. 22 February.

Paphitis, N. and G. Steinhauser (2012), 'Greek Deal Doesn't Meet Bailout Terms: Germany'. *The Globe and Mail*. 9 February. Available at http://www.cbc.ca/news/world/story/2012/02/09/greece-debt-talks.html (accessed 10 February 2012).

Paris, C., Stevis, M. and M. Walker (2012), 'Greek Clash with Germany on Bailout Looms'. *The Wall Street Journal*. 19 June, A7.

Popper, N. (2012), 'Investors in Search of Bigger Fix to Euro Crisis'. *The New York Times*, 18 June. Available at http://www.nytimes.com/2012/06/19/business/daily-stock-market-activity.html?pagewanted=all&_r=0 (accessed 20 August 2012).

Pylas, P. (2012), 'Unemployment Hits EU Record: Recession Continues to Spread Across Eurozone'. *News*. 3 May, 15.

Rachman, G. (2012), 'Greece has Won Europe a Respite—Now It Must Use It'. *Financial Times*. 19 June, 11.

Reguly, E. (2012a), 'Greek Leaders Clinch Deal on Reforms'. *The Globe and Mail*. 9 February 2012.

Reguly, E. (2012b), 'Athens Burns as Greek Austerity Bill Passes, Avoiding Default'. *The Globe and Mail*. 13 February. *Canadian Daily*. Available at http://www.theglobeandmail.com/news/world/athens-burns-as-greek-austerity-bill-passes (accessed 13 February 2012).

Reguly, E. (2012c), 'Pressure Mounts on Greece to Stick to the Austerity Plan'. *The Globe and Mail*. 9 May. Available at http://www.theglobeand mail.com/report-on-business/international-news/pressure-mounts (accessed 11 May 2012).

Rooney, B. (2012), 'Greece: One Step Forward, Two Steps Back'. *CNN Money*, 10 February. Available at http://money.cnn.com/2012/02/10/markets/greece/ index.htm?iid=EL (accessed 10 February 2012).

Rooney, B. and C. Isidore (2012), 'ECB Loans Cut €529.5 Billion to European Banks'. *CNN Money*. 29 February. Available at http://money.cnn. com/2012/02/29/markets/ecb_bank_loans/index.htm?hpt=hp_t3 (accessed 29 February 2012).

Ross, A., Wigglesworth, R., Daneshku, S. and P. Spiegel (2012), 'Euro Braced for Turmoil as Greece Fears Take their Toll'. *Financial Times*. 24 May, 1.

RT (2011), 'Italy, Spain on Bailout Precipice'. 3 August 2011. Available at http:// rt.com/news/eu-spain-italy-bailout (accessed 31 January 2012).

Rubin, J. (2012), 'Without Growth, There's Only One Ending to Euro Debt Crisis'. *The Globe and Mail*. 9 May. Available at http://www.theglobeandmail. com/report-on-business/commentary/jeff-rubins-smaller-wo (accessed 9 May 2012).

Simms, D. (2011), 'Europe's Debt Crisis: Scale of Greece Default Would be Unprecedented: Failure Would be Five Times Bigger than Argentina's'. *CBC News*. 29 September. Available at http://www.cbc.ca/news/business/ story/2011/09/28/f-greek-default-primer.html (accessed 20 January 2012).

Sivy, M. (2012), '4 Ways the Euro Could Fail'. *Time*. 2 May. Available at http:// business.time.com/2012/05/02/four-ways-the-euro-could-fail/?hpt-hp_t3 (accessed 2 May 2012).

Slater, S. and L. Laurent (2012), 'Europe's Banks Bleed from Greek Crisis'. *The Globe and Mail*. 23 February. Available at http://www.theglobeandmail.com/ report-on-business/europes-banks-bleed-from-greek-crisis/article548290/ (accessed 23 February 2012).

Spiegel, P. and K. Hope (2012), 'Greece Angrily Rejects German Plan for EU Budget Control'. *The Globe and Mail*. 30 January. Available at http://www. theglobeandmail.com/report-on-business/international-business/greece-angrily-rejects-german-plan-for-eu-budget-control/article542654/ (accessed 31 January 2012).

Steinhauser, G. and W. Horobin (2012), 'South Europe Challenge Germany's Revival Recipe'. *The Wall Street Journal*. 19 June, A8.

Szász, A. (1999), *The Road to European Monetary Union*. New York, NY: St. Martin's Press.

Telegraph (2011), 'Nicolas Sarkozy and Angela Merkel Set a Date to Save Europe'. *The Telegraph*. 9 October 2011. Available at http://www.telegraph. co.uk/finance/financialcrisis/8817053/Debt-crisis-Nicolas-Sarkozy-and-Angela-Merkel-set-a-date-to-save-Europe.html (accessed 20 January 2012).

Tymkiw C. and B. Rooney (2012), 'Greek Default is Essentially a Given: S&P'. *CNN Money*. 24 January 2012. Available at http://money.cnn.com/2012/01/24/ markets/greece_default_sandp/index.htm (accessed 29 January 2012).

Unmack, N. (2012), 'Italy and Spain on the Mend But Not Entirely Out of Danger'. *The Globe and Mail*. 1 March. Available at http://www.theglobeandmail. com/globe-investor/investment-ideas/breaking-views/italy-and-spain-on-the-mend-but-not-entirely-out-of-danger/article550272/ (accessed 2 March 2012).

USA Today (2012), 'Election Messages: Greece a Warm-up Act for Europe—and U.S.?' 19 June 2012, 6A.

Vaïsse, J. (2012), 'What Hollande's Victory Means for Europe's Economy'. *CNN*. 8 May. Available at http://edition.cnn.com/2012/05/07/opinion/vaisse-france-election/index.html?hp_bn1 (accessed 8 May 2012).

Varoufakis, Y. (2012), 'Why It's Too Late to Save Greece's Sovereignty'. *CNN*. 30 January, Available at http://articles.cnn.com/2012-01-30/opinion/opinion_ greece-germany-europe-varoufakis_1_greek-leaders-german-leaders-greece?_s=PM:OPINION (accessed 30 January 2012).

Véron, N. (2012), 'Euro Zone's Core Problem is a Bad Design'. *The Globe and Mail*. 10 February. Available at http://www.theglobeandmail.com/report-on-business/international-news/global-exchange/ (accessed 10 February 2012).

Wigglesworth, R., Giles, C. and K. Hope (2012), 'Eurozone's Greek Poll Honeymoon Short-lived'. *Financial Times*. 19 June, 1.

Wishart, I. (2011), 'Papandreou Calls New Greek Loans "Eurobonds"'. *European Voice*. 27 July. Available at http://www.europeanvoice.com/article/2011/july/ papandreou-calls-new-greek-loans-eurobonds-/71733.aspx (accessed 20 January 2012).

Zingales, L. (2012), 'The Greek Tragedy, Act II'. *Project Syndicate*. 19 March. Available at http://www.project-syndicate.org/commentary/the-greek-tragedy--act-ii (accessed 27 April 2012).

Chapter 9

Chronic Anxiety: Schengen and the Fear of Enlargement

Ruben Zaiotti

Introduction

Europe is currently in a state of turmoil. The financial crisis that has gripped the continent since 2008, and the political fallout it has provoked – most notably, the growing nervousness and inward looking attitudes of European citizens and policy-makers worried about their future – is threatening the very foundations of the European integration project and challenging the authority of the institution upholding this project, namely the European Union (EU). This is especially the case for the economic realm, as evidenced in the (not so veiled) threats by some EU member states to introduce protectionist policies in violation of Single Market principles. The gloomy political climate, however, has also affected other pillars of the European Union such as the Schengen border control regime, the institutional arrangement that has rendered possible the establishment of a free travel area across Europe. Although often hailed as a prime example of a success story of European integration, the regime is under pressure. In 2011, some EU members sparred among themselves and with the European Commission over the interpretation and application of its rules regarding the management of borders. The most serious incident pitted France against Italy over the treatment of a sudden surge in North African migrants crossing their common frontiers (see Carrera et al. 2011; Zaiotti 2011a).

Yet there are other outstanding issues affecting Europe's border control regime that may have even more serious and long term consequences for the European integration project. These matters have to do with Schengen's ongoing process of enlargement. Started as an intergovernmental arrangement among five European countries (Germany, France, the Netherlands, Belgium and Luxembourg), the regime has steadily expanded its membership and currently includes most EU countries and some non-EU members (Norway, Iceland, Switzerland, and Lichtenstein). Certain EU countries have explicitly chosen not to be part of the regime (e.g. United Kingdom, Ireland); others wish to be included, but need to meet a series of conditions (partly technical and partly political) before they can become full members. The latest group of countries undergoing this 'test' are Romania and Bulgaria. The context in which this process is taking place is a general *enlargement fatigue* that has spread across the continent in recent years (Szoulucha 2010).

There is a widespread sense that the Union should focus on deepening its achievements rather than widening further and becoming an unwieldy and ineffective entity. Since Romania and Bulgaria became EU members in 2004, their application to join the Schengen area should have been less politically charged than the issue of the Union's enlargement. Yet their accession to the European Union has turned out to be controversial and has raised concerns among current members that echo those directed against countries that are, or may become in the medium to long term, EU membership candidates (for example, Western Balkans countries such as Bosnia-Herzegovina, Macedonia and Kosovo). The Council of the European Union, the institution which has the final say in who is allowed into the club, has formally endorsed Romania and Bulgaria's candidatures but it has refrained from providing a precise date for their entry (the decision is still pending at the time of writing), despite the applicants having received the green light from the Schengen Evaluation Working Group, the group within the Council of the Europe Union in charge of assessing candidate countries' progress towards meeting the technical prerequisites for membership (i.e. adoption of Schengen *acquis*, upgrading of border controls, etc.). The main bone of contention is the mistrust of some member states (the most vocal being the Netherlands) of the candidates' capacity to uphold Schengen's standards. Particularly problematic in their eyes is the persistently high levels of corruption and the widespread presence of organized crime in these countries, phenomena which are believed to affect their capacity to effectively manage what would become *Europe's de facto* borders. The degree to which these countries have made actual progress towards overcoming these problems is a matter of debate. Both sceptics and optimists can in fact point to evidence to support their claims. Be it as it may, Romania and Bulgaria's actual or perceived shortcomings regarding border control, coupled with a growing anti-European and anti-freedom-of-movement sentiment in some Schengen member countries, have created an explosive mix that has rendered the current stalemate arguably almost inevitable.

The convergence of 'external' and 'internal' factors (respectively, the two candidate countries' reputation and Schengen members' domestic politics) is a plausible explanation for the current tensions in the Schengen regime which is shared by most commentators and policy-makers. However, the bleak conclusions that that are typically inferred from this account, namely that the regime is entering into an inward looking phase of retrenchment, with limited prospects for future enlargements, are premature. The current dispute over the accession of Romania and Bulgaria, while certainly troublesome, is not unique in the history of the Schengen regime. On the contrary, this incident can be considered the latest symptomatic example of an enduring – and so far unresolved – tension within the regime between an in-built propensity to constantly expand in order to maintain the myth of Schengen as the success story of European integration, and the fear of losing this very status because of overstretching, and, more generally, because of the fear of the unknown that the admission of new and untested members entails. This inherent tension is expressed in what I term *enlargement anxiety*.

As a psychological condition, anxiety is the result of high levels of uncertainty and over commitment that individuals might face in their everyday life.[1] Resentment often takes the form of overly critical language – including insults – and the bullying of a scapegoat. From a psychological perspective, the function of resentment is to temporarily release, in relatively controlled manner, all or part of the tension distressing an individual. Resentment in this context is in fact temporary, and does not lead the outright rejection of the object towards which it is directed. Seen in this light, the Romanian and Bulgarian situation is not only a rite of passage, in which the two candidates are enduring series of humiliating challenges in order to become a 'proper' member of the club, but it is also a cathartic process in which current Schengen members, by vocally expressing their misgivings about the candidates – yet not rejecting them outright – assuage their fears and are persuaded to accept the club's latest round of expansion.

To explore this line of argument and illustrate the recurrent nature of the present predicament involving Romania and Bulgaria, this chapter reconstructs the evolution of two of the most contentious Schengen accession negotiations, the debates involving Italy and Denmark in the 1990s, highlighting how their content, dynamics and key protagonists bear striking similarities to recent events. This reconstruction will show how, from an institutional perspective, previous expressions of enlargement anxiety represent cyclical adjustment mechanisms that have helped the regime to withstand new challenges and to consolidate its presence in Europe. As has been the case in the past, the Schengen regime, despite its current predicament, is thus likely to maintain a pragmatic and generally open policy towards countries that wish to join.

This chapter is organized as follows. The first section elaborates on the formal aspects surrounding the issue of enlargement in the Schengen regime and considers some of the technical and political problems that have been raised in the past. The second and third sections examine two historical cases of Schengen enlargement anxiety, Italy and the Scandinavian countries, respectively, detailing how this pathological condition emerged and was addressed. The concluding section examines the parallels between the regime's past and present bouts of enlargement anxiety and explores their implications for the future of Europe's border control regime.

Widening Schengen: Institutional Issues

In the early phases of the Schengen regime's history, its founding members focused mainly on establishing the legal and political foundations of the creation of a border-free Europe. It was deemed essential that a small, compact group of countries should be involved at this early stage. Once the Schengen

---

1   On 'anxiety' and the cognate concept of 'distress' as psycho-social conditions, see Thoits (1983) and Mirowsky et al. (1989).

Implementation Convention (SIC), the document outlining the practical steps that members had to take in order to render the regime operational, was agreed upon in 1990, however, the existing members felt that the initiative, in order to be fully successful, had to involve other European partners. The expansion of the regime would prove that Schengen was indeed a European project, and the precursor to the Europe of the future. The enlargement option was explicitly foreseen in the Implementation Convention. Article 140 states that all member states of the European Union (then the 'European Community') can become part of the agreement. The prerequisite to joining is that aspiring members have to accept the *acquis* as it stands at the moment of accession. Formal inclusion in the regime takes place when the Schengen Conventions enter into force in the candidate country (generally after the Conventions are ratified domestically), and all the existing members ratify a protocol of adhesion.[2] The entry into force of the Conventions does not mean that the regime can be immediately applied in the new country. Its full implementation requires a decision by existing members, which is based on both a technical and political assessment of the candidate country's fitness to be a full Schengen member.[3] There are therefore two phases in the Schengen enlargement process. The first encompasses the negotiations leading to a country's (or group of countries') formal adhesion to the regime. The second involves a debate between existing members and the candidate country over the practical implementation of the regime. These rules and procedures regarding the accession of new members were included in the Schengen *acquis* when it was incorporated in the EU institutional framework in the late 1990s and are still applied today to process new accession applications.

Formally, the negotiation process should be the same for all candidates. In practice, there have been substantial differences in the approach adopted depending on the country involved. Today, as in the past, these differences have tended to follow a North-South axis. On the one hand, this stems from the existence of different problems related to the movement of people that aspiring members have to face. Southern and Eastern European countries are more directly affected by external threats than Nordic countries, and they are believed to be less capable of mustering the technical and financial resources (and the political will) necessary to effectively control Schengen's external borders. Existing members have therefore been meticulous and particularly attentive when dealing with Southern and Eastern European countries. Nordic countries instead raised complex institutional issues. These issues, however, far from being purely formal, had important political implications, since they entailed a serious challenge to the European project's coherence. To further complicate things, these negotiations

---

2   Besides the 1990 Implementation Convention, the regime's other key legal document is the 1985 Schengen Convention.

3   In the regime's formative years, this decision was taken within the Schengen Central Committee. After the regime was incorporated in the EU in 1999, this responsibility was transferred to the EU's Justice and Home Affairs Council.

(both with Nordic and Southern countries) were influenced by existing relations between the candidate countries and individual Schengen members (and, as in the case of Nordic countries, between candidate countries themselves). As a result, the negotiations over the Schengen regime's expansion did not follow a linear path. These negotiations were mostly multi-bilateral (involving Schengen members and the individual candidate country), but they also involved bilateral and multilateral dynamics. Their timing also varied considerably. Some countries began contacting Schengen members early in the process, while others were drawn in much later. For some countries, negotiations were relatively quick, while for others they dragged on for years. The technical and political issues they raised were also different. In the next two sections I look at Italy and Denmark, two cases that I deem representative of the main controversies related to the enlargement of Schengen.

Southern Anxiety: Italy and Schengen[4]

The original group of Schengen members included countries that had the will and the capacity to carry out the task of dismantling borders across Europe. In the mid-1980s Italy lacked both, and this partly explains why it was not among the first participants of the initiative. At the same time, there was a widespread lack of confidence on the part of the five original members regarding the contribution that Rome could offer to the project (Hein 2000). This attitude also characterized the relationship with other Southern European countries. What distinguished the Italian case was that Italy, together with the then five Schengen members, was one of the founders of the European Community. Seen from Rome, not participating in a European project was considered politically embarrassing. The assumption was that Schengen was Europe, and as a self-proclaimed Europeanist country this was not acceptable (Fridegotto 1993: 17; Toffano 1989: 542). The same could be said, *mutatis mutandis*, for the existing members. For them, the inclusion of Italy into Schengen represented a legitimizing move and proof that their project was not only working by attracting new members, but that it was really a European enterprise.

It is in this context that in late 1985, soon after the first Schengen Convention was signed, that Italian officials from the Foreign Ministry contacted their French counterparts to inquire about the possibility of participating in the regime. The idea was that of a bilateral agreement (the content of which reflected that of the Schengen Conventions), whereby France would function as mandatory for all the other Schengen members (a possibility mentioned in Art. 28 of the 1985 Schengen Agreement). The dialogue was interrupted in January 1986 over problems with harmonizing visas. As is the case with the most recent crisis, the main bone of

---

4   The analysis in the present and the following section is based on Zaiotti 2011b: 100–109.

contention had to do with North Africa. Italy, in fact, wanted to maintain relations with countries in the area. However, France – together with Germany – wanted action taken immediately. The main fear was the potential mass illegal immigration that opening the borders with Italy would produce.

Discussions resumed the following year and on June 1987, Italy formally requested to be part of the agreement. The application for entry was accepted in principle, with certain conditions attached: the total acceptance of the *acquis*, and that the entry of Italy would not slow down the ongoing proceedings. Other requirements were informally demanded: the introduction of visas for Northern Africa states; the signing of an admission agreement with other members; and the denouncement of Italy's 'geographical reservation' for asylum claimants from Eastern Europe (Fridegotto 1993: 18). With the acceptance of these requests, Italy was included in Schengen as observer. As of September 1987, diplomats from the Italian Foreign Affairs Ministry as well as other national experts began to participate in various Schengen groups.

Negotiations, however, did not take off, and Italy's requests to create a working group to draft the accession agreement were not addressed. The official reason for the delay regarded a delicate phase of the negotiations between the existing members (who at the time were finalizing the SIC). It was made clear, however, that there were doubts about the Italian capacity (especially in terms of administrative structures) to join the Schengen system (Fridegotto 1993: 19). Despite the scepticism of the existing members, later that year the Italian embassy sent a letter (*note verbale*) to the Schengen ministers (28 November 1988) requesting to join Schengen. In the following meeting of 12 December 1988, the Comex took notice of the letter, demonstrating their satisfaction of the Italians' willingness to join, as an 'original founder of the Community', and put procedures in place so that negotiations could quickly lead to adhesion. Yet it asked each delegation to come up with a questionnaire about Italy's structures and practices regarding border control, in order to anticipate potential 'problems and/or difficulties' its entry might create.[5]

This request further delayed the beginning of negotiations. In May 1990 Italy gave some satisfactory technical responses to a memorandum issued by the Schengen group on issues of police and security, movement of persons, transport, customs and movement of goods. Moreover, the Italian Parliament had approved a new law on immigration (the 1990 Martelli Law), which included the deletion of the geographical reservation on asylum, and the introduction of visas for countries that were the primary sources of immigration to Europe. Official negotiations could therefore start (20 June 1990). Without further difficulties, Italy was able to the sign the accession agreement at the Comex meeting held in Paris on 27 November 1990. The French presidency, in welcoming Italy to Schengen, stressed the fact that this proved the role of Schengen as 'laboratory for the 12'.

---

5   'Conclusions of Ministers and Secretaries of State held in Brussels on December 12, 1988; Note verbale of the Belgian Presidency' (SCH/C (88)).

The Commission saw in it the proof of the role of the 'engine' of Schengen, and emphasized its function as 'precursor' to the objectives that the Community was trying to achieve.[6]

The signing of the Convention did not automatically mean the accession of Italy to the regime (which at that time had not yet entered into force). Italy had to apply the necessary preliminary measures outlined in the Convention. At its first constitutive meeting in October 1993, the Comex announced that the application of the Schengen Implementing Agreement had (once again) been postponed until 1 February 1993. Besides the issues of the control of external borders, the fight against drugs, and the setting up of the Schengen Information System, one of the reasons adduced was that Italy (together with Portugal) had not yet submitted its instruments of ratification. Some of the founding members also expressed (once again) doubts about the organizational and technical capability of Italy, Portugal and Greece to effectively implement the agreement's measures in the field of policing and external border control. The Executive Committee therefore agreed that these three countries were not going to implement the agreement on the same date as the other prospective members.[7]

These preoccupations were not new, and to a certain extent reflected the attitude of Schengen members towards Italy in other political domains. What is interesting in this context are the types of arguments that were formulated to support these criticisms. In the months that followed the application of the Schengen regime, for example, Germany became particularly vocal about the supposedly lax attitudes of the Italian authorities regarding border control. The then Interior Minister, Manfred Kanther, told the *Berliner Morgenpost* newspaper that Italy was letting hundreds of illegal immigrants into the EU from the former Yugoslavia, Albania and Turkey, who then showed up in Germany or France; he added, with words that are almost *verbatim* those used by his successor 20 years later: 'It is not right that on one side Schengen is made to function with great amounts of effort and money and on the other side streams of refugees are allowed into and through the country *against the spirit of Schengen*'.[8] Apart from the irony of the fact that Italy was not yet fully part of the Schengen regime, what the German Minister of Interior pointed to was the existence of a common understanding of what Schengen was all about, and according to those standards, Italy was breaching this 'spirit'.

It is in this 'spirit' that existing members pressured the new applicants, which at the time included Italy, Austria, Greece, Portugal and the Scandinavian countries. In the new rounds of negotiations that started in the second part of

---

6   SCH/M (90) PV 3.

7   'The long march towards the implementation of the Schengen agreement', FECL 21, December 1993/January 1994.

8   Quoted in *Statewatch* bulletin, 'Schengen: the first three months', May–June 1995, 5(3); emphasis added.

1996, however, technical issues were again raised.[9] The Italian delegation openly criticized the impression of political reservation that was given regarding the country's integration into Schengen. The Schengen presidency reiterated that, besides the worries related to the Schengen Information System, a series of questions were addressed to Italy, Greece and Austria in a questionnaire drafted by Germany and edited by France and Spain. This questionnaire aimed at better knowing and understanding the measures undertaken by these countries to prepare the application of the Convention (and thus similar to that adopted in Bonn on December 1994 for the other Schengen members). The Italian delegation agreed to comply with this request, but manifested its disapproval of the approach adopted.[10]

To ease the tension now manifested around the negotiating table, the Luxembourg presidency held a political discussion with Italy, Austria and Greece on 28 November 1996. There it announced that from a technical point of view it was not possible to apply the Convention in any of these countries before May 1997, but it suggested that the date for their inclusion in the Schengen Information System would be October 1997. In the following Comex meeting, the Italian, Greek and Portuguese delegations begrudgingly agreed to respond to the questionnaire (with the delay it would entail), wondering aloud about the rationale for the exercise.[11]

In the following months the issue of enlargement remained at the top of the Comex's agenda. The Report of the Frontier Commission – sent by Comex in February 1997 to evaluate the Italian frontiers – highlighted some problems at the Slovenian border; the Albanian crisis also raised concerns.[12] The ratification of adhesion agreements in some member states was also delayed. Despite these obstacles, following a positive report by the Portuguese Presidency on the state of the preparatory measures undertaken in Italy (and the other countries), the Comex meeting that took place in Lisbon on 24 June 1997 confirmed the date for the entry of Italy into Schengen (1 July 1997). The German delegation did not, however, approve the Presidency's assessment, and indicated the necessity of further improvement regarding the control of external borders. It also argued

---

9　In the meetings in the autumn of 1996, the Schengen presidency listed the necessary conditions for the application of the Convention to the applicants' countries. It mentioned data protection legislation, external border control having reached a required level, adaptation of airports, and the uploading of SIS.

10　GC SCH/C (96) PV 13–14 November 1996, Brussels.

11　IGC SCH/C (96) PV 15–18 December 1996.

12　In 1997, thousands of Albanian nationals were landing on the Italian coasts. At the height of the crisis (25 March 1997), Italian Interior Minister Giorgio Napolitano presented the government's counter-measure to his counterparts in the Mediterranean. Later in the year, Italy led a humanitarian operation ('Operation Alba') to stabilize the Balkan country (Perlmutter 1998). According to an Executive Decree, 16,000 Albanian refugees should have been returned before the end of August 1997, however, by mid-August only a third were back in Albania; the deadline was therefore moved to the end of November.

that, 'keeping in mind the Schengen spirit of solidarity', it was necessary to find a solution which avoided the creation of a Schengen external border between Italy and Austria.[13]

In order to overcome German doubts, a trilateral meeting between the German, Italian and Austrian heads of governments was held in Innsbruck (Austria) on 17 July. At this meeting, Italian and Austrian representatives provided the necessary political assurances that they would comply with Schengen standards, and committed themselves to improving their mutual co-operation on issues related to border control and police co-operation. As a result, the three delegations agreed that the entry into force of the Convention could take place on 26 October 1997 for Italy and 1 December of the same year for Austria, with the simultaneous abolition of controls in airports (land border control would instead be lifted on 1 July).[14]

In September, on the table of Schengen Executive Committee there were still the three draft decisions regarding the entry into force of the Convention in Italy, Austria, and Greece. The Dutch and German delegations argued that the abolition of controls at airports should occur gradually.[15] Practical measures at the borders, supported by a good dose of political pressure within the Schengen Executive Committee, persuaded the two sceptical delegations to drop their reservations. In early October, the Schengen ministers took notice of Italy's declaration specifying that all international airports would be completely functional by 26 October 1997. After a long discussion, they reached a consensus on the entry into force of the Convention for the candidate countries.[16] The Convention indeed entered into force in October 1997 (Greece had to wait until December). With the end of Italy's troubled trajectory into Europe's border control regime, the spell of enlargement anxiety that had gripped Schengen members in this period was (at least temporarily) overcome, paving the way for its further consolidation. (It was, in fact, during this period that Schengen was incorporated into the European Union institutional framework.)

Northern Anxiety: The Scandinavian Countries and Schengen

Despite the diffused Euro-skepticism characterizing Danish politics, there was broad domestic support for the Scandinavian country's entry into Schengen since the regime's very inception. Political calculations played an important part in shaping this attitude. By the early 1990s, all other continental European countries were

---

13   SCH/Com-ex (97) PV 2.

14   1998; SCH/C (97) PV 8 – 18 July 1997.

15   SCH/C (97) PV 9; 'Projets de décisions du Comité exécutif sur la mise en vigueur de la Convention de Schengen en Italie, en Grèce et en Autriche', (SCH/Com-ex (97) 27 rév. 2, 28 rév. 2 et 29 rév. 2.

16   SCH/Com-ex (97) PV 3.

either part of or had formally advanced a request to join Schengen. Copenhagen would have found itself isolated. From the existing members' perspective, the reasons to support the Danish candidature were eminently political. As was the case with Italy, this development would have reinforced the Schengen initiative and provided it with further legitimacy. Moreover, Denmark's powerful neighbour, Germany, was particularly vocal in calling for the Scandinavian country to join the regime.[17]

Overall, there was a general consensus regarding Denmark's entry into Schengen. The Danish case, however, raised complex institutional and political issues, stemming from the country's conflicting commitments with its Scandinavian neighbours (Sweden, Norway, Finland and Iceland). In the following paragraphs I examine how these questions were addressed and how, through the diplomatic practices that they spurred, the Schengen culture of border control was once again put to the test.

The idea of involving the Scandinavian countries in the common management of European borders came up not in the context of the Schengen regime, but within the European Community (EC) framework. In 1986 the European Council debated the possibility of an agreement between the Community and the Scandinavian countries on the abolition of controls at common borders. The Council referred to the 'ever closer union between the growing number of peoples in Europe' as justification for this move, while making it clear that it should not interfere with the process of easing border checks within the EC (Communication of the Secretariat General of the Council to COREPER, 8413/86).

In the months that followed, however, no concrete action was taken, and the issue remained dormant. As in the case of Italy, Schengen members became seriously interested in the expansion of the regime only after the final drafting of the SIC. The first contact between the Schengen Presidency and Denmark took place in the first part of 1991. The major issue on the table since these early stages was the compatibility of the Schengen regime with the Nordic Passport Union. This agreement, originally signed in 1957, included Denmark, Sweden, Norway, Finland and Iceland. Thanks to this agreement, since the 1960s Scandinavian countries' citizens had enjoyed free movement across their common frontiers. Joining Schengen would have meant the creation of new barriers between Denmark and the other Nordic countries; such outcome was therefore both legally and politically unacceptable for Copenhagen. To complicate matters further, unlike Denmark, none of the Scandinavian countries was then an EU member.

No major breakthrough occurred until 1993, when, unexpectedly, Denmark officially launched its candidature to Schengen.[18] The Schengen Executive

---

17   It should be noted that as early as June 1986, Denmark had signed an agreement with Germany on the easing of controls at their common frontier. However, the agreement's provisions were not implemented.

18   At the time of the first contacts in 1991, Denmark had a Conservative-led right-wing government. In January 1993 the government fell and was replaced by a Social

Committee responded positively. It drafted a questionnaire and adopted a calendar outlining the steps towards Copenhagen's successful entry into Schengen. The optimism was tamed by the worry about the compensatory measures and their compatibility with those of the other Nordic countries (Van der Rijt 1999: 30). Despite these concerns, in May 1994 Denmark requested observer status in Schengen. Meanwhile, an important development had occurred. Sweden and Finland had joined the EU, opening the door for their application as Schengen members.

It is in this context that the second stage of negotiations began. On 27 February 1995, the five Scandinavian countries' prime ministers met in Reykjavik as part of their regular multilateral meetings. The outcome was a declaration stating that the three EU members within this group would be willing to join Schengen on the condition that the free movement of people in the Nordic area was maintained. The problems rested with Norway and Iceland, who were not EU members. The first option at that time was the formal accession of the two countries to Schengen; however, this option was problematic because it was contrary to Article 140 of the Convention, which explicitly restricted admission to EU members (Van der Rijt 1997: 32). The alternative was the negotiation of a separate agreement. The Schengen Information System, however, posed serious questions regarding the access, integration and protection of data. Moreover, Norway and Iceland would have to harmonize their visa, asylum and border policies. The prime ministers eventually agreed on a compromise, whereby Norway and Iceland would remain formally outside the Schengen regime, but take charge of its external border controls.

Existing Schengen members' reaction to the proposal was mixed. In the official meetings that followed the declaration of the Scandinavian prime ministers, some delegations (the most vocal was the Italian) stressed the fact that the adhesion of Denmark was essentially a political issue, as a testing ground for the EU. Thanks to the Danish case (and the other Nordic countries), Schengen members could assess whether the objective of a 'Europe without frontiers' could be implemented within the framework of enlarged Schengen co-operation (CG 1995/00). The German position was even more radical, supporting the idea of extending Schengen even to non-EU countries (see the next section on Schengen's external relations). Others were more cautious. The Belgian delegation, for example, noted that the rapprochement with the Nordic Union, though politically important, should not have compromised the current Schengen *acquis* and its eventual incorporation in the EU. Moreover, accession '*à la carte*' would set a precedent for Switzerland

---

Democratic-led centrist government. The previous political reservations against joining Schengen, which until then had found some resonance also inside the Social Democratic Party, gradually disintegrated, leaving only the left and the extreme right in the opposition. Domestic politics thus played a role in defining the timing of the launch of Denmark's candidature, but not the decision *per se*. The Danish government had already demonstrated its interest in joining Schengen; the change of government simply speeded up the process.

and Eastern European countries. The European Commission was also wary. Its representative at the Schengen meeting stressed the importance of maintaining the article in its integrity, which therefore excluded the possibility of the inclusion of Norway and Iceland (CG 1995/00).

Without knowing whether the negotiations would be successful, Finland, then Sweden, nonetheless made a formal request for observer status in June 1995 (Van der Rijt 1999: 32). Their accession, however, was explicitly linked to a solution of the question of Norway and Iceland. The Belgian presidency made it known that the association of the two countries could not involve voting rights. The possibility of separating 'decisions shaping' and 'decision taking' powers was therefore put on the table: the Norwegian and Icelandic delegations could participate at all meetings and intervene at all levels, excluding when a vote is tabled, though they could express their opposition, a procedure that would lead to the denunciation of the accord (Van der Rijt 1999: 33).

At this stage of the negotiations an extensive exchange of information on existing legislation and policies took place. Those who held doubts were eventually convinced that no major obstacle existed for the candidate countries' accession to or participation in Schengen. As a Nordic Union official commented: 'In reality the Nordic countries have had Schengen co-operation for 40 years'.[19] In December 1995, after the Danish Government answered a comprehensive Schengen questionnaire on the country's immigration, police and border control policies to the satisfaction of the Schengen Group, the Comex granted Denmark and the other four countries observer status starting from May 1996.

Once existing Schengen members reached a political agreement on this issue, the necessary legal instruments (accession agreements for Sweden, Finland and Denmark; and co-operation agreement with Norway and Iceland) were drafted. The first meeting of Group Central with Northern countries took place in the following May (GC SCH/C (96) PV 5–7 May). On 19 December 1996 the Danish Government signed the Schengen Implementing Convention. On the same day, the other Scandinavian countries joined the regime. Without much controversy, the national parliaments supported their governments' decision and swiftly ratified the agreements. The anxiety that the possibility of extending the regime beyond the European Union had increased but also quickly dissipated. Indeed, the Nordic countries' entry into Schengen was a major success. The inclusion of non-EU members in the regime also further reinforced one of the regime's defining features, namely its commitment to pragmatism and flexibility.

---

19   *Statewatch* bulletin, May–June 1995, 5(3).

Conclusion: Living with Enlargement Anxiety

The quest to expand its geographical scope has been an integral feature of Europe's border control regime since its very beginnings in the mid-1980s. The various rounds of accession that have taken place since then, however, have not been smooth and straightforward. A combination of technical challenges and domestic political concerns has rendered these processes particularly controversial and has tainted relations between existing members and candidate countries. In this chapter I have argued that these problems are evidence of a deep seated anxiety that routinely hits Schengen members in the phase leading up to a new accession, and that this condition is the result a persistent tension within the Schengen regime between its expansionary tendencies and the uncertainty that a change in the status quo inevitably creates. Romania and Bulgaria's bids to join the regime seemed to have rekindled this tension, and that can explain the nervous reaction they have provoked among existing Schengen members.

What does this prognosis tell us about the future of Europe's border control regime? Previous manifestations of enlargement anxiety, as illustrated by the Italian and Scandinavian cases, suggests that Schengen, despite the misgivings and the delaying tactics of some of its members, is likely to maintain a pragmatic and generally open policy towards new candidates. Romania and Bulgaria, and other countries that wish to be part of the regime in the future, should nonetheless keep in mind that in previous accessions a degree of resentment against new members has lingered even after their official entry into the regime. The Italian case is once again exemplary in this regard. Since it became a member in 1997, Rome has continued to be considered Europe's soft underbelly when it comes to immigration and border control matters. Recently, this simmering mistrust has resurfaced in the spat with France mentioned earlier in the chapter. As was the case during the accession period, Italy has been the object of special scrutiny by existing members and criticized for its laxity in regard to border control. At the same time, the Italian government has repeatedly lamented the political nature of the criticism levelled against its actions and the lack of solidarity from its European partners. The bone of contention in the latest crisis was the decision by the Italian authorities to grant temporary travel permits to North African migrants fleeing the turmoil caused by the popular upraises that were taking place on the other side of the Mediterranean in early months of 2011 (Zaiotti 2011a). Due to the fear that these migrants would move *en masse* to France to join the former colonial power's well established North African community, the French government was the most vocal in criticizing the Italian decision. France promised to honour the temporary visas that Italy granted the migrants, but said it would turn away at its borders those who could not support themselves financially. The threat became a reality when, on 17 April the French government ordered the temporary closure of the Ventimiglia frontier with Italy. After numerous meetings and discussions, the two sides were eventually persuaded to tone down their animosity and to find a compromise on the issue of how to handle exceptional circumstances affecting the

Union and the EU member states' borders. By reiterating their commitment to the regime and taking practical steps to render it more viable, they also fixed (at least temporarily) some of the cracks that their dispute had created in the Schengen's edifice.

The lesson for Bulgaria and Romania from this event is that even if they achieve the ultimate prize, that of membership, their tribulations may not be over. The mutual resentment and mistrust accumulated during the accession negotiations is likely to linger for time to come. It might not reach the same feverish levels that characterized the pre-accession period, yet it will not completely disappear, potentially flaring up in the case of major crises affecting the new members' external borders, which, by virtue of their participation in the regime, are also *de facto* Europe's external borders. An 'Italian scenario', with rising tensions and reciprocal accusations between existing members, may therefore become a reality for Romania and Bulgaria as well. The impact of this enduring anxiety on the regime and its future expansion does not have to be so deleterious, however, especially in the long run. After all, in previous circumstances, the threat of a possible dilution, or even the demise of Schengen as a result of the entry of unworthy members did not materialize. Indeed, the regime not only managed to withstand new members, but also its 'spirit' came out reinvigorated. (In the aftermath of the Italian and Scandinavian accessions, for instance, the Schengen *acquis* was successfully incorporated into the European Union, becoming one of the key pillars of EU institutional architecture.)

Schengen's road ahead is certainly challenging. The persisting political and economic crisis affecting the European Union and its member states may have serious repercussions on the resolve of current members to further widen the regime. For Romania and Bulgaria, the silver lining in this predicament is that, when the issue of enlargement is raised again, the anxiety that periodically hits Schengen might be re-directed towards a new target, thus providing them brief respite in their new roles as full members of the club.

References

Carrera, S., Guild, E., Merlino, M. and J. Parkin (2011), 'A Race against Solidarity: The Schengen Regime and the Franco-Italian Affair'. *CEPS Working Paper*, April 2011.

Fridegotto, M. (1993), *L'Accordo di Schengen: Riflessi internazionali ed interni per l'Italia.* Milano: Franco Angeli.

Hein, C. (2000), 'Italy: Gateway to Europe, But Not the Gatekeeper?', in van Selm, J. (ed.), *Kosovo's Refugees in the European Union.* London: Pinter.

Mirowsky, J. and C.E. Ross (1989), *Social Causes of Psychological Distress.* New York: Aldine de Gruyter.

Perlmutter, T. (1998), 'The Politics of Proximity: The Italian Response to the Albanian Crisis', *International Migration Review* 32(1), 203–22.

Szolucha, A. (2010), 'The EU and "Enlargement Fatigue": Why Has the European Union Not Been Able to Counter "Enlargement Fatigue"?' *Journal of Contemporary European Research* 6(1), 1–16.

Thoits, P.A. (1983), 'Multiple Identities and Psychological Well-being'. *American Sociological Review* 49, 174–87.

Toffano, U. (1989), 'L'accordo di Schengen o l'Europa dei fatti', *Affari Esteri* 83, 541–54.

Van der Rijt, W. (1997), 'Schengen et les Pays Nordiques: Apercue de la Situation Actuelle', in Den Boer, M. (ed.), *Schengen: Judicial Cooperation and Policy Coordination*. Maastricht: European Institute of Public Administration.

Zaiotti, R. (2011a), 'The Beginning of the End? The Italo-French Row over Schengen and the Lessons of Past "Crises" for the Future of Border Free Europe', European Union Centre of Excellence (EUCE) Occasional Paper No. 12 (June 2011), Dalhousie University.

Zaiotti, R. (2011b), *Cultures of Border Control: Schengen and the Evolution of European Frontiers*. Chicago: University of Chicago Press.

Chapter 10

Crossroads of Integration?
The Future of Schengen in the
Wake of the Arab Spring

Kiran K. Phull and John B. Sutcliffe

Introduction

At a time of mounting concern over immigration and integration inside the European Union (EU), recent political issues surrounding new migration flows in various member states have compromised the stability of the EU border regime, raising questions about the future of Schengen and policies relating to the free movement of persons across the region's internal borders. In 2011, a series of repressive policy responses targeting incoming waves of migration highlighted the increased politicization of the EU immigration debate and revealed the difficulties that lie in the way of achieving a successful and comprehensive regional approach to integration.

No other event proved as critical in shaping EU immigration policy in 2011 as the crisis of Arab Spring migration by way of the so-called 'Franco-Italian Affair' (Carrera, Guild, Merlino and Parkin 2011). Beginning in late 2010 with Tunisia's 'Jasmine Revolution', popular uprisings and revolutions reverberating through the Arab world generated migration flows of tens of thousands in search of more stable destinations. The proximity of the Arab uprisings to Europe and the relatively low barriers to entry, directed much of this movement through the southern maritime EU border. While it was expected that the Arab uprisings would act as a push factor for immigration into Europe, the magnitude of this migratory movement and its implications for regional security were initially unclear.

Of particular interest to this analysis is the diplomatic row that emerged between France and Italy over the handling of North African migrants fleeing political unrest in Tunisia. In early 2011, thousands arriving in Italy via the island of Lampedusa were granted temporary visas by the Berlusconi administration, legally condoning their free movement across the Schengen zone. French concern over Italy's treatment of the issue resulted in the closure of the Franco-Italian border and a confrontation with the European Commission on the matters of restricting migration and the legality of reinstated border controls. At some level, it is understood that the Franco-Italian Affair degenerated into 'a "race to the bottom" on European principles of solidarity, loyal cooperation and fundamental rights' (Carrera, Guild, Merlino and Parkin 2011: 1). Between the two countries, the struggle over the power to define and govern emergency migration was justified in part by the rhetoric of fear: 'the emphasis was on the idea of an impending "humanitarian emergency," conjuring up the image of an "epochal" migratory influx about to unfold' (Campesi 2011: 5). In reality, the Arab Spring migration failed to reach the anticipated level of 'epochal exodus', yet still managed to impact EU immigration and border policies.

Other underlying factors are contributing to a general thickening of the EU's internal and external borders, for instance, the ongoing sovereign debt crisis that has threatened the very existence of the euro, sparking fears of a potential withdrawal from Greece; the growth in recent years of the European far-right and the contribution of various anti-immigration platforms to public and political debate; the role of Islam in shaping political agendas of EU member states; and the post-9/11 security climate marked by a heightened fear of terrorism. The intersection of these factors is evident in the recent reappearance of 'Euroscepticism' across the region (Harmsen and Spiering 2004; Sutcliffe 2010; Taggart and Szczerbiak 2008; Taylor 2008).

On one hand, then, it can be argued that the Arab Spring migration sparked the Franco-Italian Affair, which in turn represents a major EU crisis in this policy area (Back 2011; Carrera, Guild, Merlino and Parkin 2011). On the other hand, it may be wrong to overstate the significance of the Affair and in particular the extent to which it represents a break from the pattern evident in the development of EU policies relating to the treatment of asylum seekers and the free movement of this group within the EU. Taking the crisis of Arab Spring migration as a point of departure, this chapter examines the reintroduction of border controls in 2011 in light of the political and economic climate, arguing that the Affair is better seen as one more incident in the development of a policy sector that is frequently controversial as a result of its connection to state sovereignty and general popular unease about asylum seekers and third country nationals (TCNs). That said, it is also argued that the current economic climate, including generalized austerity measures and public perceptions linking immigrants, Islam, and more recent threats and cases of terrorism, have played a role in intensifying the situation beyond normal bounds, making issues in this policy sector potentially more politically destabilizing.

The Franco-Italian Crisis of Arab Spring Migration

Beginning in mid-December 2010, a sudden succession of political uprisings and revolutions spread through the Middle East and North African (MENA) region. The lasting impact of the so-called 'Arab Spring' on the political landscapes of these countries is yet to be seen, but as events unfolded early in 2011, certain external dimensions of the Arab Spring were immediately visible. Civilians fleeing conflict zones during the often violent process of political change instantly triggered high levels of human displacement. Of those who sought asylum in Europe, the majority arrived from Tunisia following the 'Jasmine Revolution' that saw the downfall of long-serving autocrat Zine el Abidine Ben Ali between mid-December 2010 and January 2011 (UNHCR 2011). The remaining numbers arrived mainly from Libya or from the Horn of Africa and sub-Saharan Africa via Libya.

Even prior to the arrival of migrants and asylum seekers, there were rumblings in the media and among European politicians of having to contend with an oncoming 'human tsunami' or 'biblical exodus' from the MENA region, especially into proximate receiving countries such as Italy and France (Traynor 2011). Predictions reached as high as 1.5 million flooding the Southern European region by the end of 2011 (Squires 2011). Fears over the sheer numbers of arrivals were compounded by the fact that these migratory flows were originating from predominately-Islamic nations, inciting tensions given the controversies associated with the position of the religion in Europe.

However, the mass exodus of refugees that was expected to take Europe by storm in 2011 was greatly underwhelming. Frontex, the EU agency tasked with the responsibility of managing and coordinating border security cooperation among member states, reported an influx of 20,000 irregular migrants into Europe in the first quarter of the year (Frontex 2011). In April 2011, the media reported figures in the range of 25,000 landed asylum-seekers and by the summer those numbers reached the 45,000 person mark, after which they began to plateau (Allen 2011; Fedyashin 2011; Kersten 2011). For a region comprising of some 400 million people and experiencing up to 2 million external border crossings per week, the Arab Spring migration rates seem comparatively inconsequential (Carrera, Guild, Merlino and Parkin 2011: 14).

Asylum-seekers attempting to enter the EU in early 2011 arrived mainly via the small island of Lampedusa, Italy's southernmost point and a popular transiting hub connecting Europe with North Africa. In response to the arrivals, Italy declared a national 'state of emergency' while authorities issued temporary residence permits for humanitarian protection to undocumented immigrants arriving in the country prior to 5 April 2011 (Carrera, Guild, Merlino and Parkin 2011: 14). Migrants arriving after this date were to be returned to their countries of origin on a case-by-case basis, while those permitted to stay were granted an automatic right to move freely within the Schengen zone. In response, France challenged Italy's temporary protection procedures, warning that it would impose strict national border controls in order to mitigate a potentially destabilizing cross-border security threat (Campesi 2011: 15–16). As a result, the month of April saw the forced return of trains of Tunisian migrants back into Italy after being halted at the border town of Ventimiglia. New entrants were sent back by French authorities on the basis that they had the potential to cause civil disobedience and public disorder despite their legal documentation (Carrera, Guild, Merlino and Parkin 2011: 15). Following France's move, Belgium, Austria, Germany and Denmark announced similar measures, raising concerns of a mass violation of the Schengen rules prohibiting the reintroduction of border controls (Campesi 2011: 16). Reactions from these member states to the arrival of North African nationals were exclusionary and stood in stark contrast to the EU's declared support for democratic reform in the Arab world (Emerson 2011). In this regard, a selective reneging of the principle of free movement in the Schengen zone, specifically targeting Arab Spring arrivals in 2011, exposes a measure of hypocrisy and self-interest in the EU's immigration agenda.

The Freedom Movement of People in the European Union

Facilitating the free movement of people has always been of cardinal importance to European integration. Even prior to the first treaties that led to the creation of what is now the European Union, agreements like the Benelux Customs Union were designed to promote the free movement of citizens across the borders of signatory states (Groenendijk 2004; Judt 2005). It was, however, with the signature of the 1957 Treaty of Rome establishing the European Economic Community (EEC) that the creation of a common market allowing for the free movement of people across the national borders of the participating states took centre stage in European integration, in tandem with the free movement of goods, services and capital – collectively the 'four freedoms'. This did not mean, however, with the entry into force of the Treaty of Rome in January 1958, that border checks on people moving among the participating states disappeared. In fact, this was far from the case, and one feature of this especially broad policy sector is the extent to which it has developed over time, most notably with the negotiation of the Single European Act, the Schengen agreements, and subsequent treaties (particularly the Amsterdam and Lisbon Treaties).

Differentiation represents a second notable feature of the policy sector, whereby governments individually and collectively within the European Union have traditionally developed different policies for allowing or restricting the freedom of movement of different categories of people. It has always been the case, for instance, that distinct rules have applied to EU citizens with respect to transit across the internal borders of the EU, as opposed to asylum seekers and third country nationals, who have had very different experiences of crossing national borders within the EU (Baldoni 2003; Geddes 2008; Luedtke 2011).[1] Traditionally, too, EU citizens and TCNs with offers of employment or with in-demand employment skills have been treated differently from those seeking employment (Davidson 1993; Geddes 2005a).

---

1   This difference in treatment also extends to other areas. The 2003 directive on the rights of long-term residents places different requirements on TCNs as compared to citizens of EU states with respect to securing residence rights in a state of which they are not a citizen. Member states can, for instance, impose various 'integration' measures (see Lavenex 2006b; Geddes 2008: 163–4).

A second level of differentiation with respect to the movement of individuals across EU borders concerns the location of the borders in question. Different rules and conditions have applied to different borders through time. It has often been the case that the external borders marking the boundaries between EU members and non-members have been more strictly policed and monitored than have the borders between member states, with security from external threats often used to frame policies and actions at external borders (Freudenstein 2000; Neal 2009). Related to this, asylum policies have differed among EU member states and refugees and asylum seekers have not received uniform treatment regardless of where they have sought asylum within the European Union (Luedtke 2011; Geddes 2008; Monar 2001).

Differentiation based upon the border in question has been, and indeed remains, particularly evident as a result of the prevalence of 'variable geometry' within the European Union. When the Schengen Agreement was originally signed in 1985, not all member states agreed to participate in the initiative to remove internal border barriers. The United Kingdom and Irish governments secured the right to opt in to only those aspects of the developing proposals that they supported; this remains the case since the incorporation of the Schengen *acquis* within the European Union following the 1999 ratification of the Treaty of Amsterdam (Geddes 2005b). As a result, the borders between the UK, Ireland and other EU member states function differently from borders between the full participants in the Schengen *acquis*.

A third element of differentiation concerns the specific procedures used to make decisions affecting freedom of movement into and within the EU. These decision-making procedures, and thus the central actors, vary (and continue to vary) depending upon the precise issue area and the category of person moving within or into the European Union (Geddes 2008). They have also changed over time, with a number of policy areas beginning as intergovernmental agreements outside of the main EU framework and subsequently being incorporated into EU decision-making (Lavenex 2006a; Monar 2001). Furthermore, successive treaties have changed the scope and institutional arrangements of decision-making relating to freedom of movement of persons, first through the Maastricht Treaty's creation of the Justice and Home Affairs pillar and then through the 'communitarization' of this pillar's policies by the Treaties of Amsterdam and Lisbon (Geddes 2008; Lavenex 2006a, 2006b; Monar 2010, 2011).

The operation of borders within the European Union has always, therefore, been characterized by a level of complexity surrounding the questions of who is seeking to cross a border; where and when; the rules that are in place to regulate such crossings; the manner in which they are implemented or not; and who has authority over establishing and implementing these rules. This complexity stems in part from the variety of issues that are affected by the movement of persons across borders. The questions of who gains entrance into a state's territory, and how easily, impact upon policies relating to employment access, welfare benefits, education, healthcare, security, and national identity (Geddes 2005a, 2008; Joppke

2007). The interaction of these issues becomes clear when the Franco-Italian Affair is re-examined with reference to the rules relating freedom of movement of persons across internal EU borders and EU asylum policies.

The Schengen Agreements and Asylum Policies in the EU

The controversy surrounding the 2011 Franco-Italian Affair revolved around two central issues: Italian authorities' handling of the influx of asylum seekers from Tunisia – particularly the decision to grant temporary residence visas to those arriving prior to 5 April 2011 – and the French authorities' decision to reintroduce border checks at its border with Italy (Carrera, Guild, Merlino and Parkin 2011). Analysis of the affair therefore requires attention to the EU's policies relating to the freedom of movement principle and the process of granting asylum. This analysis, in particular, must also examine the terms of the Schengen agreements within the EU, to which both France and Italy are signatories.[2]

The original Schengen Agreement was signed in 1985 by the governments of France, West Germany, and the three Benelux states (Belgium, the Netherlands and Luxembourg), which had a pre-existing travel-free mandate in place (Groenendijk 2004; Schutte 1991). This agreement contained within it a commitment to examine the steps necessary in the fields of immigration, police cooperation, judicial cooperation and asylum, among others, to secure the eventual abolition of border controls among the participating states and move their functions to the external borders of the Schengen area. It did not, however, immediately establish the practical steps to achieve these objectives. These were gradually developed over an extended period of time, beginning with the Schengen Implementing Convention signed in June 1990 (Geddes 2008; Hailbronner and Thiery 1997), followed by a series of regulations and directives based on this agreement and negotiated over the subsequent years (Lavenex 2006a). Major revisions include the growth in the number of participants within the Schengen area – now numbering 26 participating states and four non-EU member states – and the adoption of the 2006 Schengen Borders Code (European Parliament and the Council of the European Union 2006).

The Schengen agreements began as a process of intergovernmental cooperation outside of the EU's institutional framework. Importantly, the commitments outlined in these agreements overlapped with key developments within the EU itself (Monar 2001). First, Schengen had a central relationship with the EU goal of creating an area without internal frontiers, as revised and restated in the Single European Act (Hailbronner and Thiery 1997; Swann 1992). Second, it overlapped with developing activities in the fields of immigration and asylum policies, as

---

2   France was one of the original signatories to the Schengen Agreement, while Italy made a formal application to join in 1987 but did not become a full member until 1997 (Zaiotti 2011).

well as policing and judicial cooperation, particularly within the Justice and Home Affairs pillar created by the Maastricht Treaty Geddes 2008; Monar 2001). The 1999 Amsterdam Treaty subsequently incorporated the Schengen agreements into the EU within its Area of Freedom, Security and Justice (AFSJ) and the revised third pillar of the European Union (police and judicial cooperation in criminal matters) (Lavenex 2010). The 2009 entry into force of the Lisbon Treaty altered the policy landscape once again by abolishing the pillar structure first established by the Maastricht Treaty and moving police and judicial cooperation in criminal matters into the Treaty on the Functioning of the European Union. This particular decision removed the earlier restrictions on the role played by the European Parliament and the European Court of Justice in these areas (Monar 2010).

The complexity of the situation persists, in large part because not all EU member states are party to the Schengen agreements – some, like the United Kingdom and Ireland, because they have opted out, and others (Bulgaria and Romania) because their acceptance has yet to be ratified by the participating states. Thus, the situation in 'Schengenland' remains different from that of the European Union.

At the heart of the original Schengen Agreement and its subsequent implementation is the commitment to the removal of barriers to the free of movement of persons across the internal borders of the participating states, 'irrespective of their nationality' (Article 20, Schengen Borders Code; European Parliament and the Council of the European Union 2006). The Schengen agreements are therefore built upon the principle that there should be no distinction between EU nationals and third country nationals who have the legal right to enter a member state when it comes to crossing internal borders, and though spot checks are permissible, neither category of entrants should be subjected to systematic border controls at internal borders.

In order to achieve this goal, the Schengen agreements emphasize the importance of maintaining strong external borders and procedures, ensuring that only those legally permitted can cross. Several elements are of note here. First, the Schengen agreements place limits on who can enter 'Schengenland' while the Schengen Borders Code states that 'third-country nationals shall be subject to thorough checks' at external borders (Article 7.3 Schengen Borders Code; European Parliament and the Council of the European Union 2006). It has always been the case that third country nationals must secure a valid visa to enter a Schengen state, and that participating states have been at liberty to attach different conditions to these visas, such as proof of sufficient financial means (*Economist* 2011a; *Economist* 2011b; Article 7.3 Schengen Borders Code; European Parliament and the Council of the European Union 2006; Schutte 1991: 553). Second, the Schengen agreements led to the creation of the Schengen Information System (SIS) in order that participating states keep a database of individuals who should be prevented from entering an external border. Third, the Schengen agreements emphasized the importance of developing a common approach to the treatment of asylum seekers – a commitment that became central to the EU's Area of Freedom, Security and Justice Monar 2001; Geddes 2008).[3] Of key importance here is the 2003 Dublin II regulation that further developed the principle that the responsibility of handling an asylum request belongs to the country that is a refugee's first port of entry (Geddes 2008; Monar 2011). It is also emphasized that states should demonstrate solidarity in dealing with flows of people into the Schengen area, a notion that has not always been observed (Carrera, Guild, Merlino and Parkin 2011).

Finally, the Schengen agreements allow for the temporary reintroduction of internal border controls in the face of exceptional circumstances relating to serious threats 'to public policy or national security' (Article 23, Schengen Borders Code). The Schengen Borders Code lays out the procedures that national governments must follow in the event that they seek to reintroduce systematic border controls (European Parliament and the Council of the European Union 2006).[4] Each of these procedural mechanisms has been implemented to guide decision-making in the area of external migration, so as to avoid diplomatic failures between member states over the handling of new entrants, as evidenced in the Franco-Italian Affair. The French and Italian governments' treatment of the situation thus demonstrated a strong disregard for some of the guiding principles underlying these procedural elements in the Schengen agreements.

Schengen Compromised?

The Franco-Italian affair raises two key questions, namely the legality of the actions taken by the Italian and French governments and the long-term consequences of these actions for the Schengen *acquis*.

With respect to the first of these questions, there is little doubt that the actions taken by the governments concerned were highly contentious and stretched the limits of the terms of the Schengen *acquis*. Indeed the European Commission found that the Franco-Italian Affair revealed cracks in the Schengen system and violated 'the *spirit* of the Schengen agreements' (Campesi 2011: 16). The French government, in particular, acted contrary to the agreements reached in closing

---

3   The creation of a common asylum policy is central within the European Council's 1999 Tampere Programme, the 2004–2009 Hague Programme and the 2010–14 Stockholm Programme dealing with the Area of Freedom, Security and Justice. It has, however, yet to be achieved.

4   Article 2 of the 1990 Schengen Implementing Convention established the principle that a national government could reintroduce internal border checks for limited periods on grounds of public policy or national security. The Schengen Borders Code suggests that these should last no longer than 30 days, and also indicates the procedures to follow in the event that further 30-day periods are required (European Parliament and the Council of the European Union 2006; Groenendijk 2004).

its border with Italy, while the Italian government was accused of irresponsibly processing North African asylum seekers.

As Carrera, Guild, Merlino and Parkin identify, a participant government is entitled under the Schengen Borders Code to issue temporary residence permits to third country nationals and, when accompanied by a legitimate travel document or passport, these permits allow the TCNs to travel anywhere within the Schengen area (2011). Before there was any clear indication that migratory pressures from North Africa would overburden the Italian border management system, the Berlusconi administration declared a state of national emergency until 31 December 2011, granting immediate and temporary protection to all arrivals on humanitarian grounds under Article 20 of Italy's Consolidated Immigration Law (Campesi 2011; Nascimbene and Di Pascale 2011: 344). As Campesi notes, 'the Italian government wasted no time resorting to its extra-constitutional emergency powers in managing the Lampedusa crisis', the reasons for which were in reality more security-related than humanitarian, given Italy's efforts to crack down on irregular immigration of late (2011: 9).

Not until the permits were issued on 5 April 2011, when Italy signed an agreement with Tunisia granting temporary protection to all landed immigrants, was the legal status of migrants landing at Lampedusa clarified, with Italy opting for 'a clear humanitarian framing of the crisis' against the view of member states like France (Campesi 2011: 11). Italy's decision to stall on the matter of defining the legal status and treatment of migrants was in clear violation of the basic rights of those affected. At the same time, European partners and institutions, including the European Commission and the Office of the United Nations High Commissioner for Refugees (UNHCR), challenged the legality of Italy's decision to issue the documentation, intimating that Italy was exporting the situation to the European level with no clear indication of an impending humanitarian crisis (Campesi 2011). Ultimately, Italy's unilateral decisions raised the question of whether temporary protection and a humanitarian framing of the issue were compatible with the Schengen agreement. The situation was viewed as a violation of the 'Schengen spirit' and diverged from the guiding principles that seek to develop political solidarity amongst member states and a shared approach to migration management.

At the time of Italy's actions, French authorities announced that border security would be strictly enforced to keep out those arriving via Lampedusa. Under the terms of Article 21 of the Schengen Borders Code, a state may authorize the facilitation of spot checks at internal Schengen borders, however, these police checks may not be 'systematic' and have 'border control as an objective' or 'be considered equivalent to the exercise of border checks' (European Parliament and the Council of the European Union 2006: 11). In this case, the French authorities' actions at its border with Italy went beyond spot checks and took the form of systematic border controls targeted against Tunisians carrying temporary residence permits granted by the Italian government (Carrera, Guild, Merlino and Parkin 2011; Carrera 2012).

Similarly, the French government did not comply fully with the Schengen Borders Code with respect to the temporary reinstatement of internal border controls. Article 23(1) of the Schengen Borders Code states that the 'scope and duration of the temporary reintroduction of border control at internal borders shall not exceed what is strictly necessary to respond to the serious threat' (European Parliament and the Council of the European Union 2006: 12). The subsequent articles establish the procedures that a national government is expected to follow when reinstating controls – these include notifying the Commission, the other member states, and the European Parliament of the reasons for the reintroduction of border controls, as well as providing a report (Article 29) on the operation of the border controls and their effectiveness.

The French government did not act in accordance with these specified terms. First, as noted above, there is the singularly important and very real question of whether the volume of third country nationals seeking to secure entry in 2011 actually constituted a serious threat to public policy or internal security and called for the reinstatement of internal controls (Carrera, Guild, Merlino and Parkin 2011, 16). Second, even if it can be argued that the movement of TCNs in this instance constituted a serious threat, the French authorities did not follow the procedures by way of providing a report to the Commission, the European Parliament, or member states on the operation of the border controls and their effectiveness. The French government also explicitly stated that it did not recognize the Italian government's right, as the first port of entry, to issue the temporary residence permits (Carrera, Guild, Merlino and Parkin 2011).

Taken in isolation, the Franco-Italian Affair can be viewed as a major challenge to the terms of the Schengen *acquis* and its commitment to a border-free area. The extent of this challenge is more pronounced when it is examined in relation to decisions that were taken simultaneously in other states with respect to internal borders, and in relation to proposed changes to the Schengen *acquis*. In 2011, the Danish government announced the unilateral re-establishment of customs controls on internal borders in an effort to stave off an immigration 'emergency', and authorities took some initial steps in this direction. Though this bid to reinstate controls was terminated with the change in government to the center-left coalition of Helle Thorning-Schmidt in September 2011, the timing of the initial decision, backed by the traditionally Eurosceptic Danish People's Party, intensified the debate about a potential threat to the free movement of people within the EU (Hobbing 2011; Kirby and Petrou 2011). Adding to this, more recent efforts by the Dutch administration to increase surveillance at its German and Belgian borders to curb illegal immigration are currently underway (Carrera 2012).

At a bilateral reconciliation summit in Rome in April 2011, former leaders Sarkozy and Berlusconi agreed jointly to press for revision of the Schengen rules on the reintroduction of border controls (Back 2011; Ministry of Foreign Affairs Italy 2011). This was followed by the conclusions of the European Council summit in June 2011 calling for revisions to the Schengen Borders Code so as to allow more flexibility in responding to pressures at external borders (European Council 2011).

In September 2011, the European Commission brought forward two measures proposing reforms to the Schengen Borders Code (European Commission 2011a, 2011b; Pascouau 2012).

It is impossible to deny that the Franco-Italian Affair challenged certain principles of the Schengen *acquis* and holds the potential for a long-term impact on the border-free arrangement; however, one must be cautious about overstating the uniqueness of the 2011 Affair and its potential reach. While the idea of establishing an area allowing the free movement of people has always been central to the process of European integration, the removal of these border controls has been treated with some caution by the national governments because of the strong relationship between border control and state sovereignty. This is evident insofar as some national governments continue to refrain from participating in the Schengen agreements. Additionally, to the extent that national governments have been willing to negotiate the removal of internal borders, they have traditionally done so in intergovernmental contexts – that is, in decision-making settings where the governments themselves remain of central importance to policy making and have reserved for themselves the right to reverse course should they feel it appropriate, having limited the role played by supranational institutions such as the European Commission and the Court of Justice (Monar 2001). As noted above, the institutional context has not remained static (Geddes 2008; Monar 2010, 2011), yet national governments are still principal actors in this policy field. With this in mind, it is not altogether surprising that the French government should take it upon itself to close its border with Italy and demand reforms to the Schengen Borders Code to allow for more flexibility in reinstating controls.

The second reason for caution is that even as decisions have been taken to reduce or eliminate the presence of internal border controls, and even as the institutional context for policy making in this area has changed, national governments have retained for themselves the right to reinstate controls in certain circumstances (Groenendijk 2004). Moreover, as the Schengen *acquis* has developed and undergone revisions, governments have not hesitated to make use of this right.[5] It is by no means the case that the French government has acted alone in reinstating controls during the lifetime of the Schengen agreements. Indeed, Groenendijk (2004) identifies 33 occasions between 2000 and 2003 when national governments temporarily reintroduced border controls.[6] National governments also frequently

---

5   The French government announced in April 1996 that it would maintain border controls with Belgium and Luxembourg due to concerns about the flow of drugs from the Netherlands (Geddes 2008: 84–5; Groenendijk 2004; Monar 2001; Zaiotti 2011), and also reintroduced controls in March 1999 to bar the entry of Italians and Albanians seeking to participate in pro-migrant demonstrations in Paris (Carrera, Guild, Merlino and Parkin 2011).

6   As Groenendijk (2004) notes, the most frequent reasons for the reinstatement of internal border controls are to maintain security at political summits or large-scale sporting events.

fail to report on the reinstatement of controls and the effectiveness of these controls as demanded in Article 29 of the Schengen Borders Code, indicating that they are prepared to do so without consultation with other member states or the European Commission on the matter (see Groenendijk 2004: 163). The French government's actions in April 2011 are therefore not unusual in this regard.

A third reason to be cautious in interpreting the Franco-Italian Affair as a long-term threat to the Schengen *acquis* relates to the targeting of third country nationals. Without comment on the normative aspect of the French government's actions, the decision to prevent asylum-seekers with temporary permits from entering was not entirely unique (Geddes 2008: 138–9; Wolff 2008). Increasingly over the last two decades, EU states have demanded and reached agreements with non-EU states to secure their participation in efforts to prevent legal and illegal migration (Lavenex 2006a; Wolff 2008), including provisions for non-EU states to accept the return of failed asylum seekers and to participate in efforts to prevent potential migrants from departing for Europe (Boswell 2003; Geddes 2005b). These efforts have occurred jointly through the European Union and also in separate bilateral agreements. In 2004–5, Frontex was created with the specific goal of fostering cooperation and coordination of EU border management. Since it became operational, Frontex has facilitated several joint missions geared at securing the EU's external borders with a focus on the prevention of illegal migration (Lavenex 2010; Monar 2011, 2009). European governments have also independently taken action to limit immigration, as in 2004 and again in 2009, when the Italian government concluded agreements with the then-Libyan leader General Qaddafi to conduct naval patrols and establish reception centres in Libya to prevent would-be asylum seekers and other migrants from reaching Italy (see *Economist* 2009; Lavenex 2006a).

In sum, attempts to prevent third country nationals (or at least certain categories of TCNs) from entering EU territory are not new phenomena. Concerns over illegal migration often raise issues of national security (Geddes 2005b; Salter 2004), and in cases concerning both the internal and external borders of the European Union or the Schengen area, measures taken to exclude illegal migrants or limit the numbers of asylum seekers are often linked to member states' domestic policy agendas.

An Uncertain Time

By September 2011, the Franco-Italian Affair had brought about proposed revisions to the Schengen Borders Code and inspired debate over Schengen governance moving forward. In absolute numbers, the Arab Spring migration movement remained small and relatively contained, and yet the movement was politicized to a high degree. After France and Italy called for revisions to the Schengen Borders Code to further facilitate the reinstatement of internal border checks in exceptional circumstances, the European Commission issued a proposal that introduced the possibility of enacting such a mechanism (Pascouau 2012). In response to the conclusions of a European Council summit in June 2011, two legislative measures were proposed by the Commission in September 2011. The first was an amended proposal for a regulation on a revised Schengen evaluation mechanism (European Commission 2011a), where a safeguard clause was introduced for 'truly critical situations' in which a member state is no longer able to comply with their obligations under the Schengen rules. Here, the Commission declared its commitment to lending additional support to member states experiencing border difficulties and opened the possibility of the reintroduction of internal controls where a serious threat to public policy or internal security exists.

This change implied the second amendment to Regulation (EC) No. 562/2006 of the Schengen Borders Code, which lays down the rules for controls at external borders and mandates the abolition of controls at internal borders. This amendment now allows for the reinstatement of controls by member states for a maximum of six months (European Commission 2011b). In unforeseeable events, member states retain the right to unilaterally reintroduce controls at internal borders limited to a period of five days, which can be prolonged based on negotiations with the Commission (European Commission 2011b). Under Article 15, these provisions are intended as a measure of last resort.

These changes raise questions relating to the parameters of the reintroduction of controls. For one, 'exceptional circumstance' is left undefined (Carrera 2012), which becomes especially problematic in cases such as the 2011 Affair where the classification of North African migrants as an exceptional security threat was never unanimously agreed upon. Furthermore, these proposed amendments come in direct response to a migration event. The Schengen Borders Code inherently maintains provisions for the reinstatement of controls in special circumstances; until now, however, these provisions have not normally been used in an effort to restrict migration (Carrera 2012; Groenendijk 2004). Ambiguity therefore exists in understanding what constitutes a serious threat to public policy or internal security with respect to migration and where the authority lies with regards to internal and external border policy-making.

The September 2011 proposed changes were released as part of the Schengen Governance Package, designed to verify the application of Schengen rules by member states in the wake of events that challenge the provisions for freedom of movement in 2011 (Carrera 2012). Beyond the Franco-Italian Affair, the Danish government's proposed reintroduction of stringent border checks in May 2011 and more recent efforts by the Dutch administration to increase checks and surveillance at its land border crossings have tested member states' commitment to the Schengen rules. As Carrera notes, the ongoing Schengen debate is 'characterised by a prevailing logic of nationalism' and a struggle between reinforcing security and ensuring the freedom of movement of persons (2012: 23). A further example of this is the fact that many national governments reacted negatively to the Commission's proposal to give itself a larger role in monitoring the operation of external borders (Carrera 2012: 7–9; European Commission 2011a).

Arguments in the EU migration policy debate are also being shaped to a great degree by the populist setting in which they are unfolding. A notable feature in the party politics of many European states is the electoral successes of various right-leaning parties with xenophobic tendencies and anti-immigration political platforms (Mudde 2011). Like the Front National (FN) in France and Italy's Lega Nord (LN), the radical right are represented to varying degrees in European countries, and in many instances have been responsible for capitalizing on public susceptibility to fear the immigrant 'other'. Some of these parties have experienced considerable success in this regard – the right-leaning Danish People's Party played a key role in precipitating the 2011 Danish border closure incident. In other instances, anti-immigrant rhetoric is employed as prevailing theme for political gain. This was more recently visible with Nicolas Sarkozy's vow to curb immigrant admissions and crack down on extremism in France as part of his failed bid for re-election in 2012 following the race-related Toulouse shootings in March of this year.[7]

In the public sphere, 'Eurosceptic' sentiment questioning the validity and viability of EU integration altogether has risen as the sovereign debt crisis persists (Sutcliffe 2010; Taylor 2008). With a growing list of member states facing budget deficits, rising unemployment and costs of unemployment, budget cuts, and downgraded debt ratings, talks abound of a salient threat to the very existence of the common euro currency and the future role of countries like Greece in the EU. Public perceptions and misconceptions of the social and economic impact of immigrants become particularly acute during periods of austerity and economic duress, explaining in part the pattern of push-back on recent external migration flows (Eurobarometer 74 2011; European Union Agency for Fundamental Rights 2010; Papademetriou, Sumption, and Somerville 2009).

The popular emphasis on a cultural conflict between Europe and its Muslim populations is another contributing factor to the climate in which these policy events are unfolding. The dialogue of conflict between Islam and 'the West' has facilitated xenophobic preconditions linking immigration with cases of reactionary violence and home-grown terrorism, further alienating Europe's Muslim and ethnic populations and making the successful integration of ethnic nationals seem insurmountable from a cultural perspective. In many ways, recent patterns of border closures targeting new entrants have negatively impacted the cultural dimension of EU integration, and although measures taken to prevent TCNs from entering for cultural reasons are neither new nor uncommon, the underlying factors above have played a significant role in intensifying the 2011 Franco-Italian Affair beyond normal bounds. In effect, controversial events in the border policy sector become more unstable and potentially more politically and culturally destabilizing when viewed in relation to the current economic and

---

7   Sarkozy also threatened a French withdrawal from the Schengen zone during his unsuccessful 2012 campaign if the rules on free movement and the policing of borders were not revised (Carrera 2012).

political climate. In this respect, it becomes difficult to assess the value and future impact of the Schengen Governance Package – created in response to pressures by member states like France and Italy to amend border regulations they themselves did not fully comply with. The task of avoiding similar political dilemmas in the near future hinges on member solidarity during a time of increasing economic, political, and cultural introspection.

Conclusions

The EU's response to Arab Spring migration in 2011 incited controversy over the management of external immigration and internal mobility in the region. In resorting to exceptional powers by declaring a national state of emergency and issuing temporary residence permits to Arab Spring asylum seekers that sent them freely into greater EU territory, Italy incited a bitter debate over 'the power to control the political and legal framework by which to define and govern emergency in migration policy' (Campesi 2011: 1). At the same time, France's restoration of systematic border controls and refusal to grant entrance to incoming migrants resulted in a momentary disruption of the Schengen framework. The cross-border incident prompted a request for the modification of Schengen rules in order to allow member states to immediately reinstate controls in situations where a threat to public order or national security is perceived. The Commission's decision to process these requests has undoubtedly placed strain on Schengen (Pascouau 2012), and new initiatives governing emergency migration vis-à-vis the Schengen Governance Package released in September 2011 have so far been met with reservation by member states, who regard regional approaches to ensuring the proper application of Schengen rules as an encroachment of national sovereignty (Carrera 2012: 1).

The impact of the 2011 Franco-Italian Affair on the Schengen border regime has been subject to different interpretations. Some analysts interpret it as evidence of a major watershed moment for this aspect of European integration, and suggest that it may be a harbinger of renationalized border control (Carrera, Guild, Merlino and Parkin 2011; Carrera 2012; Hobbing 2011). The analysis here presents a more mixed view of the Affair and its potential impact on the EU. The dramatic turn of political events following the arrival of undocumented migrants in early 2011 is not an isolated event. Indeed, it may be wrong to overstate its significance and better to analyse it as part of a pattern in the development of EU policies relating to migration, mobility, and the treatment of asylum seekers and TCNs. The 2011 Affair is not unusual in a policy sector that touches closely on matters traditionally at the heart of state sovereignty (Zaiotti 2011). National governments have always retained for themselves the right to reinstate controls for short-term emergencies and have frequently been prepared to use this power without consulting their partner governments or the EC. In addition, national governments within the EU have always treated TCNs (and particularly illegal immigrants and asylum seekers) differently from EU citizens or TCNs with firm employment prospects. As the Schengen agreements have developed, it is not unusual for the participating states, either individually or collectively, to limit the flow of third country nationals into their territory. In this respect, the actions of the French and Italian governments are not unique.

For these reasons, the future impact and success of the Schengen Governance Package remains unclear, and it is not difficult to imagine similar reactionary responses by European states to future flows of migration given the political and economic climate in which these events are unfolding. In sum, while actual levels of EU immigration from the Arab Spring have had an imperceptible impact, a pervasive climate of anxiety relating to immigrants, as well as austerity measures, have allowed the issue to become securitized and politicized beyond normal bounds. Furthermore, whether the Franco-Italian Affair is seen as a major challenge to the idea of border free travel within the Schengen area or more narrowly as just the most recent of a list of attempts to control cross-border movement, it does highlight the prevalence of opposition to immigration within European states. In evaluating the external dimensions of Arab Spring migration as they pertain to EU policy-making in migration and mobility, the outright abrogation of the spirit of the Schengen triggered by the Franco-Italian Affair and other recent European cases demonstrates how these issues become more sensitive and therefore potentially more destabilizing.

References

Allen, P. (2011), 'Arab Spring' Camp Set Up in Calais as Thousands of North Africans Vie to Get to Britain. *Daily Mail*, [online] 23 May.

Back, L. (2011), 'Fortress Europe? There is a Better Way'. *The Guardian*, 27 April.

Baldoni, E. (2003), 'The Free Movement of Persons in the European Union: A Legal-Historical Overview'. Pioneur Working Paper no. 2, July.

Boswell, C. (2003). 'The External Dimension of EU Immigration and Asylum Policy'. *International Affairs* 79(3), 619–38.

Campesi, G. (2011), 'The Arab Spring and the Crisis of the European Border Regime: Manufacturing Emergency in the Lampedusa Crisis'. European University Institute Working Paper RSCAS 59.

Carrera, S. (2012), 'An Assessment of the Commission's 2011 Schengen Governance Package: Preventing Abuse by EU Member States of Freedom of Movement?' CEPS Paper in Liberty and Security in Europe. Brussels: Centre for European Policy Studies.

Carrera, S., Guild, E., Merlino, M. and J. Parkin (2011), 'A Race against Solidarity: The Schengen Regime and the Franco-Italian Affair'. CEPS Paper in Liberty and Security in Europe. Brussels: Centre for European Policy Studies.

Davidson, S. (1993), 'Free Movement of Workers', in Lodge, J. (ed.), *Institutions and Policies of the European Community*. London: Frances Pinter, 110–16.

Economist, The (2009), 'A Mess in the Mediterranean'. *The Economist*, 16 May, 58.

Economist, The (2011a), 'Keep Out'. *The Economist*, 31 December, 38.

Economist, The (2011b), 'Take My Migrants, Please'. *The Economist*, 16 April, 58.

Emerson, M. (2011), 'Summary and Conclusions', in Emerson, M. (ed.), *Interculturalism: Europe and its Muslims in Search of Sound Societal Models.* Brussels: Centre for European Policy Studies, 1–16.

European Commission (2011a), Commission Communication, *Schengen Governance – Strengthening the Area without Internal Border Control,* COM(2011) 561, 16.9.2011, Brussels.

European Commission (2011b), *Commission Proposal for a Regulation Amending Regulation (EC) No. 562/2006 in Order to Provide for Common Rules on the Temporary Reintroduction of Border Control at Internal Borders in Exceptional Circumstances*, COM(2011)560, 16.9.2011, Brussels.

European Council (2011), *Conclusions: 23/24 June 2011*. EUCO 23/1/11. Brussels.

European Parliament and Council of the European Union (2006). *Regulation (EC) No 562/2006 of the European Parliament and of the Council of 15 March 2006 Establishing a Community Code on the Rules Governing the Movement of Persons across Borders (Schengen Borders Code)*. Brussels.

Eurobarometer 74 (2010), 'Public Opinion in the European Union'. Brussels.

Fedyashin, A. (2011), 'Europe Shuts Doors to Illegal Immigration'. *RIA Novosti*, [online] 13 May.

Freudenstein, R. (2000), 'Río Odra, Río Buh: Poland, Germany and the Borders of Twenty-First-Century Europe', in Andreas, P. and Snyder, T. (eds), *The Wall Around the West: State Borders and Immigration Controls in North America and Europe*. Oxford: Rowman & Littlefield, 173–83.

Frontex (2011), *Risk Analysis Network Quarterly*, Issue 1. January–March (2011).

Geddes, A. (2005a). 'Europe's Border Relationships and International Migration Relations'. *Journal of Common Market Studies* 43(4), 787–806.

Geddes, A. (2005b), 'Getting the Best of Both Worlds? Britain, the EU and Migration Policy'. *International Affairs* 81(4), 723–40.

Geddes, A. (2008), *Immigration and European Integration: Beyond Fortress Europe?*, 2nd edn. Manchester: Manchester University Press.

Groenendijk, K. (2004), 'Reinstatement of Controls at the Internal Borders of Europe: Why and Against Whom?' *European Law Journal* 10(2), 150–70.

Hailbronner, K. and C. Thiery (1997), 'Schengen II and Dublin: Responsibility for Asylum Applications in Europe'. *Common Market Law Review* 34, 957–89.

Harmsen, R. and M. Spiering (eds) (2004), *Euroscepticism: Party Politics, National Identity and European Integration*. Amsterdam: Rodopi.

Hobbing, P. (2011), *A Farewell to Open Borders? The Danish Approach*. CEPS Paper in Liberty and Security in Europe. Brussels: Centre for European Policy Studies.

Joppke, C. (2007), 'Beyond National Models: Civic Integration Policies for Immigrants in Western Europe'. *West European Politics* 30(1), 1–22.

Judt, T. (2005), *Postwar: A History of Europe since 1945*. London: Penguin.

Kersten, M. (2011), 'France and Italy Call for Closed EU Border: An Abrogation of Moral Responsibility'. *Justice in Conflict*, [online] 28 April.

Kirby, J. and M. Petrou (2011), 'States of Disunion'. *Maclean's*, 5 September, 32–4.

Lavenex, S. (2006a), 'Shifting Up and Out: The Foreign Policy of European Immigration Control'. *West European Politics* 29(2), 329–50.

Lavenex, S. (2006b), 'Towards the Constitutionalization of Aliens' Rights in the European Union'. *Journal of European Public Policy* 13(8), 1284–301.

Lavenex, S. (2010), 'Justice and Home Affairs: Communitarization with Hesitation', in Wallace, H., Pollack, M. and Young, A.R. (eds), *Policy-making in the European Union*, 6th edn. Oxford: Oxford University Press, 457–77.

Luedtke, A. (2011), 'Uncovering European Union Immigration Legislation: Policy Dynamics and Outcomes'. *International Migration* 49(2), 1–27.

Monar, J. (2001), 'The Dynamics of Justice and Home Affairs: Laboratories, Driving Factors and Costs'. *Journal of Common Market Studies* 39(4), 747–64.

Monar, J. (2009), 'Justice and Home Affairs'. *Journal of Common Market Studies*, 47(Annual Review), 151–70.

Monar, J. (2010), 'Justice and Home Affairs'. *Journal of Common Market Studies*, 48(Annual Review), 143–62.

Monar, J. (2011), 'Justice and Home Affairs'. *Journal of Common Market Studies* 49(Annual Review), 145–64.

Mudde, C. (2011), 'Radical Right Parties in Europe: What, Who, Why?' *Participation* 34(3), 12–15.

Nascimbene, B. and A. Di Pascale (2011), 'The "Arab Spring" and the Extraordinary Influx of People Who Arrived in Italy from North Africa'. *European Journal of Migration and Law* 13, 341–60.

Neal, A.W. (2009), 'Securitization and Risk at the EU Border: The Origins of Frontex'. *Journal of Common Market Studies* 47(2), 333–56.

Papademetriou, D.G., Sumption, M. and W. Somerville (2009), 'Migration and the Economic Downturn: What to Expect in the European Union'. *Migration Policy Institute.*

Pascouau, Y. (2012), 'The Schengen Evaluation Mechanism and the Legal Basis Problem: Breaking the Deadlock'. *European Policy Centre Policy Brief*, 31 January. Brussels: European Policy Centre.

Salter, M.B. (2004), 'Passports, Mobility, and Security: How Smart Can the Border Be?' *International Studies Perspectives* 5, 71–91.

Schutte, J.J.E. (1991), 'Schengen: Its Meaning for the Free Movement of Persons in Europe'. *Common Market Law Review* 28, 549–70.

Squires, N. (2011), Italy Fears Up to 1.5 Million North African Migrants. *The Daily Telegraph*, [online] 24 February.

Sutcliffe, J.B. (2010), 'Critical Interpretations of Integration in North America and the European Union: A Comparative Evaluation', in Laursen, F. (ed.), *Comparative Regional Integration: Europe and Beyond*. Farnham: Ashgate, 63–82.

Swann, D. (1992), 'The Single Market and Beyond – An Overview', in Swann, D. (ed.), *The Single European Market and Beyond: A Study of the Wider Implications of the Single European Act*. London: Routledge, 3–25.

Taggart, P. and A. Szczerbiak (2008), 'Introduction: Opposing Europe? The Politics of Euroscepticism', in Szczerbiak, A. and Taggart, P. (eds), *Opposing Europe? The Comparative Party Politics of Euroscepticism, Volume 1: Case Studies and Country Surveys*. Oxford: Oxford University Press, 1–15.

Taylor, P. (2008), *The End of European Integration: Anti-Europeanism Examined*. London: Routledge.

Traynor, I. (2011), 'Arabic Exodus Likely to Lead to Tighter Border Controls in Europe'. *The Guardian*, [online] 8 May.

UNHCR (2011), 'Update no. 28: Humanitarian Situation in Libya and the Neighbouring Countries', 10 June.

Wolff, S. (2008), 'Border Management in the Mediterranean: Internal, External and Ethical Challenges'. *Cambridge Review of International Affairs* 21(2), 253–71.

Zaiotti, R. (2011), 'The Beginning of the End? The Italo-French Row Over Schengen and the Lesson of Past "Crises" for the Future of Border Free Europe'. *European Union Centre of Excellence, Dalhousie University Occasional Paper*, no. 12, June. Halifax: Dalhousie University.

PART V
Concluding Chapter

Chapter 11

Equilibrium, Further Deepening or More 'Variable Geometry': Reflections on the Future of European Integration

Finn Laursen

Introduction

Scholars may focus on explaining the past as well as understanding the present, but we may also reflect on the future. That is what policy-makers and journalists expect us to do. The better our theories, the more informed such speculations can be. If we have detected general patterns in the past they may help us think about the future, or likely futures. Our problem is of course that we do not have single factor explanations of the past. We use a number of independent variables and intervening variables to construct a causal model of European integration. The big theoretical debates are about finding the variables with most explanatory power.

In my studies of regional integration I have taken a fairly rationalist approach as a point of departure, but have also recognized the importance of creating trust and solidarity among integrating units. According to the rationalist perspective, integration requires demand and supply (Beach 2005; Laursen 2003; Laursen 2010; Mattli 1999; Moravcsik 1998). Demand comes from society, including various organized interests. Supply must be provided by politicians who in turn are constrained by the domestic and international political systems. Integration is about overcoming 'collective action' problems, i.e. situations where there are temptations to cheat or defect from cooperation or where distribution problems have some actors feeling that they get too little from common endeavours. Whether actors take a positive gains or relative gains perspective on this is one of the debates between liberal and realist international relations scholars (Baldwin 1993). However, it seems fair to expect that even in integration schemes among like-minded states, governments do pay attention to what other member states get from cooperation compared with what they get themselves. This becomes very clear in budgetary politics, for instance, but even when weighting of votes in the Council of Ministers has been on the agenda of some treaty reforms member states compare themselves with other member states.

As I tried to outline in the introductory chapter of this book European integration has had ups and downs, but overall there has been a trend towards expanding the functional scope and the geographical domain of integration. At the same time there have been continuous efforts to improve institutional capacity, as demonstrated especially by successive treaty reforms. Arguably this new integration trajectory in Europe started with the Schuman Plan in 1950. The so-called Community method invented at the time put emphasis on supranational institutions, based on the conclusion that classical intergovernmental institutions were inadequate. The method was efficiency oriented. Results were supposed to produce legitimacy. However, gradually there emerged a concern for the democratic nature of the institutions, leading to a steady empowerment of the European Parliament (Rittberger 2005). In due course these paths took us into the efforts to produce and adopt a constitutional treaty after the disappointing results of the Treaty of Nice in 2000.

The Debacle of the Constitutional Treaty

The efforts to adopt the so-called Constitutional Treaty however did not succeed. The method was novel, preparing the new treaty in a so-called convention with important participation of politicians from national governments as well as the European Parliament (EP), and deliberate effort to generate greater openness and debate. Arguably the Convention took important steps beyond what the governments had been able to agree upon four years earlier in Nice, and the members accepted most of the draft treaty in the Intergovernmental Conference (IGC) that followed (Beach 2005).

At least 10 of the 25 member states then decided to use referendums to ratify the treaty. Given the history of referendums this was a risky strategy. Most member states ratified the treaty by parliamentary vote, and referendums in Spain and Luxembourg had positive outcomes. But the French and Dutch voters rejected the treaty in May and June 2005. The No vote from France in particular – it being one of the leading founders of the European Communities – signalled that the treaty was dead (Laursen 2008).

After a 'reflection period' the Lisbon Treaty was adopted including many of the same provisions as the failed Constitutional Treaty. The methodology changed. This time it was not a completely new treaty, but an amendment to existing treaties. 'Constitutionalist' terminology was removed. The treaty was negotiated in relative secrecy under German leadership (Laursen 2012a). However, the alleged advantages of openness, debate and involvement of the people in history-making decisions did not materialize on this occasion. Could it be that representative democracy is better than direct democracy to adopt complex treaties that even experts can find difficult to decipher?

Has Integration Reached a Plateau?

Andrew Moravcsik has argued that a constitutional equilibrium has been reached by the EU (Moravcsik 2005, 2006, 2007). According to him, 'The Treaty of Rome has long provided the EU with a de facto constitution' (Moravcsik 2007: 33). Although the EU's constitutional structure has federal elements it is essentially confederal, and the 'EU does not (with a few exceptions) enjoy the power to coerce, administer, or tax'. Constitutional change requires unanimity but '[s]uch a system is deeply resistant to any fundamental transformation without consensus among a wide variety of actors'. So, despite some features of federalism, many of its most important elements are missing. Thus, 'the EU has no police, no army, no significant intelligence capacity – and no realistic prospect of obtaining any of them' (Ibid.: 34–5). He argued that the Constitutional Treaty was not in fact a revolutionary document:

> Recent constitutional deliberations underscored the stability of existing constraints on political, coercive, fiscal, and administrative capacity. Notwithstanding its high-minded Philadelphian rhetoric, the proposed draft consolidated, rather than fundamentally reformed, the 'European constitutional settlement.' Few in recent constitutional debates called the EU's essentially confederal structure into question (Ibid.: 36).

The proposed reforms were incremental as earlier reforms of the treaties had been.

According to Moravcsik, the main reason why people do not take a bigger part in EU debates is the fact that most salient political issues such as health care, pensions, taxation and education remain overwhelmingly national. What the EU can do about another issue that people care about – namely unemployment – is also limited because fiscal, labour market and education policies remain largely national. It is this problem of saliency of the issues dealt with at the EU level which also explains the low turn-out in elections to the EP. Further institutional changes will not be able to get citizens to become more involved. Moravcsik argues:

> Forcing the issue onto the agenda via a constitutional convention and referendum is counterproductive. This is the deepest lesson of the constitutional episode: from the very beginning with the Laeken Declaration – not simply at the end in a set of mismanaged referenda – the constitution utterly failed to inspire, engage, and educate European publics (Ibid.: 43).

The alternative to conventions and referendums about history-making decisions is more attention to and politicization of the day-to-day decision making process in Brussels. Of course, the problem here is the saliency of the issues. As long as the most important issues for the citizens are decided nationally it will be difficult to 'politicize' EU decision-making. How political parties approach the elections to the EP is an important variable.

Lisbon and Post-Lisbon

As mentioned the Lisbon Treaty adopted many of the new institutional provisions suggested by the Constitutional Treaty. The European Council now has a semi-permanent president. There is a new High Representative of the Union for Foreign Affairs and Security Policy, who runs a new European External Action Service (EEAS). Voting in the Council of Ministers will in the future be based on a double majority formula, at least 55% of the member states representing at least 65% of the EU's population. Efficiency is expected to improve by the extended use of qualified majority voting (QMV) in the Council, and legitimacy is expected to improve by making the EP a co-legislature in many more policy areas (Laursen 2012b).

When the Lisbon Treaty was adopted in 2007 there was widespread expectation that this was the last treaty reform for many years. The Constitutional Treaty debacle had clearly produced treaty reform fatigue. However, by the time the treaty entered into force the financial crisis had already started to hit Europe. The Economic and Monetary Union (EMU) parts of the treaty had not been an issue in the deliberations on, and negotiations of, the Constitutional Treaty, and subsequently the Lisbon Treaty. There were talks of improving economic governance in the Convention and IGCs, but changes were minor, such as explicitly recognizing the existence of the Eurogroup consisting of the finance ministers from the 'Member States whose currency is the euro' (Piris 2010: 304–5).

Since the entry into force of the Lisbon Treaty there have already been two formal changes in the treaty, one dealing with seats in the EP, and the other one dealing with the permanent rescue fund, the European Stability Mechanism (ESM). In general the financial crisis has rekindled the discussion about the need for further treaty reforms to deepen integration at least among the eurozone countries. German Chancellor Angela Merkel has become a leading spokesperson for deepening of integration in the form of fiscal and political union, although whatever these terms mean exactly remains unclear. The Commission has also been moving on this issue. In his State of the Union address to the EP on 12 September 2012, Commission president José Manuel Barroso said: 'Let's not be afraid of the words: we will need to move towards a federation of nation states. This is what we need. This is our political horizon'. He recognized, 'Creating this federation of nation states will ultimately require a new Treaty' (Barroso 2012).

Will the Eurozone Survive?

The biggest question about the future of European integration is the survival of the eurozone. At the moment the approach to the crisis is one of muddling through, which has included the questionable emphasis on austerity at a time where growth and competitiveness should have the highest priority. The steps taken by the last European Council meeting at the end of June 2012 moves a little in that direction, but only baby steps. The eurozone needs more decisive strides by the governments, EU institutions and the European Central Bank (ECB).

The rational strategy – seen from a European point of view – is 'more Europe'. Many agree on that, but they have different ideas of what it means. In the current debate, fiscal union often means more fiscal discipline, not more fiscal federalism in the sense of a union budget that could make a difference. Also, clearly the ECB should be allowed to issue Eurobonds to mutualize sovereign debt and become a lender of last resort. It is also important to make sure that the ESM has enough firepower. In the end this is all about solidarity among the countries in Europe. The EU must have a real sense of community as its foundation.

As has been suggested in a number of contributions to this book, there is a risk of a Greek exit from the eurozone, possible even being followed by other eurozone members. This would undoubtedly have both economic and political costs, in the end threatening the EMU construct. The worst case scenario would be the disintegration of the eurozone, an important part of the EU. The alternative is for the eurozone to move towards banking, fiscal and political union (the three Us), as discussed by Kurt Hübner in his chapter in this book. If this is not possible in the short run, a 'rationalized' muddling through might gradually take EMU in that direction, eventually to be crowned by a new treaty. Figure 11.1 illustrates some of the possible directions EMU and the eurozone could take.

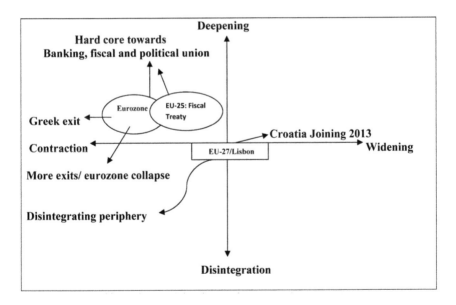

Figure 11.1   Future of deepening and widening

Source: Designed by author, with inspiration from Wessels 1996 and 2008.

Will We Get More Variable Geometry?

The move towards various forms of flexible integration or variable geometry became more visible in connection with the Maastricht Treaty in 1992, when the United Kingdom (UK) secured opt-outs from EMU and social policy, and Denmark from EMU, defence policy as well as Justice and Home Affairs (JHA) cooperation. As the EU expanded its agenda and membership, it became more difficult to keep it all together. Subsequently as the Schengen cooperation consolidated, later becoming part of the EU by the Amsterdam Treaty in 1999, the UK and Ireland stayed out. The Danish opt-out from JHA concerned supranational JHA, not intergovernmental cooperation where Denmark, formally speaking, would have a veto. Therefore Denmark took part in the pillar 3 portion of the Maastricht Treaty initially, but when part of pillar 3 was moved to pillar 1 by the Amsterdam Treaty, Denmark could not take part in JHA except for Police and Criminal Justice, which stayed in a slimmer intergovernmental 3rd pillar. With the entry into force of the Lisbon Treaty all JHA now falls under the Community method, so Denmark is excluded. However, the country secured an opt-in arrangement similar to the British solution, allowing for selective participation.

Figure 11.2 gives a somewhat simplified overview of the current situation. It does not include CFSP where Denmark still has an opt-out from the Common Security and Defence Policy (CSDP) and where there is a tendency for *ad hoc* 'coalitions of the willing' to form. Nor does it include the European Economic Area (EEA), the agreement that allows Norway, Iceland and Lichtenstein to take part in the internal market, arguably the most important part of the EU. Switzerland, which has joined Schengen, does not take part in the EEA. It should not come as a surprise that students of European integration find all this a bit confusing.

Seen from a European integration perspective the main problem with variable geometry is the way it can affect decision making. Often major decisions are packet-deals including a variety of issues. Political scientists talk about linkage strategies. Decision-makers link various issues in the hope of reaching a deal where everybody feels that there is something in it for them. If linkage takes place within the same policy area American political scientists talk about log-rolling. If the link is with a different policy area the term used is side-payment (Lindberg and Scheingold 1970). Obviously a significant amount of variable geometry can make the use of side-payments more difficult.

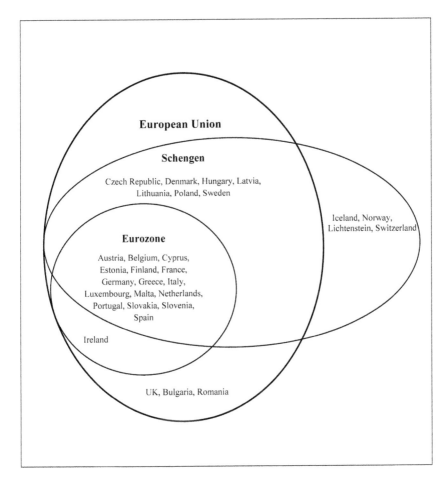

Figure 11.2   Variable geometry of European integration
Source: Designed by the author.

Is There a Leadership Deficit?

If variable geometry can make the use of side-payments more difficult, sometimes it does have one clear advantage. It allows a smaller group to move ahead without waiting for the laggards. In this way it can facilitate leadership, which is seen by many as an important and sometimes necessary ingredient in the integration process (Beach 2005; Lindberg and Scheingold 1970; Mattli 1999; Tallberg 2006).

It is therefore relevant to ask whether the EU has the leadership required to overcome current challenges, including – especially – the eurozone crisis. The European Commission does try to put forward proposals. The President of the European Council has also tried to exercise leadership. But in the end, when we face major crises national leadership is probably more important that supranational leadership. In history-making decisions the EU tends to become intergovernmental (Moravcsik 1998). In the past Franco-German leadership has been important (Pedersen 1998). In today's EU Germany has become the most powerful country, for better or worse. Arguably Germany, led by Chancellor Merkel, played an important and positive role in reaching an agreement on the Lisbon Treaty in 2007 (Laursen 2010a). But history may be more critical when Chancellor Merkel's role in the euro crisis will be assessed in the future. As any rational political leader she has the next national election in her mind. If the national mood is not in favour of generosity it becomes difficult to be a regional paymaster. Integration is a two-level game (Evans et al. 1993; Putnam 1988).

***

In the end, should we then be optimistic or pessimistic about European integration? There can be no doubt that the EU, and the eurozone in particular, is under great stress. But the EU has faced crises before and in the end has sorted things out. Interdependence and common interests are important. If historical institutionalists are right about path dependency we may see more deepening and widening in the future, albeit at a slower pace than European federalists would like.

References

Baldwin, D.A. (ed.) (1993), *Neorealism and Neoliberalism: The Contemporary Debate*. New York: Columbia University Press.

Barroso, J. and M. Durão (2012), 'State of the Union 2012 Address'. Available at http://europa.eu/rapid/pressReleasesAction.do?reference=SPEECH/12/596&format=HTML&aged=0&language=EN&guiLanguage=en (accessed 13 September 2012).

Evans, P.B., Jacobson, H.K. and R.D. Putnam (eds) (1993), *Double-Edged Diplomacy: International Bargaining and Domestic Politics*. Berkeley: University of California Press.

Laursen, F. (ed.) (2003), *Comparative Regional Integration: Theoretical Perspectives*. Aldershot: Ashgate.

Laursen, F. (ed.) (2006), *The Treaty of Nice: Actor Preferences, Bargaining and Institutional Choice*. Leiden: Martinus Nijhoff Publishers.

Laursen, F. (ed.) (2008), *The Rise and Fall of the EU's Constitutional Treaty*. Leiden: Martinus Nijhoff Publishers.

Laursen, F. (ed.) (2010), *Comparative Regional Integration: Europe and Beyond*. Farnham: Ashgate.

Laursen, F. (ed.) (2012a), *The Making of the EU's Lisbon Treaty: The Role of Member States*. Brussels: P.I.E. Peter Lang.

Laursen, F. (ed.) (2012b), *The EU's Lisbon Treaty: Institutional Choices and Implementation*. Farnham: Ashgate Publishing.

Laursen, F. (ed.) (forthcoming), *Designing the European Union: From Paris to Lisbon*. Farnham: Palgrave.

Mattli, W. (1999), *The Logic of Regional Integration: Europe and Beyond*. Cambridge: Cambridge University Press.

Moravcsik, A. (1998), *The Choice for Europe*. Ithaca, NY: Cornell University Press.

Moravcsik, A. (2005), 'The European Constitutional Compromise and the Neofunctionalist Legacy', *Journal of European Public Policy* 12(2) (April), 349–86.

Moravcsik, A. (2006), 'What Can We Learn from the Collapse of the European Constitutional Project?' *Politische Vierteljahresschrift* 47(2), 219–41.

Moravcsik, A. (2007), 'The European Constitutional Settlement', in *The State of the European Union. Vol. 8. Making History: European Integration and Institutional Change at Fifty*. Oxford: Oxford University Press, 23–50.

Pedersen, T. (1998), *Germany, France and the Integration of Europe: A Realist Interpretation*. London: Pinter.

Putnam, R. (1988), 'Diplomacy and Domestic Politics: The Logic of Two-Level Games', *International Organization* 42 (Summer), 427–60.

Rittberger, B. (2005), *Building Europe's Parliament: Democratic Representation beyond the Nation State*. Oxford: Oxford University Press.

Tallberg, J. (2006), *Leadership and Negotiation in the European Union*. Cambridge: Cambridge University Press.

Wessels, W. (1996), 'Evolution possible de l'Union européenne. Scénarios et stratégies pour sortir d'un cercle vicieux', *Politique Étrangère* 1, 139–50.

Wessels, W. (2008), *Das politische System der Europäischen Union*. Wiesbaden: VS Verlag für Sozialwissenschaften.

Index

Accession 13, 20, 95, 162, 164, 167,
      171–3
Accountability 18, 58
Adjustment 52
Administrative burden 91
Afghanistan 76
Africa 179
Agriculture 18, 85–6, 88–91, 93–4, 97–8,
      103
Albania 13, 20
Amsterdam Treaty 4, 7, 10, 13, 20, 181,
      183, 204
Arab Spring 178–80, 192
Area of Freedom, Security and Justice
      (AFSJ) 183–4
Argentina 145
Asia 151
Asylum 178–82, 188
Austerity, automatic 54
Austria 3, 14, 150, 167–9, 179
Autonomy 5, 50

Bailouts 11, 45–6, 50, 52, 144–8, 150, 152
Balanced budget rule 48
Barroso, José Manuel 151
Belgium 3, 14, 150, 161, 179, 182
Berlusconi, Sylvio 46, 177, 185–6
Black Wednesday 72–3
Blair, Tony 67–8, 75–6
Border controls 20, 162, 169–70, 173,
      182, 186
Border security 179, 185
Bosnia-Herzegovina 13, 162
Breton Woods 101
Britain 1, 3–4, 7, 11, 14, 18–19, 27, 48,
      65–74, 76–80, 116, 119, 128, 140,
      204
Brown, Gordon 68, 76, 78
Bulgaria 3, 14, 19–20, 161–3, 174, 183
Bundesbank 70, 147

Burden sharing 40–41
Bureaucratic burden 90
Business Europe 47, 53

Cameron, David 68, 78
Canada 17, 88–9, 107–8, 110–11, 116–18
Canada-US Free Trade Agreement
      (CUFTA) 117
Candidate countries 95, 162, 164–5, 169,
      172–3
CAP *see* Common Agricultural Policy
CFSP *see* Common Foreign and Security
      Policy
Charest, Jean 110
Charter of Fundamental Rights 129, 135
Chirac, Jacques 132
Climate change 89
Cohesion Fund 12
Cold War 8, 146
Comex 166–8, 172
Common Agricultural Policy (CAP) 9, 19,
      12, 18, 66, 85–93, 95, 97, 99–106,
      151
Common currency 57
Common Foreign and Security Policy
      (CFSP) 4–5, 12–13, 16, 204
Common Security and Defence Policy
      (CSDP) 19, 16, 204
Commonwealth 69
Communitarization 181
Community method 15, 5, 204
Competition 53, 90
Comprehensive Economic and Trade
      Agreement (CETA) 12, 18–19,
      107–19
Conditionalities 37, 42, 51, 56
Constitutional Treaty 13, 16, 200–202
Controlled depreciation 36
Convergence criteria 10
COPA-COGECA 103

Correction mechanisms 49
CRAs *see* credit rating agencies
Credit rating agencies (CRAs) 19, 152
Crisis management 31, 33, 36, 40, 68, 72,
      74, 90, 92, 94, 98, 118, 134, 136,
      160
Croatia 13–14
Currencies, common 57, 70
Currency risk 27
Currency war 36
Current account balances 47
Cyprus 3, 14, 19, 145, 150, 152
Czech Republic 3, 11, 14, 48, 78, 128, 147

DDR *see* Doha Development Round
De Gaulle, Charles 66
Debt brake 37, 48, 54
Debt redemption funds 41, 55
Deficit 54, 125, 129, 131, 133, 137
Deficits, structural 48, 54–5
Delegated decision-making 57
Delors Committee 70–71, 77
Delors Report 69, 71
Democracy 5, 18, 45–6, 50, 52, 55, 57–8,
      61, 63, 126–8, 133, 140, 142, 146
   delegated 57
   representative 49, 200
Democratic accountability 49, 59
Democratic deficit 19, 50–51, 125, 127
Democratic legitimacy 15, 46, 52, 57
Denmark 3, 14, 20, 72, 76, 91, 128, 163,
      165, 170–72, 179, 204
Department of Foreign Affairs and
      International Trade (DFAIT) 115
Deutschmark 38, 70
Devaluation 10, 72
Direct democracy 19, 125–6, 137–9, 200
Doha Development Round (DDR) 112
Dumping 18
Durable convergence 10

ECB *see* European Central Bank
ECOFIN *see* Economic and Financial
      Affairs Council
Economic and Financial Affairs Council
      (ECOFIN) 3, 11

Economic and Monetary Union (EMU)
      3–4, 7–12, 17–18, 33, 69–71, 74,
      78, 146, 202–4
Economic crisis 49, 104
Economic cycle 79
Economic governance 15, 55
Economic policies 43, 47–9, 69, 73, 91
ECSC *see* European Coal and Steel
      Community
ECU *see* European Currency Unit
Education 181
EEA *see* European Economic Area
Elections 72–3, 76
Empowerment 49, 52
EMS *see* European Monetary System
EMU *see* Economic and Monetary Union
Energy 89
Enforcement 19, 108
Enlargement 12–13, 15–16, 18–19, 43, 95,
      129, 137, 161–3, 165, 168, 174
Enlargement fatigue 13, 19, 161, 175
EP *see* European Parliament
ERM *see* Exchange Rate Mechanism
ESM *see* European Stability Mechanism
Estonia 3, 14
ETUC *see* European Trade Union
      Confederation
EU-Canada Summit 110
EU-Canada Trade Initiative (ECTI) 109,
      117
EU citizenship 136
Euro bills 55
Euro group 3, 51
Eurobonds 12, 55–6
European Central Bank (ECB) 4, 9–11,
      25–6, 29, 33–4, 36–9, 42–3, 46–8,
      51, 54, 56, 143, 147, 149, 203
European Coal and Steel Community
      (ECSC) 5, 15, 125
European Communities (EC) 3, 5, 8, 12,
      20, 68–9, 86, 88, 109, 164–5, 170,
      189, 191, 193, 200
European Constitutional Settlement 201
European Council 12, 25, 32, 35–6, 38,
      58, 68

European Court of Justice (ECJ) 4–5, 58, 147, 183
European Currency Unit (ECU) 19
European Economic Area (EEA) 19, 204
European Economic Community (EEC) 4–5, 15, 18, 65, 87, 180
European Financial Stability Fund 78
European Financial Stability Mechanism (EFSM) 28
European Free Trade Association (EFTA) 13, 19, 65
European Integration 7, 3, 5, 20, 34, 52, 57, 66–9, 78–9, 138, 180, 206
European Investment Bank (EIB) 12, 56
European Monetary System (EMS) 8–9, 69–70
European Parliament (EP) 15, 4, 12–13, 15–16, 34, 50, 52, 54, 58, 126, 132, 139, 183, 186, 200–202
European Political Cooperation (EPC) 12
European Social Model 53
European Stability Mechanism (ESM) 11, 28, 33, 36–7, 42, 45–6, 48–9, 53, 55–6, 202–3
European Trade Union Confederation (ETUC) 53–4
Eurosceptic critics 77
Euroscepticism 125, 127, 178
Eurosceptics 72
Eurozone 15, 3–4, 8, 11, 16–17, 19, 25–30, 32–43, 45–9, 57–8, 65, 76–7, 144–5, 148, 202–3
Exchange rate 36, 39
Exchange Rate Mechanism (ERM) 9–10, 69–74, 79
Exchange rate stability 10, 70
Expertocracy 49
Export subsidies 87–8
Extremism 146

FCO *see* Foreign Commonwealth Office
Federalism 17, 201
Financial crises 27–8
Financial institutions 31, 48, 57, 59
Financial markets 19, 25–6, 29, 33, 35–6, 39, 43
Financial products 27
Financialization 29, 43

Finland 3, 13–14, 20, 33, 36, 148, 170–72
Fiscal pact 48, 51–3, 55, 59
Fiscal policy 11, 45, 53, 56, 58
Fiscal Treaty 53–4, 59, 77, 79
Fiscal union 33–4, 47, 50, 55
Foreign Commonwealth Office (FCO) 20, 75–6
Foreign exchange 145
Foreign policy 65, 74
Former Yugoslavia 167
Four freedoms of the internal market *see* Free movement of goods, services, capital and people
Framework Agreement for Commercial and Economic Cooperation 109, 111
France 3, 14, 46, 55, 66, 128, 132, 137, 147–8, 150, 152, 165–8, 173, 179, 182
Franco-Italian Affair 177–8, 182, 184, 187–9, 192
Free movement of goods, services, capital and people 6, 20, 171, 177–8, 180, 187
Free Trade Agreements (FTAs) 18, 112–13, 117–19
Frontex 179
FTAs *see* Free Trade Agreements

General Agreement on Tariffs and Trade (GATT) 86
Germany 3, 11, 14, 19, 33–5, 37–8, 40, 42, 56, 58, 70–72, 103, 147–50, 166–8, 170
Gexit (German exit) 33
Global economy 27, 29, 34, 36
Global Europe 111
Global market 91
Global trade strategy 18
Globalization 53
Golden Dawn 146
Government bonds 26, 38, 42
Great Crisis 26, 28, 30
Greece 3, 11–14, 17, 25–6, 30, 32, 34–8, 41–2, 46–7, 49, 55–6, 143–6, 148, 167, 169
Greek default 19, 144, 152
Grexit (Greek exit) 33, 36–8, 148

Growth, economic 25, 30, 70
Growth and Stability Pact 10

Haircuts 11, 37, 144, 147, 149
Harper, Stephen 110
Healthcare 181
Herzegovina 162
Humanitarian emergencies 178
Hungary 3, 14, 66, 88, 95, 146

Iceland 13, 19–20, 161, 170–72, 204
IMF *see* International Monetary Fund
Immigration 20, 130, 146, 166, 173, 177,
    182, 185–6, 188, 190, 192
    migration 177, 188–9, 192
Implementation 37–8, 47, 51, 90, 92, 101,
    103, 109, 116, 164, 183
Implementation Convention 164
Incentives 52
Income Stabilization Tool 100, 103
India 104
Industry, dairy 89
Inflation 30
Input legitimacy 52
Institutional capacity 6, 8, 15–16, 200
Integration 5–6, 34, 42, 57–8, 67–8, 70–
    71, 116–17, 125–7, 129, 136, 143,
    177, 179–80, 189–91, 199–200
Intellectual property rights (IPRs) 110,
    113–14, 116, 119
Inter-governmentalism 143
Inter-state 153
Interdependence 17, 206
Interest rates 30
Intergovernmentalism 15
Internal Border Control 184, 186–7
Internal borders 177, 180, 183, 187–9
Internal market 13, 15, 17, 48, 70, 204
International banking 27, 29
International Monetary Fund (IMF) 11, 26,
    34, 36, 41, 46, 49, 51, 144–5, 151
International trade 18–19, 93
Investment 19, 51, 74, 97, 107–8, 110,
    116, 118
Investment agreement 111
IPRs *see* Intellectual property rights

Ireland 3, 11–12, 14, 28, 30–32, 35, 46,
    55, 76, 128, 131, 134, 137, 145,
    149
Islam 178, 190
Italy 11–12, 20, 35, 38, 46–7, 56, 148–50,
    152, 163, 165–71, 173, 177, 179,
    182, 184–8

Jasmine Revolution 177, 179
JCC *see* Joint Cooperation Committee
JHA *see* Justice and Home Affairs
Joint Cooperation Committee (JCC) 108–9
Juncker, Jean-Claude 3, 51, 147
Justice and Home Affairs (JHA) 4–5, 16,
    181, 183, 204

Karel, De Gucht 148
Keynesian stimulus policies 50
Kosovo 13, 162

Labour market reforms 56
Labour markets 53–4, 90, 201
Lampedusa 179, 185
Latvia 3, 14, 102
Leadership 205
Legitimacy 15, 18, 51, 57, 170
    indirect 51
    output 45, 52
    parliamentary 51
    political 32
    procedural 51
Less favoured areas (LFAs) 100, 102–3
LFAs *see* Less favoured areas
Liabilities, contingent 144
Liberalization, economic 27, 53–4, 57
Libya 20, 179
Lichtenstein 19, 161, 204
Lisbon Treaty 4–5, 7, 11, 13, 16, 68, 116,
    130, 183, 200, 202, 204, 206
Lithuania 3, 14
Long-Term Refinancing Operations
    (LTRO) 42
LTRO *see* Long-Term Refinancing
    Operations
Luxembourg 3, 14, 126, 128, 130–32, 135,
    137, 148, 161, 182, 200

Maastricht criteria 47
Maastricht Treaty 4–5, 7–10, 15–16, 72–3,
        136, 148, 183, 204
Macedonia 13, 16, 162
MacSharry, Ray 88
MacSharry reforms 88
Major, John 67–8, 70–73, 78
Malta 3, 14, 102, 152
Media 19, 65, 79, 94, 103, 108, 146, 179
Members of the European Parliament
        (MEPs) 13, 68, 132–3
MEPs *see* Members of the European
        Parliament
Merkozy plan 146
Migration *see* immigration
Mobility 57
Monetary policy 9, 68, 70, 78
Monetary union 9, 27, 33, 65, 67, 70–73,
        76–8
Monitoring 48
Montenegro 13
Monti, Mario 35, 46
Moral hazard 26

NAFTA *see* North American Free Trade
        Agreement
National identity 181
Nationalism 19, 189
Neo-functionalism 127, 149, 152–3
Neo-liberalism 52–3
Netherlands 3, 14, 33, 36, 42, 126, 128,
        130, 133–5, 137, 150, 161–2, 182
New governance instruments 47
Nordic area 171
Nordic Passport Union 20, 164–5, 170–72
North Africa 166, 179, 185, 194
North American Free Trade Agreement
        (NAFTA) 117
Norway 19, 161, 170–72, 204

OECD *see* Organization for Economic
        Co-operation and Development
Organization for Economic Co-operation
        and Development (OECD) 53

Pan-European deposit guarantee schemes
        36
Papademos, Lucas 46

Papandreou, George 46, 144
Path dependency 206
Paying Agencies 92, 96–7, 101, 103
Peace 57
Petersberg tasks 13
PIIGS 11
Poland 9, 3, 14, 66, 95, 97, 99–103, 128
Political union 12, 33–4, 36–7
Pompidou, Georges 66
Portugal 3, 11–12, 14, 30, 32, 47, 66, 128,
        145, 149–50, 152, 167
Price stability 10
Privatization 54, 146
Procurement 19, 107–8, 110, 116, 118
Public debt 17, 25–6, 28, 30–31, 48
Public sector layoffs 56

QMV *see* Qualified majority vote
Qualified majority voting (QMV) 4–6, 10,
        13, 15, 202

Recapitalization 48
Recessionary conditions 46
Referendum debates 129, 135–6
Referendums 13, 19, 46, 52, 55, 66, 73,
        76, 78, 129–30, 134–5, 137–8,
        200–201
Refugees 181
Regionalism 151
Rehn, Olli 51
Rome 71, 165
Round, Doha 107
Rules
        balanced budget 48–9
        technocratic 45, 55

Samparas, Antonis 144
SAPS *see* Single Area Payment Scheme
Scandinavian countries 163, 167, 170, 172
SCG *see* Stability, Coordination and
        Governance
Schengen 3–4, 19–20, 161–74, 177,
        179–92, 195, 204
Schengen acquis 165, 181–2
Schengen Borders Code 182–9
Schengen Conventions 164–5, 172, 182
Schengen Evaluation Working Group 162
Schengen Governance Package 189, 192

Schengen Information System 167–8, 171,
        183
Schengen ministers 166
Schengen spirit 185
SEA *see* Single European Act
Security 39, 66, 166, 181, 189
Serbia 13
Services 19, 107–8, 110, 116
SGP *see* Stability and Growth Pact
Shadow economy 150
Side-payments 204–5
Single Area Payment Scheme (SAPs) 101
Single currency 15, 3–4, 11, 52, 69, 71–6
Single European Act (SEA) 6–7, 9, 12, 15,
        67–8, 70, 77, 180, 182, 195
Single Payment Scheme (SPS) 89, 93, 101
Slovakia 3, 14, 152
Slovenia 3, 14, 150, 152
Social cohesion 48, 52–3, 58
Social inclusion 53
Social movements 54
Social policy 68, 77, 129, 204
Social security 53
Sound public finance 10
Sovereign debt defaults 27, 31
Sovereign debt levels 31
Sovereignty 34, 58, 65, 129, 144, 151
Sovereignty supranational 152
Spain 3, 11–12, 14, 26, 28, 30, 32, 46–7,
        55–6, 128, 130, 135–6, 148, 150,
        152
Species biodiversity 89
Spillover 146
SPS *see* Single Payment Scheme
Stability 47, 57, 70, 145, 177, 201
Stability, Coordination and Governance
        (SCG) 48–9, 52, 78, 146
Stability and Growth Pact (SGP) 46, 48,
        52, 55
Stimulus policies 50
Structural funds 12, 51, 56
Structural reforms 11, 49
Subsidies 88, 97, 100, 151
Sustainability, fiscal 49
Sustainable public finance 10
Sweden 3, 13–14, 20, 170–72

Switzerland 19, 150, 161, 171
Systematic border controls 183–5

Tariffs 110
Tax evasion 54
Taxation 12, 50, 201
TCSs *see* Third country nationals
Technocratic governance 59
Technocratic legitimacy 51
Technocrats 51
Temporary protection 179
Temporary residence 20, 185–6
Terrorism 178
Third country nationals (TCNs) 178, 180,
        183, 185–6, 188, 190–92
Three Us 17, 34, 36–7
Trade 18, 47, 79, 93, 107, 110, 116–17,
        119
Trade and Investment Enhancement
        Agreement (TIEA) 110
Trade liberalization 107, 109–10, 152
Trade negotiations 86, 107–8, 110, 112,
        114, 119
Trade policy 18, 118–19
Trade unions 50
Transaction costs 90
Transatlantic Economic Partnership
        Agreement 117
Transnational constitutionalism 54
Transparency 90, 94
Treaty Establishing a Constitution for
        Europe (TCE) 126, 128–30,
        132–3, 135–7
Treaty of Maastricht 11
Treaty of Nice 7, 76
Treaty of Paris 7
Treaty of Rome 4, 6–7, 18, 85–6, 180, 201
Treaty on European Union (TEU) 72
Treaty on the Functioning of the European
        Union (TFEU) 183
Tripartite Social Summits for Growth and
        Employment 53
Tunisia 177, 179, 182, 185
Turkey 13, 16, 132, 151, 167
Two-Level Games 206

UK *see* Britain
United Nations High Commissioner for
　　Refugees (UNHCR) 185
United States (US) 9, 11, 26–7, 36, 39, 88,
　　107, 113, 115–18, 136, 152
US *see* United States

Value Added Tax (VAT) 15, 66, 145
Van Rompuy, Herman 151
Variable geometry 7, 3, 17, 20, 181, 199,
　　201, 204–5

VAT *see* Value Added Tax
Visas 166, 171, 173, 183

Water resources management 89
White Paper on European Governance 58
World Trade Organization (WTO) 18, 86,
　　107, 112
World War I (WWI) 116
World War II (WWII) 65, 86, 117
WTO *see* World Trade Organization

THE INTERNATIONAL POLITICAL ECONOMY OF NEW REGIONALISMS SERIES

Other titles in the series

Roads to Regionalism
Genesis, Design, and Effects of
Regional Organizations
Edited by Tanja A. Börzel,
Lukas Goltermann, Mathis Lohaus and
Kai Striebinger

New Regionalism or No Regionalism?
Emerging Regionalism in the
Black Sea Area
Edited by Ruxandra Ivan

Our North America
Social and Political Issues beyond NAFTA
Edited by Julián Castro-Rea

Community of Insecurity
SADC's Struggle for Peace and Security
in Southern Africa
Laurie Nathan

Global and Regional Problems
Towards an Interdisciplinary Study
Edited by Pami Aalto, Vilho Harle
and Sami Moisio

The Ashgate Research Companion to
Regionalisms
Edited by Timothy M. Shaw, J. Andrew Grant
and Scarlett Cornelissen

Asymmetric Trade Negotiations
Sanoussi Bilal, Philippe De Lombaerde
and Diana Tussie

The Rise of the Networking Region
The Challenges of Regional Collaboration
in a Globalized World
Edited by Harald Baldersheim, Are Vegard
Haug and Morten Øgård

Shifting Geo-Economic Power of the Gulf
Oil, Finance and Institutions
Edited by Matteo Legrenzi
and Bessma Momani

Building Regions
The Regionalization of the World Order
Luk Van Langenhove

National Solutions to Trans-Border
Problems?
The Governance of Security and Risk
in a Post-NAFTA North America
Edited by Isidro Morales

The Euro in the 21st Century
Economic Crisis and Financial Uproar
María Lorca-Susino

Crafting an African Security Architecture
Addressing Regional Peace and Conflict
in the 21st Century
Edited by Hany Besada

Comparative Regional Integration
Europe and Beyond
Edited by Finn Laursen

The Rise of China
and the Capitalist World Order
Edited by Li Xing

The EU and World Regionalism
The Makability of Regions in the 21st
Century
*Edited by Philippe De Lombaerde
and Michael Schulz*

The Role of the European Union in Asia
China and India as Strategic Partners
*Edited by Bart Gaens, Juha Jokela
and Eija Limnell*

China and the Global Politics
of Regionalization
Edited by Emilian Kavalski

Clash or Cooperation of Civilizations?
Overlapping Integration and Identities
Edited by Wolfgang Zank

New Perspectives on Globalization and
Antiglobalization: Prospects for a New
World Order?
Edited by Henry Veltmeyer

Governing Regional Integration for
Development: Monitoring Experiences,
Methods and Prospects
*Edited by Philippe De Lombaerde,
Antoni Estevadeordal and Kati Suominen*

Europe-Asia Interregional Relations
A Decade of ASEM
Edited by Bart Gaens

Cruising in the Global Economy
Profits, Pleasure and Work at Sea
Christine B.N. Chin

Beyond Regionalism?
Regional Cooperation, Regionalism and
Regionalization in the Middle East
*Edited by Cilja Harders
and Matteo Legrenzi*

The EU-Russian Energy Dialogue
Europe's Future Energy Security
Edited by Pami Aalto

Regionalism, Globalisation
and International Order
Europe and Southeast Asia
Jens-Uwe Wunderlich

EU Development Policy
and Poverty Reduction
Enhancing Effectiveness
Edited by Wil Hout

An East Asian Model for Latin
American Success
The New Path
Anil Hira

European Union and New Regionalism
Regional Actors and Global Governance
in a Post-Hegemonic Era.
Second Edition
Edited by Mario Telò

Regional Integration and Poverty
*Edited by Dirk Willem te Velde
and the Overseas Development Institute*

Redefining the Pacific?
Regionalism Past, Present and Future
*Edited by Jenny Bryant-Tokalau
and Ian Frazer*

Latin America's Quest for Globalization
The Role of Spanish Firms
*Edited by Félix E. Martín
and Pablo Toral*

Exchange Rate Crises
in Developing Countries
The Political Role of the Banking Sector
Michael G. Hall

Globalization and Antiglobalization
Dynamics of Change in the New
World Order
Edited by Henry Veltmeyer

Twisting Arms and Flexing Muscles
Humanitarian Intervention and
Peacebuilding in Perspective
*Edited by Natalie Mychajlyszyn
and Timothy M. Shaw*

Asia Pacific and Human Rights
A Global Political Economy Perspective
Paul Close and David Askew

Demilitarisation and Peace-Building
in Southern Africa
Volume II – National and
Regional Experiences
*Edited by Peter Batchelor
and Kees Kingma*

Demilitarisation and Peace-Building
in Southern Africa
Volume I – Concepts and Processes
*Edited by Peter Batchelor
and Kees Kingma*

Persistent Permeability?
Regionalism, Localism, and Globalization
in the Middle East
*Edited by Bassel F. Salloukh
and Rex Brynen*

The New Political Economy of United
States-Caribbean Relations
The Apparel Industry and the Politics
of NAFTA Parity
Tony Heron

The Nordic Regions and the European Union
*Edited by Søren Dosenrode
and Henrik Halkier*

www.ingramcontent.com/pod-product-compliance
Ingram Content Group UK Ltd.
Pitfield, Milton Keynes, MK11 3LW, UK
UKHW020355010325
455677UK00021B/471